Plato on Virtue and the Law

Continuum Studies in Ancient Philosophy
Series Editor: James Fieser, University of Tennessee at Martin, USA

Continuum Studies in Ancient Philosophy is a major monograph series from Continuum. The series features first-class scholarly research monographs across the field of Ancient Philosophy. Each work makes a major contribution to the field of philosophical research.

Aristotle and Rational Discovery, Russell Winslow
Aristotle's Theory of Knowledge, Thomas Kiefer
The Enduring Significance of Parmenides, Raymond Tallis
Happiness and Greek Ethical Thought, M. Andrew Holowchak
The Ideas of Socrates, Matthew S Linck
Plato's Stepping Stones, Michael Cormack
Pleasure in Aristotle's Ethics, Michael Weinman
The Socratic Method, Rebecca Bensen Cain
Stoic Ethics, William O. Stephens

Plato on Virtue and the Law

Sandrine Berges

continuum

Continuum International Publishing Group
The Tower Building
11 York Road
London SE1 7NX

80 Maiden Lane
Suite 704
New York NY 10038

www.continuumbooks.com

British Library Cataloguing-in-Publication Data
A catalogue record for this book is available from the British Library.

ISBN-13: 978-1-4411-1150-0

Library of Congress Cataloging-in-Publication Data
Berges, Sandrine.
Plato on virtue and the law / Sandrine Berges.
p. cm.
Includes bibliographical references.
ISBN 978-1-4411-1150-0
1. Plato. Dialogues. Selections. 2. Ethics. 3. Virtue. 4. Law. I. Title.

B395.B435 2009
179′.9092–dc22 2008035215

Typeset by Newgen Imaging Systems Pvt Ltd, Chennai, India
Printed and bound in Great Britain by the MPG Books Group

For Max and Charlotte

Contents

Acknowledgements

I am grateful to those who have helped me put together a proposal for this book, by their comments and encouragements: Christopher Bobonich, Geoff Bowe, Sarah Broadie, Tim Chappell, Christopher Gill, Richard Kraut, David Sedley, Christopher Gill.

I would also like to thank all those who have commented on the material presented in this book, in particular my colleagues: Sandy Berkovski, Radu Bogdan, Josh Cowley, Andrea Rehberg, Ulrich Steinvorth, Lucas Thorpe, Lars Vinx, Simon Wigley.

I am particularly indebted to Bill Wringe for reading through the manuscript countless times, discussing the arguments with me, and providing invaluable feedback on every aspect of the writing.

Introduction

The study of ancient philosophy is no longer an isolated part of the discipline of philosophy. The past 30 years or so have witnessed the growth of a dialogue between scholars whose primary interest is in ancient philosophy and philosophers writing on central issues in contemporary moral or political philosophy. What is particularly interesting to these moral and political philosophers is the ancients' emphasis on virtue. In the early phases of analytic philosophy, the main focus was on moral rules and principles following the influence of Kant and Mill. But now, moral philosophers are again interested in the concepts first introduced by the Greeks, concepts pertaining to the character, what makes it good or bad, and how it may be developed. Not that these concepts and theories ever dropped out of philosophical thought altogether, but in analytic philosophy, at least, they were no longer mainstream. But with the revival of virtue ethics, philosophers are again looking at ancient writers, and in particular, Aristotle whom they perceive as their key inspiration.[1]

Of course it is not clear to everyone that there is such a thing as a 'virtue ethics revival', in that some philosophers do not believe that there is a cohesive branch of modern moral philosophy that calls itself 'virtue ethics', or that whatever now calls itself virtue ethics has much to do with whatever Plato or Aristotle were doing.[2] I take my cue from Hursthouse and Slote in claiming that there is a new branch of ethics that should rightly be called 'Virtue ethics', that it is inspired by what the ancients had to say about virtue and the good life, and that insofar as there was a revival, it was started by the writings of Elisabeth Anscombe and Philippa Foot – even if they would not necessarily approve of the current state of modern virtue ethics.[3] But granted that modern virtue ethics is influenced by ancient virtue ethics, it tends to be Aristotle rather than Plato. In this introduction, I want to cast some doubt as to whether going back to Aristotle is always the right thing for virtue ethicists to do. I want to suggest that sometimes, they should instead turn to Plato.

Surprisingly, given his extensive discussions of the virtues, Plato remains very much in the background of this virtue ethics revival. This neglect can be traced to the beginnings of the revival of virtue ethics, when one of the movement's most influential figures, Philippa Foot, wrote in her seminal paper 'Virtues and Vices':

> I myself have found Plato less helpful [than Aristotle] because the individual virtues and vices are not so clearly or consistently distinguished in his work. (1)[4]

This careless statement of preference has set the tone for research in virtue ethics which sometimes calls itself 'neo-Aristotelian',[5] at least until very recently when writers like Michael Slote, David Wiggins, Christine Swanton have started to turn to other sources of writings on the virtue such as Hume's, Hutchinson's and Nietzsche's.[6]

But even with this move away from Aristotle, Plato's contribution to virtue ethics has been neglected.[7] This maybe not terribly surprising, as he seems to have been cast out from the very beginning. But what should we make of Foot's reason for not looking at Plato? What are Plato's so called Socratic dialogues if not lengthy discussions of individual virtues? True, these dialogues are aporetic, and Plato does not pretend to define the virtues for us, but he does give us enough that we understand what they are almost certainly not. The *Euthyphro's* elenctic examination of piety, may not tell us what piety is, but it tells us what bigotry and pedantry are, and why they are not admirable.

Certainly, Plato's writings on the individual virtues is not to be ignored and has been taken very seriously by ancient philosophy scholars.[8] So what could Foot mean? There are, I think, two clues in her brief dismissal of Plato. The first is the claim that what is unhelpful about Plato's writings is his failure to *distinguish* between the virtues, the second, is her mention of Plato's *work*, in the singular. Although these choices of words do not point unilaterally to the interpretation I am about to suggest (after all it is perfectly normal to refer to a body of writings as someone's 'work'), it is nonetheless suggestive. I believe that what Foot meant by Plato's 'work' was the *Republic*, and that by Plato's failure to distinguish between the virtues, she meant his contention that no single virtue can exist without the others.

An almost exclusive focus on the *Republic* would have meant that Foot missed the discussions of the virtues of the *Laches*, *Charmides* and *Euthyphro*, but also that she came across arguments for the unity of the virtue thesis, i.e. the thesis that holds that no one can be courageous who is not at the same time wise, temperate and just. But of course, Aristotle also held the thesis of the unity of virtues, and claimed that 'as soon as someone has practical wisdom, which is a single state, he has all the virtues as well'.[9] So if one were to reject Plato on the grounds that he holds the unity of virtue thesis, one would also have to reject Aristotle. But maybe Foot and others could object that Aristotle is more discreet, in his holding of the thesis, that this particular belief does not obscure other things he has to say on the virtue, and that maybe that is not true of Plato in the *Republic*. We may answer two things here: first, once again, the *Republic* is not the only significant dialogue Plato has written on the virtues – I mentioned three dialogues as dealing with specific virtues in details, but very few dialogues have nothing significant to say about the virtues, how we acquire them, and what role they should play in our lives. Secondly, there are at least some philosophers who believe that a version of the unity of virtues thesis is defendable. I shall look into some of their arguments in Chapter 2.[10]

Having cast some doubt, I hope, on the fairness of Foot's dismissal of Plato from her work on the virtues, I want to turn to what is I think a compelling reason why we should in fact turn back to Plato.

In their introduction to an influential collection of articles on virtue ethics, Michael Slote and Roger Crisp write:

> If virtue ethics cannot produce some plausible conception of social justice and of political morality more generally, then its main contemporary rivals, consequentialism and Kantianism, will have a distinct advantage.[11]

The question of whether a virtue politics can be evolved from virtue ethics has become particularly urgent in recent years.[12] If it cannot, then doubts can be raised as to its overall usefulness, and there will be grounds for preferring ethical theories, such as consequentialism and Kantianism, which can. Not only is it judged a failing that an ethical theory cannot address questions of political relevance, but it is certainly an internal failing of virtue ethics. Justice, for the ancients, was one of the central virtues. Neither Plato nor Aristotle ever had any thought of doing ethics without politics. The two were inextricably linked. Yet, modern virtue ethics hardly focuses on the virtue of justice. As Chris Coope points out, justice is likely to be lost in long tedious lists, right between 'fondness' and 'concern'.[13] Unless virtue ethics can somehow redress this and bring justice back to the foreground, it does seem that it is in some serious trouble, at least as regards its claims of continuation with the ancients.

One aspect of virtue politics that has received special attention recently, is virtue jurisprudence, a set of questions regarding the virtue ethical understanding of the law. So an account of how a virtue ethicist may answer central questions regarding laws will go quite some way towards vindicating the possibility of extending virtue ethics to the political domain.

In this book I argue that a distinctive virtue theoretic account of the law is clearly presented in Plato's political dialogues: the *Crito*, the *Menexenus*, the *Gorgias*, the *Republic*, the *Statesman* and the *Laws*. In the *Crito* and *Menexenus*, Plato develops two versions of an analogy between parents and laws, claiming that the role of laws is to promote and secure an environment in which it is possible to live a virtuous life. In the *Gorgias* he raises questions as to the relationship between laws pertaining to punishment and promoting virtue of the soul. In the *Republic* he discusses the possibility of a state in which the leaders are so virtuous that they do not need laws, except for those laws that focus on educating the young. He reassesses this possibility in the *Statesman* and proposes a more realistic relationship between the leaders and the laws. In his last dialogue, the *Laws*, he proposes a detailed account of how laws promote virtue in the state, and what specific laws will be more successful.

But can we read these dialogues as a developing project? Granted, it is not controversial that the *Statesman* and the *Laws* were written at a later date than the *Republic*, the *Gorgias*, the *Crito* or the *Menexenus*. But the *Crito* and the *Gorgias* are often referred to as Socratic dialogues, and together with other dialogues which fall in that category, they are said to be separate from the rest of the Platonic corpus. On this view, the Socratic dialogues are a rendition of Socrates' philosophy, but dialogues from the *Republic* onwards express Plato's own ideas, and these are significantly different from Socrates'. Without wanting to dismiss altogether the thought that some dialogues are in some sense 'Socratic' while others are not, I want to stress that on any reading of the dialogues I listed, it is clear that Plato addressed similar problems in all of them, and that he tried out some potential answers in the earlier dialogues and revised these answers in the later ones. To say that the ideas he discussed in the early dialogues were Socrates', rather than his, is not to say that he did not think on these ideas, and that they did not influence his later thoughts. This is all I mean by the need to see these dialogues as being part of a project, and my claim should not be taken to imply that the early dialogues were intended as the beginning of a project. I mean instead that Plato remained preoccupied by the problems he first raised in these dialogues and that he sought to improve his solutions throughout his works.

Another question that can be put about my decision to look at these dialogues for insights as to what a virtue ethicist might have to say about laws, is whether we might not do better to look at books seven and eight of Aristotle's *Politics* instead. It is true that the virtue ethicist interested in applying her way of thinking to political philosophy might do well to study these books. There Aristotle addresses the questions of what role the law plays in promoting virtue amongst citizens, and in particular, in habituation. But the text is too short to be very satisfying, and a contrast between this and, say, the *Laws*, shows that Aristotle's views in these books are little more than a summary of what Plato has already said. I will discuss this in more details in Chapter 6. One would have to be very prejudiced against Plato indeed to choose the last two books of the *Politics* over the many dialogues in which Plato discusses the law as a source of ideas for the role of virtue in political philosophy.

The dialogues that I choose to focus on all display innovative, and provocative arguments about the relationship between virtue and law. But as well as being a rich showcase for arguments in the philosophy of law, the *Crito*, *Menexenus*, *Gorgias*, *Republic*, *Statesman* and *Laws* also help us find answers to several problems that might arise for a virtue-centred account of the law. Here are two of these challenges.

First it seems prima facie difficult for a virtue ethicist to have anything interesting to say about the laws. A virtuous agent will act according to what she perceives as the morally relevant features of the particular situation she finds herself in. But the law requires that she follows the same rules as everyone else, no matter what the fine details of her situation might be. This apparent incompatibility makes is difficult to imagine that a virtue ethicist might have anything useful to say on the topic of laws. Note that I am not claiming that virtue ethicist reject general rules, or indeed absolute rule (Aristotle claims that certain types of actions, such as adultery, are always wrong). A virtue ethicist would not want to consider whether rape, for example, is ever acceptable.[14] But generally, virtue ethics does emphasize particular judgment over general rule.

Secondly, one might easily feel that giving a virtue ethical account of the law would constitute a threat to autonomy.[15] Laws tell us what we should do in order not to be punished. We know that they are necessary in order for society to function well. We choose to be part of a well-functioning society, and so we respect the laws. But a virtue ethical account of laws might also state that laws are good for our characters, and that someone who disobeys them is not just a dissenter, but a bad person, and, possibly, a mentally unhealthy one.

By looking at the arguments of the *Crito, Menexenus, Gorgias, Republic, Statesman* and *Laws*, I will show how Plato proposes several ways in which we can understand the law from the perspective of virtue ethics and at the same time respond to the two challenges above. I will argue that Plato worked on these questions throughout his career, and that not until his later works in political philosophy, the *Statesman* and the *Laws*, does he succeed in addressing the challenges of incompatibility of law and virtue, and paternalism satisfactorily.

Chapters overview

I will focus on six dialogues: *Crito, Menexenus, Gorgias, Republic, Statesman* and *Laws*. Each of the following six chapters will be devoted to one of these in order.

Chapter 1 offers preliminary remarks on the central themes of the book, starting with a discussion of what ancient virtue ethics is, its role in the revival of virtue ethics, an attempt to define virtue jurisprudence, and lastly, a brief analysis of the two problems I take Plato to solve in his later dialogues: the incompatibility problem and the paternalism problem.

In Chapter 2, I begin to discuss the apparent incompatibility between virtue ethics and allegiance to laws. I will then argue that the *Crito* offers a deep and subtle answer to the question: 'why should a virtuous agent obey the law?', and that this answer is couched in terms of the law/parent analogy presented by the Personified Laws of Athens at *c*.50–*c*.51. This answer is controversial in that it refutes two schools of thought: one is that the *Crito* lends itself to an authoritarian interpretation, we must obey the law no matter what[16] (this is clearly not compatible with a virtue ethical reading) and the second is that the *Crito* presents the laws' claims as authoritarian but does not recommend that we should obey the law at all, and claims instead that Socrates obeys for moral reasons which are independent of the belief that one owes allegiance to the law.[17] I shall argue sets of interpretations are wrong and that a correct interpretation of the argument of the *Crito* must rely understanding the parent analogy as claiming that the purpose of the law is to promote and maintain an environment in which it is possible for the virtuous agent to flourish.

The *Menexenus* takes up again the parent/law analogy introduced in the *Crito*. In Chapter 3, I show how the analogy enables Plato to answer further questions about the virtue ethical understanding of laws, namely, what is it for a law to be a good law from the point of view of the virtuous agent? This goes further than the argument of the *Crito*, as in that dialogue, Plato tells us why a virtuous agent has reasons to obey a law, even if it is a bad law. My interpretation of the *Menexenus* draws on Plato's beliefs that a good law, like a good parent, will educate citizens, and therefore promote virtue. This interpretation lends itself to charges of paternalism: if the law shapes citizens' characters, then it is not clear that citizens ever decide autonomously whether a law is good or not. I will show how one might respond to these objections.

Up to Chapter 3, I discuss laws from the perspective of the virtuous agent, focusing on why a virtuous agent would want to obey a law, and what makes a good law from the point of view of the virtuous agent. However, problems tend to arise when we try to apply a virtue theory of law to the non-virtuous agent, in particular, to agents who disobey the law, i.e. criminals. The virtue theory propounded by Plato equates virtue with psychological health. This can be taken to mean that those who are not virtuous, and those who disobey the law, are mentally unhealthy. A consequence of this view is to say that criminals should be cured, rather than punished, a claim that Plato supports sometimes. Chapter 4 will explore the significance of the health analogy with reference to punishment. I will argue that the medical model Plato is proposing in the *Gorgias* is based on the elenctic method, i.e. that to become psychologically healthy is an intellectual process involving dialectic. I will then show that Plato's medical model has interesting implications for modern penology, in that it would encourage a predominance of community service sentencing. In that chapter I will also address the plausibility of Plato's claims on character development in the light of recent criticisms of virtue ethics from social psychology.

Chapter 5 explores the extent to which in the *Republic*, Plato fails or succeeds in addressing the paternalistic worry raised by the very idea of virtue promoting laws. I will argue that although he does present us with the means of partly resolving the problem, by insisting that laws should focus on education, his insistence that different classes of his ideal society should be educated in different ways, and in particular that only the smallest part should be given the means to develop their reasons, and therefore the ability to decide for themselves what the good life consists in, means that in the *Republic*, Plato remains staunchly paternalistic.

Chapter 6 examines Plato's mature attempt in the *Statesman* at resolving the incompatibility problem. I start by considering the dialogue's two very controversial and apparently contradictory claims about laws:

1. That a true king will not rely on laws except as convenient shorthand to avoid having to review each individual case, and as guidelines for his people on occasions when he has to go away.[18]
2. That in the absence of a true king, states must do their best to imitate the rule of the true king and that to do so, they must stick to their written laws, whatever they are, and not attempt to change them or write new ones.[19]

It seems that Plato is saying that either a virtuous ruler must do without laws, or that, in the absence of such a ruler, citizens must forget about a system of laws that is compatible with virtue. However, I will argue that in fact, the image of the true king, who relies on written laws for convenience only, provides a model for a more realistic appeal to virtue in jurisprudence, that is, a respect of laws that is compatible with equity. The *Statesman*, I will show both sets out clearly the dilemma facing those who wish to explain legislation and jurisprudence in terms of virtue, and makes some very plausible claims about how one might deal with these dilemmas.

Plato's last dialogue, the *Laws*, has been read as the product of his disillusion with politics. He no longer believes that kings are capable of becoming philosophers and ruling justly. This would explain the emphasis he places on the nitty-gritty detail of the laws in that dialogue. Men are not to be trusted – laws are, as one interpretation of the *Statesman* might suggest.

However, in Chapter 7, I will show how the *Laws* is in fact the mature product of Plato's reflection on the possibility of understanding laws from the point of view of virtue, and in particular, that he is now able to answer the paternalism worry. What Plato proposes is that all laws should be prefaced by a preamble, such that when citizens obey the law, it is because they have been rationally persuaded that these laws are in fact good laws. But several writers have argued that in fact, the preambles of the *Laws* fail to persuade rationally. I will attempt to explain why some of them appear to be unpersuasive, and at the same time, defend Plato against accusations that he is interested in propaganda, not persuasion.

In the concluding chapter, I retrace the main lines of Plato's thought on virtue and the laws as well as the various links between his proposal and contemporary virtue ethics. I ask how democratic institutions, focusing on the problem of discrimination, may use Plato's teachings to our benefit.

Chapter 1

Some Key Concepts in Ancient Virtue Ethics

Before getting on with the business of presenting Plato's contribution to a virtue ethical understanding of the law, it is necessary to introduce certain key concepts and give some background information on the state of the relevant debates. Many of the themes introduced here are taken up again in later chapters.

This chapter begins by introducing ancient virtue ethics: asking whether there is such a thing, and arguing that if there is, it had better be the ethical writings of Plato and Aristotle. In the first section I focus on three central doctrines shared by Plato and Aristotle: (i) that philosophers should seek to answer the question 'how should we live?', (ii) that central to the answer is an account of the virtues as stable character traits developed through habituation, and (iii) that holding the virtues and the good life together is the argument that human beings have a function, to flourish, or be happy, and that to fulfil that function successfully they must be virtuous. In (i) I focus on the relationship between the good life and the happy life for Plato and Aristotle. In (ii) I try and deal with the problem of the unity of virtue thesis: did Plato and Aristotle really hold it? And is the thesis they held so strong that we cannot possibly accept it? In (iii) I analyse Plato's and Aristotle's functional arguments, explain their weaknesses, and suggest why these flaws may not matter too much as far as my project is concerned.

In Section 2, I turn to modern virtue ethics, and particularly, Plato's place in the debate. I present Michael Slote's distinction between agent-based and agent-focused virtue ethics, and take issue with his description of Plato's ethics as belonging to a third category, agent-prior. I argue that if we are interested in agent-based virtue ethics, then we had better turn to Plato, not Aristotle. The distinction between agent-based and agent-focused virtue ethics is useful in order to understand Plato's moral psychology, as we shall see in Chapter 4. At the end of Section 2, I discuss two worries that arise from agent-based virtue ethics, but I will deal with these worries in Chapter 4.

Section 3 introduces virtue jurisprudence as a potential way into virtue politics. By virtue politics I mean the application of the tenets of virtue ethics to central questions in political philosophy. Virtue jurisprudence applies these theories to legal philosophy.

1. Plato and Aristotle's virtue ethics

It sometimes seems as though virtue ethics is simply a modernization, or a revamping of ancient ethical theories. Indeed some modern virtue ethicists call their theories 'neo-Aristotelian'.[1] But as Roger Crisp points out,

> Although virtue theory does have ancient roots, it is far from mere revivalism. Modern writers on the virtues, however keen they are on bridge-building, are not unaware of the vastness of the gulf that lies between us and the ancient Greeks.[2]

Indeed, one of the first question we need to ask when attempting this sort of bridge building, is whether it is right to characterize the ancients in general as doing virtue ethics? Certainly, one thing that ancient Greek and Roman thinkers have in common is the emphasis they place on virtues when they discuss the question 'how should one live?' This is true not just of Plato, and Aristotle, but also the Epicureans, the Sceptics and the Stoics. But virtue ethics does not just mean that one talks about the virtues. When it is used by writers like Michael Slote and Rosalind Hursthouse,[3] it also means that the virtues should be the focus of ethical judgement, instead of moral rules or calculations of consequences. In other words, the virtue ethicist is supposed to ask 'what makes a person good?' and give an answer in terms of virtues. They are not supposed to ask 'what makes an act right?' and appeal to universal rules or consequences in order to answer.

But in that case, not all ancient philosophers are virtue ethicists. Epicureans are in a sense consequentialists – they, more clearly than any others, believe that ethical judgement is a function of happiness.[4] The Stoics do not merely rely on an account of the virtues to determine what right and wrong are. They believe in universality, and the need for every agent to follow certain rules of behaviour, such as 'do not harm others'. In that sense they are much closer to Kant than they are to modern virtue ethicists.[5]

If I am right about the Stoics and Epicureans, then it is a mistake to view ancient ethics as monolithic, and to see modern virtue ethics merely as a revival of what was done by the Greeks and Romans.[6] But we can take a different view when it comes to discussing Plato and Aristotle. Perhaps because they worked alongside each other – Aristotle was a student, and then a teacher in Plato's Academy.[7] As we shall see, many characteristic Aristotelian themes are anticipated by Plato, and while many people may not be surprised by this general claim, they might be surprised to find out which particular views these are.

So how can we characterize the central doctrine Plato and Aristotle argued for? I believe that their ethical theories have three tenets in common. First both believed that the question philosophers should try to answer was 'how should we live?' And they both understood this question in two ways.[8] On the one hand, to state how one should live was to understand how one could be happy. On the other hand, it would also tell us what it took to be an admirable, praiseworthy individual. In different degrees, and more so for Plato than Aristotle, to be a good individual and to be happy were inextricably linked. Secondly, both philosophers also believed that central to the question how one should live was an account of the virtues, or stable, acquired character traits which together make up a good individual. Both also adhered to versions of the unity of the virtue thesis, which holds that to have one virtue is to have them all. One question I shall address is whether this claim is so implausible that we may be tempted to reject their moral psychologies wholesale. The third important doctrinal point Plato and Aristotle have in common is a version of the functional argument claiming that human beings, like bodily parts, or artefacts, have a function, namely to be happy or flourishing, and that to fulfil that function, one must be virtuous. Let us turn to each of these points.

i. In the closing argument of Plato's *Gorgias*, Socrates tells Callicles that 'this is the best way to live – to live and die in the pursuit of justice and the other virtues' (427e). This was 'revealed' to them by their arguments, and if they can be persuaded by that conclusion, they will avoid the shame of failing to agree on the 'most vital question' on which subject 'even a man of slight intelligence' could not fail to be serious, i.e. the question 'what kind of life one should live' (500c). Plato is not alone in finding this question a suitable topic for ethical discussions. In the beginning of Book I of the *Nicomachean Ethics*, Aristotle lists a few possible answers to that very question, thus setting the background of common beliefs against which he can philosophize. Should we live a life of action? Or study? Or money-making?

What is the ultimate good for a human life? What do we mean by happiness? Considering this passage stood as the introduction to a series of lectures on Ethics, we can take it that Aristotle, like Plato, took very seriously the question how one should live.

Not only did Plato and Aristotle share the conviction that the central question of ethics was how one should live, but their answers were not dissimilar. 'To live well' Socrates tells Crito, 'is the same as to live honourably and rightly' (*Crito*, 48b). This is echoed by the last paragraph of the *Gorgias*: the best life is the just and virtuous life, and anything else is worthless. But perhaps more famous is Socrates' other comment on the kind of life that is worthless in the *Apology*: 'the unexamined life' (38a). There it seems Plato is giving a different account of 'the good life', one in which what matters is not to be virtuous, but to spend time reflecting on what virtue is. At the same time, it is much more consistent with the portrait Plato draws of Socrates: Socrates does not tell people how to be virtuous, he asks them to reflect on what the virtues are and whether they are beneficial. In a way it seems that the life of philosophical inquiry, rather than the life of virtue, is what we should aim for.

To anybody not familiar with Plato's dialogues, this would look like a contradiction. However, the *Protagoras* gives us a clue as to what is happening: inquiry is not a pursuit separate from virtue, but rather, it is the means to acquire knowledge, and, according to the Socrates of the *Protagoras*, virtue is knowledge. It is a single whole, not a set of separate qualities, and each one of the virtues can be understood as a form of wisdom (361b). So there is no contradiction. To enjoin the Athenians to inquire is to enjoin them to become wiser, and hence more virtuous. To say that there is relationship between philosophical inquiry and virtue is not to say that by engaging in the elenchus, the Socratic method of philosophical inquiry, one *ipso facto* becomes virtuous. The elenchos can make one wise, but it takes time, and while we are still at the stage where we are sorting out what we truly believe from what we don't, we are not wise. So what we might say is that doing philosophy is a pre-requisite for virtue and hence happiness. If we cannot do philosophy, we cannot become virtuous, hence a life without philosophy is not worth living.

Note that the argument hangs some suggestion that the virtues are unified. It has to be that each virtue is identical with wisdom for the argument to work. If we thought, as Protagoras suggests at 349d, that it is possible to be courageous, and at the same time unjust, ignorant and intemperate, then we might also believe that it is possible to be wise, and at the same time lacking in the other virtues. If that were the case, then the life lived in pursuit of wisdom and the life lived in pursuit of virtue would be very different indeed. I will come back to the question of the unity of the virtues later in this section.

For Plato, the good or happy life is the virtuous life, and this turns out to be a life of philosophical inquiry. Aristotle offers a similar answer: at the beginning of the *Nicomachean Ethics* he tells us that the good life is that which is led in accordance with 'the most complete' virtue (1098a17–20). Throughout the rest of the text, Aristotle maintains how the virtues are necessary, and sufficient, for eudaimonia (1099b25–28). But external goods, good luck and material resources also help, he says. Not because they too are necessary for happiness, but because they help us achieve virtue (1099a31–b8; 1100b7–11). So in a sense, Aristotle agrees with Plato that certain things are necessary in order to become virtuous. He differs as to what these things are: for Plato it is the practice of the elenchus, but for Aristotle, it is definitely more tangible goods, goods which enable us to hold a place in society from which we can exercise the social and political virtues.[9]

Does Plato also believe that material external goods have a role to play in attaining happiness? When in Book II of the *Republic* (360e–361d) Glaucon dresses a portrait of the successful unjust man, and of the ill-treated just man, Socrates does not reply that the just man will be just as happy if he is ill treated as if he is not – simply that he will be happier than the unjust man despite being ill treated. When Callicles makes a similar case in the *Gorgias* (487a) depicting the life of a virtuous man who has had everything taken from him, Socrates does not claim that this man would be as happy as he would be if he had not been ill-treated. He answers, much later at 509b, that the real harm is to commit an injustice, not to be the victim of one. This is not to say, however, that there is no harm at all in being treated unjustly – just that it is not significant in comparison to the harm to one's soul that is perpetuated by acting unjustly.

The above claims rely on the supposition that what Plato is defending in the *Gorgias* is the thesis that virtue is necessary and sufficient for happiness, rather than an identity thesis. That would allow for degrees of happiness in the life of the virtuous individual. No matter what external goods she lacks, as long as she is virtuous, she will be happy. But if she is not lacking in external goods, she will be happier still. The stronger identity thesis implies that no matter what else is going on in her life, her happiness is determined entirely by virtue. Do we have any grounds for supposing that Plato's thesis is the weaker, rather than the stronger one? Some of the things he says in the *Gorgias* suggest not. When discussing the tyrant

Archelaus, Polus asks Socrates whether he thinks happiness rests entirely upon education and justice. Socrates replies 'Yes, in my opinion, Polus, for the man and woman who are noble and good I call happy, but the evil and base I call wretched.' (470e). But at 477b, he does acknowledge that there are lesser evils, besides injustice: poverty and disease. Evil in the soul is described as 'the greatest of all evil' (477e), not the only one, or even, the only one we need to worry about. At 504e, he goes even further, and states that 'it is not worthwhile in my opinion for a man to live with a diseased body'. This makes it quite clear that Plato is not defending a strong identity thesis of virtue and happiness, but merely the claim that virtue is both necessary and sufficient for happiness.[10]

ii. I will now show that Plato and Aristotle offer a similar view of the virtues as stable character traits obtained through habituation.

Stability

In chapter 4 of Book II of the *Nicomachean Ethics*, Aristotle sets out the prerequisites for an action to be a virtuous one:

> The agent also must be in a certain condition when he does [virtuous actions]; in the first place he must have knowledge, secondly he must choose the acts, and choose them for their own sakes, and thirdly his action must proceed from a firm and unchangeable character.

It is clear why virtues should be firm, and unchangeable if we want to attribute the praise for an action to the agent's character.[11] Someone who simply acts a certain admirable way because they're subject to a temporary emotional state does not deserve the same praise as someone who acts in the same way because that is what they always consciously do. The father who praises his daughter to the skies because he has just acquired a new mistress, or gotten a promotion at work, is not to be admired in the same way (or indeed at all) as the father who praises his daughter whenever she has done something good. The person who comes home in a good mood after an evening out drinking and gives a large note to a passing beggar is not charitable in the way that the person who gives a little everyday is. All this makes perfect sense, but how does Aristotle support his claim that virtues are, in fact, firm character traits, while other dispositions are not? Before turning to the answer he in fact gives, that virtues are the result of habituation, and that this is why they are stable, let us look at the psychological background Plato offers.

According to the famous thesis of the *Republic*, to become virtuous is to achieve psychic harmony, i.e. to make oneself 'a unit, one man instead of many, self-controlled and in unison' (*Republic*, 443e).

Virtue is about control – some parts of the soul must be controlled so as not to create disunity, both because to have several independent sources of motivation is itself a cause of disunity, but also because the 'lower' part of the souls themselves lack unity, whereas the higher part, reason, is able to set goals for the entire soul and organize the lower parts in accordance with these goals.

The internal disunity of the lower parts is discussed in the *Gorgias*, where the appetites are described as 'that part of the soul in which dwell the desires is of a nature to be swayed and to shift to and fro' (493a). By nature the appetites, and presumably, although Socrates does not make that distinction clearly in the *Gorgias*, the emotions, are incapable of being firm or stable. The only way for them to become so is to subject them to the authority of reason. As a result, the character of someone who is guided by reason will be stable and reliable. We can expect the virtuous individual to behave in certain ways and be confident that they will always act virtuously. (*Republic*, 442b–443c).

Habituation

One feature of Aristotle's views that is often remarked on is his emphasis on habituation. But many of the key themes of this are in fact anticipated by what Plato says in the *Laws*. To become virtuous is to develop our character through habituation,[12] that is, to make a conscious effort to perform the kind of actions that someone with a good character would perform, until we develop a liking for that kind of behaviour. If I am by nature lazy, I should force myself to sit at my desk from morning till night until I have developed a liking for sustained work. When my baby daughter offers one of her toys to another toddler, I must reward her with a kiss, so that she chooses to repeat the action until she finds out that sharing is not only the right thing to do, but that it is pleasurable in itself.

These dispositions, however, must be distinguished from virtues, in that virtues are the result of a process of conscious and systematic habituation.[13] Natural disposition are just the raw material on which habituation must be set to work. No one is naturally virtuous (although virtues are not 'against nature' either – you cannot habituate a stone to fall upwards) because no one is naturally in possession of a firm character. A natural disposition is something that can be improved or worsened, and unless it is made firm, there is no reason to suppose that it will display cross-situational consistency. The way to make these dispositions firm, habituation is not, as commonly thought, a concept introduced by Aristotle (in the *Nichomachean Ethics*, Book II), but was first discussed by Plato in the *Laws*.

> I call 'education' the initial acquisition of virtue by the child, when the feelings of pleasure and affection, pain and hatred, that well up in his soul are channeled in the right courses before he can understand the reason why. Then when he does understand, his reason and his emotions agree in telling him that he has been properly trained by the inculcation of appropriate habits. Virtue is this general concord of reason and emotion. But there is one element you could isolate in any account you give, and this is the correct formation of our feelings of pleasure and pain, which makes us hate what we ought to hate from first to last, and love what we ought to love. Call this 'education', and I, at any rate, think you would be giving it its proper name. (Book II, 653)

So when Aristotle claims that 'moral virtue comes about as a result of habit' (1103a13) he is building on the arguments that Plato had already put forward, interestingly, at a time when Aristotle was still a member of the Academy.

The problem of unity of virtues

Both Plato and Aristotle defend a version of the unity of the virtues thesis. Plato's most famous discussion of the unity of the virtues is in the *Protagoras*:

> Is virtue (1) a single whole, and are justice and holiness and self-control a part of it, or (2) are these latter all names for one and the same thing? (329c). (3) Do they [the virtues] stand for a single reality, or (4) has each term a particular entity underlying it, a reality with its own separate function, each different from the other? (349a)

According to Terrence Irwin, Socrates' own view is reflected by (2) and (3). He calls it the strong unity thesis.[14] But Vlastos in 'The Unity of Virtues in Plato's Protagoras' claims that (2) is too strong to be Socrates' view, but that (3) is a better candidate. (1), he says, also reflects some kind of unity thesis that Socrates might well accept, but (4) definitely does not.[15]

Given that Socrates and Protagoras's ensuing disagreement is about whether it is possible to have one of the virtues, namely courage, but not the rest, it is perfectly possible that Socrates would adhere to (1) which states that virtue is a whole, and therefore, that we cannot separate out one virtue from the rest. Therefore, I believe that Vlastos is right, and that Plato's view is better reflected by (1) and (3), than by the stronger (2).

Aristotle also holds a unity thesis as stated in the *Nicomachean Ethics*:

> As soon as someone has practical wisdom, which is a single state, he has all the virtues as well. (1145a2)

It is not clear that there is much of a difference between what Plato and Aristotle believe here. In a nutshell, both think that if a person has one virtue, she has them all. Both would disagree that it is possible to be, say, courageous, if one is not also just, wise and temperate. This is what so many commentators have found hard to digest. It has to be possible, they say, to have some virtues but not the others. The often-quoted examples of the courageous tyrant (e.g. Hitler), or the temperate dictator (e.g. Stalin) may not be all that convincing. After all, we do not have to believe that they are perfectly courageous or temperate. Maybe it is true that in some situations, they have succeeded in acting as a courageous or temperate person would. But would we be surprised to learn that Hitler was afraid of spiders (or his mother) and that Stalin had an irrepressible fondness for chocolate (or little boys)? A large part of the attribution of virtues to historical figure is after all mythical: we do not know them well enough to decide whether they in fact had these virtues perfectly or completely. More convincing examples would be the ones closer to us. We might be happy to say of a close relative that they are generous, but feel that on the whole they are rather cowardly. Or a friend might strike us as just in his dealings with everyone, but intemperate when it comes to food and drink.

Several writers have tried to reinterpret or modify the unity thesis so as to render it more palatable. Susan Wolf in 'Moral Psychology and the Unity of the Virtues' suggested that the unity thesis turns on the claim that virtue essentially involves knowledge, and that knowledge is unified.

> The kind of knowledge that is required for the virtues, on this conception, is knowledge of what's important. A person who has this kind of knowledge we may describe as 'having her priorities straight'. As the reference to 'priorities' suggests, however, such knowledge of value seems to be essentially unified. (150)

What Wolf is saying is that if I have a good grasp on what kind of things matter, then that will be true whether I am in a battlefield, a courthouse or dining with friends. What makes her version of the unity thesis appealing is that it only appeals to the kind of common sense emotional knowledge that is accessible to all.

> A person who has her priorities straight may well see in a flash what needs to be done, whether it involves rushing into a burning building or try to save a child, or stopping along the highway to help an accident victim. (155)

Unfortunately, this is not, either on Plato or Aristotle's account – or indeed on any account – what being virtuous is. Certainly, Wolf is right that in order to act virtuously, we need to be able to see what matters. Her suggestion that the right thing to do may come to us in a 'flash' is right: one of the features of the virtuous agent is that she should know what to do and when to do it. If a situation requires immediate action, then the virtuous agent will be able to make up their mind what to do very quickly. But at the same time, that we should know what to do 'in a flash' has certain unfortunate implications. One thing that may come to mind when we read Wolf's examples is not the virtuous agent setting things to right, but the fool rushing into a situation she can only make worse, because she has not stopped to think what special skills or attentions may be required of her. Wolf is right also when she says that being virtuous need not be overly intellectual – certainly one should not have to study astronomy and mathematics in order to help an accident victim! But one needs at least to be familiar with first aid, and the virtuous agent will have made sure she took a course in that just in case she is one day called upon to act in a medical emergency (as indeed we all are). Her virtuous agent will also need to know something about burning buildings before she rush into one. And if she is saving a child from what she believes is an abusive family situation, she had better have a very good grasp of what is going on in that family, and what kind of situations are harmful to children. In other words, there's a lot more knowledge involved than a simple matter of priorities. Someone could have their priorities straight without having any ideas about how to bring them about in their actions. This would not be a virtuous person by a long call.

Neera Badhwar tried to do something different, namely, to offer a weaker version of the unity thesis. Although she believes that Plato and Aristotle's claims that to have one virtue is to have them all is false, she thinks that the unity thesis holds within particular domains or spheres. One particularly convincing example of what she has in mind is that of the good parent. Parenting requires that one should act virtuously, i.e. fairly, wisely, courageously, generously, etc. But being a good parent usually means that one exercises these virtues within the family circle, specifically towards one's children. But the virtues need not extend beyond that sphere. So a good father, for instance will be generous towards his children. He will make sure they are well provided for, and give them gifts of appropriate value as rewards, or for their birthdays and Christmas. But this same father need not be generous to the world at large. The fact that he does not give to charity, or that he does not treat his co-workers particularly well will not make him any less of a good father. This sounds, prima facie, convincing.

Unfortunately, again, the attempt to make the unity thesis more palatable to its detractors is not failsafe. Say that the good father is oblivious to hard ups around him, and that he only exercises his virtues within his family circle. What happens when one of his children is unpleasant to another child because, say, of that child's skin colour or social background? Will the father then have to step out of his sphere and see that the child receives an apology, or will he simply let his own child become a racist? It is unclear, even, whether his intervention may not be too late. Had he shown proper care and respect for those outside his family circle habitually, the situation may not have arisen, or if it did, it would be more easily dealt with.

The problem with Badhwar's proposal is that no spheres of action are so isolated that one will not be called upon to act in one at some point, and how we act in those spheres is bound to influence our virtue in the spheres we commonly inhabit.

It seems that the unity thesis cannot be watered down. However, this need not be a tragedy. First, let us note that the thesis holds only as far as perfect and complete virtues are concerned. One can be on one's way to becoming virtuous, and be closer to achieving virtue where, say, courage is concerned than temperance. Or one can be naturally more disposed towards one virtue than another. In neither case is it right to say that a person possesses a particular virtue, but it might be useful, nonetheless, to be able to point out that this person is closer to being, say, courageous, than she is to being temperate. This will not be taken to imply that she is going to become fully courageous before she becomes temperate, but that before she can become fully courageous, i.e. fully virtuous, she will have to work on her temperance. It is only once one has a perfect virtue that one has them all.

Secondly, as Wolf rightly points out, there is nothing wrong with the claim that to be virtuous, one has to know what is worthwhile, and that this has to be a unified sort of knowledge that can in principle be applied to any situation given the right mastery of the particulars. On the whole the unity thesis seems more like something we should embrace than reject.

iii. The third important doctrinal point Plato and Aristotle have in common is a version of the functional argument claiming that human beings, like bodily parts, or artefacts, have a function, namely to be happy or flourishing, and that to fulfil that function, one must be virtuous.

The function argument holds a place of honour in the *Nicomachean Ethics.* Aristotle presents it in Book I as part of his discussion of the concept of happiness (eudaimonia). He starts by stating his conclusion that happiness is the supreme good at which all actions aim.

But to talk of happiness as an end requires that we see human life as having an end. For Aristotle, just as artefacts and other living things have ends, so must human beings. The function of a human being must be specific to human beings, and not something shared with other living things such as animals or plants. He deduces that the function of human beings must be the exercise of their rational faculties which, alone, they do not share with other beings or artefacts. But just as there is a distinction between a flute player and a good flute player, so we must be able to distinguish between a human being who functions and one who functions well. Aristotle concluded that a good or happy human being is one who exercises his rational faculties in accordance with the virtues.

Plato offers his version of the argument at the end of Book I of the *Republic* (352d–354a), in order to convince Thrasymachus that in order to be happy one should be virtuous. He uses analogies with a knife, a horse and an eye. The argument is not widely discussed in the literature[16] despite Annas commenting that it is the most notorious of the arguments of Book I (53).

The argument has four premises. First, Socrates establishes that the function of something (e.g. horse, eye, ear, pruning knife) is that which it can perform better than anything else (353a). Secondly, to each function corresponds a virtue, i.e. a trait which enables a functioning object to perform in the best possible way (e.g. an eye deprived of its virtue, clear-sightedness, will not work as it is supposed to, nor will a pruning knife with a blunt blade) (353b–c). Thirdly, the first two premises must apply alike in all cases (353d). Fourthly, the soul' s function is to live well (or happily), and its virtue is justice (353d–e). He concludes that to live well, is to live a just life (354a).

Given that the second half of premise four is simply introduced as already settled on, it is not surprising that Thrasymachus rejects the conclusion that a happy life is a just life (and therefore that injustice can never be more profitable than justice). It is simply not clear enough that when Thrasymachus agrees that justice is a virtue of the soul he means what is implied by the argument at 353–354, and if it is not, then he has no reason to accept the conclusion drawn by Socrates.

Annas's comment on the argument is that it is 'formally all right, and succeeds in making its point on a high level of abstraction'. But as Socrates' claim at 353e that 'we have agreed that justice is excellence of the soul' is simply untrue, 'in the end the argument is futile, for it depends on a premise which there is not the faintest change that anyone would accept unless they already accepted the conclusion' (55).

If the argument's sole purpose is to convince Thrasymachus, then it is indeed futile, and it fails to achieve its purposes. But it would be strange if Plato at the same time portrayed a Socrates trying his best to convince, using what he thought of as a powerful argument, and a Thrasymachus who is completely untouched by anything he says. A more plausible interpretation of what is going on at the end of Book I is that Socrates is announcing his view on an important matter, not to Thrasymachus, but to an audience who is sympathetic to the claims that the just life is happier than the unjust one. In a sense, that is preaching to the converted. This claim is supported by a reading of the beginning of Book II where Glaucon says 'I don't believe it [that the unjust life is more profitable than the just one], yet I am disconcerted when my ears are tinned by the arguments of Thrasymachus and innumerable others' (358b). What Glaucon is saying is that he is converted, but that he also needs some arguments to consolidate his beliefs. Obviously the function argument of Book I isn't it, otherwise he would not challenge Socrates to offer one at the beginning of Book II.

So what is the purpose of the function argument? My thought is that it offers an insight into the worldview that Plato is trying to develop, and into which he will construct his arguments about justice. This worldview is teleological, and it is the same as he announces in the Phaedo at 97b:

> mind in producing order sets everything in order and arranges each individual thing in the way that is best for it. Therefore if anyone wished to discover the reason why any given thing came or ceased or continued to be, he must find out how it was best for that thing to be, or to act or be acted upon in any other way.[17]

In this passage Plato is making it very clear that he believes the world to be arranged according to a teleological understanding. For everything, there is a way in which it is best for that thing to be, and that includes the human soul. So even though Plato is not offering as yet any argument for his belief that what is best for the human soul is justice, he is explaining why he is going to argue that justice is best, by telling us that according to his worldview, something has to be. And indeed, we need to have understood this basic assumption when Plato takes up the argument again in Book IV to define a just soul as a healthy soul. The function argument in Plato is meant to prepare us for this (443d–444c).

Because neither Plato's nor Aristotle's function arguments are terribly persuasive as they stand, it makes sense in Plato's case not to look at it as intended to persuade. Whereas Aristotle's function argument plays an important role in his ethics, we should probably understand Plato's arguments as a statement that Plato has certain teleological beliefs that underline his ethical theory, rather than as an intended demonstration that those beliefs are true. We might expect to find further defence of these beliefs in the texts, but the short argument presented in *Republic* I is not intended to be conclusive. In other words, less argumentative weight is placed on Plato's function argument than on Aristotle's. And given that the teleological aspect of ancient virtue ethics is one that proves uncomfortable for modern virtue ethicists, it is probably a good thing that Plato's is very much in the background of his defence of the virtuous life.

I have said that it makes sense to read Plato's and Aristotle's ethical writings as gravitating around three central tenets that they have in common: first that the central question in ethics is 'how should one live?', second that an account of the virtues as properties of the character is central to an answer to that question, and third, that virtue and the good life are linked by a teleological theory expressed in Plato's and Aristotle's function arguments. We must now turn to an important difference in their accounts.

2. Agent-focused and agent-based virtue ethics

The previous section introduced the common tenets of Plato and Aristotle's ethics. In this one I want to discuss an important difference between them. This difference is best expressed in terms of a distinction drawn by Michael Slote between agent-based and agent-focused virtue ethics. An agent-based virtue ethics is one in which the value of actions is derived entirely from the character of the agent who performs it. An act is fine or honourable if and only if the agent who performs it is virtuous. There are no external points of reference for ethical value outside of character. An agent-focused virtue ethics, on the other hand puts forward the less ambitious claim that the virtuous agent is the measure of actions. Acts have an ethical value independently of the character of the agent who performs them, and a virtuous agent is one who is good at perceiving that value. Slote believes that agent-based virtue ethics is 'purer' and 'more radical' than agent-focused virtue ethics.[18]

Slote argues that Aristotle's virtue ethics is agent-focused: the status of actions as fine or noble is independent of the evaluation of the agent's character. Virtuous agents are simply better at perceiving which acts are fine. On Slote's interpretation, Aristotle does not believe that an act is made good simply because it is performed by a virtuous agent. What the virtuous agent does is to show us which acts are good and which we should emulate:

> The good person . . . is the measure of things; what appears pleasures to him will also be pleasures . . . If what he finds objectionable appears pleasant to someone, that is nothing surprising since human beings suffer many forms of corruption and damage.[19]

Indeed, if we take seriously Aristotle's claim that some kinds of acts such as adultery, are always wrong, then it appears inevitable that we should conclude that for Aristotle the moral status of an act is not derived from the moral character of the agent performing it, but is truly independent: 'In cases of this sort, say adultery, the mere fact of committing such action at all is to do wrong' (1107a15–17).

For Slote, Plato's ethics is more radical (on his terms) than Aristotle's as it is not agent-focused, but it is not quite agent-based either; he calls it agent-prior:

> But Plato, for example, is in the above terms a less pure instance of virtue ethics. Plato does insist, certainly, that we evaluate actions by reference to the health and virtue of the soul, but he seems also to think that (appreciation of) the Form of the Good represents a level of evaluation prior to the evaluation of souls, with souls counting as virtuous when properly appreciating and being guided by the value inherent in the Form of the Good. (Crisp and Slote (eds) 1997, 240–41)

I disagree with Slote's analysis and believe that Plato's ethics would be more properly termed agent-based. It is not surprising that Slote believes that for

Plato, the character derives its value from the forms as this is a common reading of Plato based in particular on what he says in the *Phaedo* 97e:

> It seems to me that whatever else is beautiful apart from absolute beauty is beautiful because it partakes of that absolute beauty and for no other reason.

This passage suggests that for Plato, all value derives from the forms. So if an agent's character is good, then it is made good by the Form of the Good. But the passage needs to be read in conjunction with what precedes it. What immediately precedes it is a discussion of Anaxagoras's failure to come up with a good theory of the cosmos and knowledge. But this failure is only mentioned because of his original intentions, which, to Socrates, sounded very promising.

> I once heard someone reading from a book, as he said, by Anaxagoras, and asserting that it is mind that produces order and is the cause of everything. This explanation pleased me. (97c)

Socrates goes on to disagree with what Anaxagoras makes of this thesis. He is disappointed by Anaxagoras's emphasis on physical explanations – what is the point of that if everything originates from the mind? But the original thoughts still hold and Anaxagoras is for Socrates 'an authority on causation who was after my own heart'.

If Socrates does indeed take 97c seriously, then it looks as though the forms themselves must be produced by the mind. They are the mind's tools for ordering things, not external entities that determine what the mind should be like. If that's the case, and I believe it is, then Plato's ethics is not agent-prior. On Slote's definition, it is agent-based.

This fits quite well with several features of Plato's account of how we should attribute value. According to him an act is praiseworthy only if it promotes or sustains or creates psychic health or harmony, only if it has a beneficial effect on the agent's character. Justice itself is a state of complete harmony, whereby the agent is brave, wise and temperate, which means that all her sources of motivation (irrational desires, emotions and reason) are in harmony with each other under the guidance of reason. Whatever such an agent does is virtuous and there is nothing more to ethics than moral psychology. In the *Republic*, for example, he writes that justice and injustice

> are in the soul what the healthful and the diseaseful are in the body; there is no difference. [. . .]

> Virtue then would be a kind of health and beauty and good condition of the soul, and vice would be disease, ugliness and weakness. [20]

In Book IV he then elaborates as to what this health might be:

> attained to self-mastery and beautiful order within himself, and [. . .] harmonised these three principles [the three parts of the soul: reason, the emotions or high spirit, and the appetites], the notes or intervals of these three terms quite literally the lowest, the highest, and the mean, and all the others there may be between them, and [. . .] linked and bound all three together and made himself a unit, one man instead of many, self-controlled and in unison.[21]

Unfortunately, agent-based virtue ethics, and in particular Plato's version of it, has met with some very serious criticisms. The source of the objections is captured by the following dilemma.[22] A platonic agent-based virtue ethics requires that we have an account of character and human flourishing: we need to be able to say why it is good for the agent to develop certain character traits, virtues, and bad for her to develop others, vices. The dilemma follows directly from this requirement: either the moral psychology which is behind the ethical claims is indeterminate, or it is bound to be unacceptable. It may be indeterminate in the sense that we are unable to come up with a working moral psychology to back up our theory that character traits should form the basis of moral discourse. In that case, the theory is unsupported. We may also believe that there is no unified account of human character and flourishing. In that case if we still want to support agent-based virtue ethics, then we end up with a rather unattractive kind of relativism which would enable us to make claims like this one: 'My character flourishes when I commit regular acts of violence, so, for me, violence is a virtue'.

The other horn of the dilemma is this. We are, it seems, reluctant to put the stamps of approval on any theory of human character and flourishing. This for two main reasons. First, we do not think that any such theory can be objective in a hard scientific way. We may think psychology is a science, but character and flourishing don't exactly hold a place of pride in psychological theories these days.[23] Secondly, it is feared that to derive moral praise or blame from a unique conception of what is good for a human being is downright authoritarian, and ought to be resisted on moral grounds. To sum up, either the agent-based virtue ethicist can't come up with a theory of flourishing and we have no reason to accept her moral theory, or she can come up with one which either fails to convince or is morally unacceptable. The agent based virtue ethics might as well pack her bags and return to the study of Aristotle – there are just too many ways to lose. I shall address these worries in Chapter 4, and show how Plato in fact does offer an account of character and flourishing which is both coherent and acceptable to the modern virtue ethicist.

Another reason why modern virtue ethics, and in particular versions that derive value solely from the agent's character, is not always regarded as a serious competitor to Kantian or Utilitarian theories, is that it supposedly cannot do politics. Utilitarianism slips naturally into welfarism, and Kantian ethics into resourcism. Both also have things to say about rights and about the best forms of government. But can virtue do any of that? Virtues are personal: they are properties of an individual's character traits. This means that they grow with the individual: the story of a virtue is a tale of character development. One becomes courageous, fails to get any wiser, achieves peace of mind and happiness through justice, tries to be more temperate, etc. An individual's relationship with virtue is thus always fuzzy, in movement and it is personal.

One way of expressing what the above is to say this: the main concern of the agent, from the point of view of virtue ethics, is that she should be virtuous. Sometimes, this appears to stand in the way of a concern for others, as in Socrates' decision, in the *Crito*, that he will not escape for fear of harming his soul, despite Crito's claim that he has a duty to others to survive. It seems as if Socrates' concern for his own soul overrides any concern he may have for the well-being or just treatment of others. If this sounds dubious for an ethical theory, it is downright impossible as a political one! How could one derive any political arguments from a theory which has no concern beyond the agent's care of her own soul? This absence of other regarding concerns in the virtue theories of the ancients has led contemporary ethicists to believe that virtue ethics simply cannot do politics. And, if it cannot, then it is not as useful as Kantian or Utilitarian theories which can. The example of these two show that an ethical theory is only full-blown if it can deploy itself in the political domain. If virtue ethics cannot do that, then it is not a serious competitor.[24]

Some writers, including Michael Slote, have suggested that virtue ethics is not inherently exclusively self-regarding. The ancients did focus on the health of the soul, but more recent virtue ethicists shared our concern for the welfare of others. Slote mentions Hume and Hutchinson, as perhaps more likely models for a virtue politics. However we need not give up altogether on the ancients, for after all, most of Plato's writings about the virtues are political in whole or in part. In fact, Plato has much more to say about the behaviour of the city than he has about the behaviour of the individual. Dialogues which start off with a question as to what a particular individual should do about something inevitably end in *aporia* with the individual in question no closer to a decision than he was at the beginning. On the other hand, political dialogues such as the *Crito, Republic, Statesman* and the *Laws*, all end with a fairly clear political proposal, whether it is about something specific, i.e. that a virtuous agent should obey the law, or a complete and detailed political program such as the Athenian offers in the *Laws*. It is no wonder that this aspect of Plato's writings has been overlooked since the focus of study in Ancient Virtue Ethics, has, from the beginning, been Aristotle. But once again, a return to Plato might prove highly beneficial for modern virtue ethics, here because it might actually give us some useful ideas as to what a virtue ethicist could say about at least some aspects of politics.

3. What is virtue jurisprudence?

Although legal philosophy was long dominated by consequentialist and Kantian ways of thinking, recently, it has begun to take virtue ethics into consideration.[25] In general terms, virtue-based jurisprudence appeals to the virtues in order to understand the law, that is, legislation or judging. For example, an advocate of virtue jurisprudence could claim that a good legal system is one which promotes virtue and eliminates vice, which is more or less what both Plato and Aristotle seem to think.[26] However, to a mind more accustomed to a liberal conception of the law, this can seem uncomfortably paternalistic and reminiscent of certain totalitarian conceptions of the law.[27]

The main proponent of virtue jurisprudence, Laurence Solum proposes something less threatening, namely, that virtue should play a role, if not in legislating, at least in judging.[28] He claims that what makes a judgment good, is that it should be brought by a virtuous judge. In that sense, his claim is agent-based. The judgment derives its value from the character of the judge, it is not simply the case that the virtuous judge perceives that this particular judgment is the right one to make. His claim is especially convincing in cases of equitable judgment, where it is not always clear what the law dictates in a particular set of circumstances. Often we may feel that the right judgment in a hard case is not predetermined, but that it comes out of the virtuous judge's deliberation. Take the example of King Solomon who when faced with two women each claiming that a child was theirs, judged that the child should be cut in half and shared between the two women, unless they were able to resolve their differences. This daring and contentious judgment clearly would not have been acceptable coming from anyone but the virtuous Solomon of the story – we certainly would not accept it from any living judge. It was the right judgment for Solomon to make, because he was confident of the outcome, namely that the real mother would back down and thereby reveal herself. Even though this confidence comes from Solomon's superior ability to perceive certain features of the case, these features do not constitute the rightness or the wrongness of the outcome. What it comes down to is that Solomon is simply better at understanding human psychology, and successfully applies this knowledge to his ethical deliberations. So in this case, the judgment is simply made right by the wisdom of the judge. A less virtuous judge, would not have known that such a judgment would not result in the death of the child, and therefore, it would have been wrong for him or her to give that judgment.

Anthony Duff, replying to an article in which Solum propounds the view that what makes a judgment good is the virtue of the judge objects that a judgment may be good even though it was given by a corrupt judge. For example if I was a millionaire who cared to see that justice was done, I may bribe a judge to look into a case fairly and not to accept other bribes. If the judge accepts my bribe and honours its terms, we may be able to say that the judgment he or she arrives at is just, while remaining in no doubt that the judge himself or herself is not. One may not be entirely persuaded by this objection, maybe because the example Duff uses to illustrate it is somewhat implausible – would one rely on such a corruptible judge to come up with the right judgment in a difficult case? It may still cast reasonable doubt on the possibility of coming up with an agent-based account of judging, and on the whole idea of virtue jurisprudence. For to say that a virtuous judge will be better equipped to perceive the justice of a case and come up with a good judgment does not necessitate a switch from Kantian or consequentialist ethics to virtue ethics. Both those theories leave room for saying that a virtuous agent will be better at doing the right thing.[29]

It seems that a small window of opportunity for applying virtue ethical thinking to the law is being shut by Duff's doubts. Duff claims that virtue jurisprudence can only address itself to judging, and not legislating, and that moreover, it does not have much to say about judging that cannot be said within the context of a consequentialist or Kantian theory. I propose that in order to rescue virtue jurisprudence from Duff's criticisms, we need to turn to Plato.

If we think of jurisprudence in ancient philosophy, the first (and maybe last) thing that is bound to come to mind is Aristotle's account of justice and equity.[30] Indeed, the only writer so far to have made any reference to the ancients with reference to virtue jurisprudence is Roger Shiner, and this is what he refers to.[31] Yet it seems that a significant philosophical source has been overlooked: many of Plato's political works are concerned with the law, and they are concerned with it from the point of view of virtue. The *Crito* asks why a virtuous agent might want to obey the law, the *Menexenus* gives a rational for a system of law that is virtue promoting, the *Gorgias* explores an analogy between law, in particular penal law, and medicine, the *Republic* outlines a lawless state ruled by virtue alone, the *Statesman* argues that such a state is not viable, and the *Laws* gives a detailed picture of a state that is ruled by virtue and the law. Here I must make two concessions.

First, it is true that these dialogues are not usually interpreted as being part of a program, least of all a program in virtue jurisprudence. One of my tasks will be to make this claim plausible and to show that there is enough apparent development in these dialogues to legitimize seeing them as part of a same endeavour.

Secondly, many readers will have reacted to my claim by thinking that even if Plato does have a virtue-centred account of the law, it is highly unlikely that such an account will be acceptable to the modern reader. Plato's views are famously anti-democratic and paternalistic. Given that a good virtue-centred account of the law will have to fight a tendency to paternalism anyway, to start it off with Plato's views seems unpromising. Yet I am confident that this is only so because close enough attention has not been paid to Plato's specific arguments on virtue and the law. My aim in the following chapters is to show that such attention is rewarding, and that many of the problems that arise from Plato's views can be solved from within his own perspective.

Chapter 2

Obedience and Persuading the Laws in the *Crito*[1]

1. Introduction

One central issue in political philosophy is that of political obligation: what arguments can be given why we should, under normal circumstances, obey the law, and conversely, are there any circumstances under which we are morally justified in disobeying? So if virtue ethics is to cast any light on issues in political philosophy, it will need to be able to say something about these questions. I have chosen the *Crito* as the first of Plato's dialogues to discuss because it does just that: it answers a form of the question why should we obey the law? Typically, the *Crito* is read as giving a bad answer to that question, to put forward an authoritarian justification of unconditional obedience based on weak arguments.[2] But I will argue that the *Crito* has in fact been misinterpreted by those who have seen its argument as authoritarian and that the *Crito* gives us a very good beginning for an investigation of the authority of law from a virtue ethical perspective. But I will also argue that for the complete story to be told we need to take into account the way Plato develops his position in later dialogues.

In Plato's dialogue, Socrates, enjoined by his wealthy friend Crito to bribe the prison guard and escape his death sentence, refuses on the grounds that to disobey the laws of the city would be unjust, and that he had rather die than commit an injustice. Socrates' attitude seems at odds with his other beliefs. Why should Socrates, who believes no Athenian is truly wise or virtuous, pay so much attention to their laws when they have condemned him unjustly? Is blind obedience to the law really compatible with the belief that what matters is not to commit injustice?

My interpretation of the dialogue means that I depart from the way in which it is often discussed in two ways. First, I refocus the question slightly. The Crito does not just ask: 'why should we obey the law?' but 'why should we obey the law given that what we care about is virtue?' This difference is important, as it means that in order to understand the answer Plato gives, we need to concentrate on the virtue ethical aspects of the dialogue, something which has not generally been done before.

My second departure from traditional interpretations concerns the argument in the dialogue I choose to focus on. I argue that the most significant argument of the *Crito* is the parent/law analogy given at 50c–51c, an argument usually regarded as weak and tangential. I will argue that the arguments regarded as central by other writers, such as the argument from agreement, and the 'persuade or obey' clause to the Laws' demands, only derive their significance from the parent analogy. When they stand alone, they are weak, and readings of the dialogue as centred on these arguments has contributed to the wide spread belief that the arguments of the *Crito* are not only authoritarian, but also unconvincing.

One of the advantages of a virtue ethical interpretation of the *Crito* is that it makes sense, not just of why Socrates obeys the law when he is condemned to die, but as importantly, it explains why in the *Apology* Socrates shows that he is prepared to disobey the law under other circumstances. Explaining these apparent inconsistencies between the two dialogues is one of the most troublesome aspects of interpreting the *Crito.* I believe my interpretation will show that there are in fact no inconsistencies.[3]

By examining 50c–51c, I argue that the *Crito* answers the question 'why should an agent who cares about virtue (i.e. who either is virtuous or wants to become it) obey the law?' by suggesting the following very general principle:

> VGP An agent who cares about virtue will obey the laws, provided they do not demand that she act in a way incompatible with remaining a virtuous agent, if their purpose is to guarantee the conditions needed for flourishing, in the same manner that a parent's claims to obedience is justified by the need to educate the children's character.

This principle helps explain why Socrates decided to obey the laws and die, while he made it clear that under different circumstances he would or did disobey them. In particular, it makes sense of two occasions on which Socrates tells us he would not or did not obey. It tells us under what circumstances he would disobey: had the laws ordered him to give up philosophy he would have disobeyed; and did disobey: when he was a member to the council and voted against the trial of the ten commanders, and again when the government of the Thirty ordered him to bring

Leon of Salamis for trial.[4] In both these cases, the laws would be destroying the environment necessary for flourishing, either by putting a ban on a citizen's freedom to do philosophy, thereby decreasing his potential flourishing, and that of his interlocutors; or by instituting unjust and life threatening practices.

But the principle also explains why Socrates felt obliged to obey when the laws of Athens condemned him to die: because the laws of Athens promote and protect the flourishing of the Athenian citizens.[5]

The structure of this chapter is as follows. The next section introduces what I call the incompatibility problem, a difficulty facing a virtue ethicist who wants to say anything useful about the law simply because virtue requires that we decide how to act independently of general rules.

In the third section, I address a substantial objection to my argument, namely that Socrates obeys the laws because he believes he owes them unconditional obedience. In other words, the argument of the *Crito* is not a virtue ethical one, but it is authoritarian. I will reply that Socrates does not believe he should obey the laws no matter what. I will argue that aside from the inconsistencies such an interpretation would raise between *Crito* and *Apology*, it would also run counter to an important argument in the *Crito*, i.e. that one must never act unjustly.

In Section 4, I show that the Laws present themselves through the parent analogy at 50c, not as absolute masters, but as the guarantors of flourishing and the virtues. I will argue that it is for this reason that Socrates will not risk destroying them.

2. The incompatibility problem introduced

One noticeable omission in the otherwise copious literature on Plato's *Crito* (and one might say on the early Platonic dialogues in general) is the recognition that Plato is presenting a problem from a virtue ethical angle. This is no doubt due to the fact, which I highlighted in my introduction and Chapter 1, that Aristotle, rather than Plato is regarded as the originator of Virtue Ethics as a branch of philosophy.[6] Plato's own contribution to the discipline is more often than not bypassed.[7] This has unfortunate consequences not only for Platonic scholarship, but also for the study of Virtue Ethics. What the latter loses by not considering the *Crito* as a central text is specifically an opportunity to expand into the domain of political philosophy, something which, we saw, should be regarded as somewhat of a priority by virtue ethicists.

One particular problem facing the virtue ethicists who wish to do virtue politics is what I call the incompatibility problem, namely, the difficulty in reconciling certain virtue ethical beliefs with the laws' claim to obedience. A virtue ethicist believes that to be a good person is to have certain character traits which enable us to perceive or decide (depending on whether we are proponents of agent-focused or agent-based virtue ethics) for each situation what the proper thing to do is without having to rely exclusively on moral rules, because exclusive reliance on moral rules prevent us from perceiving special, morally relevant features of a situation. These features, again depending on whether we account for them from the perspective of agent focused or agent based virtue ethics, either determine, or help us decide what the proper course of action is. What may Solomon (from the example in Chapter 1) have noticed, when confronted with the true and the fake mothers? That at least one of the women seemed genuinely distressed at the possibility of losing the baby, and was not acting. Recognizing human emotions, thus, is one of the skills that a virtuous person will have. But had Solomon relied on a more 'legal' judgment, he would not have been able to act on this perception of the emotions at play. He would have had to say that, in the absence of conclusive evidence, the baby had to be either taken into care, or given to the woman best able to bring it up, or whatever the local laws might have said on such issues. This dependence on recognizing the 'details' of a situation makes it awkward for the virtue ethicist to say anything sensible about laws. As Slote (1995b) has noted:

> Because virtue ethics is supposed to concentrate more on the inner life of the individual than either consequentialism or deontology, one can easily wonder whether the former is really capable of doing justice to law or to any sort of objective or real constraint upon human action.[8]

There seem to be two problems here. First, how can we transfer the psychological theory which is central to virtue ethics into an account of the law? Whether an agent is just depends on her character, or psychic health, i.e. whether she has achieved harmony amongst the different sources of her motivation. It seems that it would be difficult to transfer such an account to laws without an unacceptable degree of anthropomorphism, that is, treating laws as if they had characters which could evolve out of their own accord through habituation.[9]

The second problem is the thought that reliance on written laws cannot yield justice in all cases as 'justice is blind' and laws fail to take into consideration aspects of situation which may be relevant to its justice or injustice. As the Eleatic Stranger puts it in the *Statesman*:

> Law can never issue an injunction binding on all that really embodies what is best for each; it cannot prescribe what is good and right for each member of the community at any one time. The differences of human personality, the variety of men's activities, and the inevitable unsettlement attending all human experience make it impossible for any art whatsoever to issue unqualified rules holding good on all questions at all times.[10]

This thought is echoed by Aristotle's more famous words:

> And this is the nature of the equitable, a correction of law where it is defective owing to its universality. In fact this is the reason why all things are not determined by law, viz. that about some things it is impossible to lay down a law, so that a decree is needed. For when the thing is indefinite, the rule also is indefinite, like the leaden rule used in making the Lesbian moulding; the rule adapts itself to the shape of the stone and is not rigid, and so too the decree is adapted to the facts.[11]

So Plato and Aristotle describe the perspective that virtue ethics, whether agent-based or agent-focused, will almost inevitably take on laws, and at the same time outlines a possible solution to the problem which faces the virtue ethical account. Laws, because they are universal and do not pay heed to the particular, cannot ensure that justice will be done. Therefore they must be supplemented with decrees or judgments that will adapt themselves to the particulars of a situation just as the Lesbian rule adapts itself to the shape of the stone.[12]

What Aristotle says about equity, although powerful and insightful, does not provide much in the way of argument or analysis of the question how a virtue ethicist should think about the law. Plato, on the other hand, addresses the problem at greater length, first in the *Crito*, where he attempts to show that a virtue ethicist should see the law as securing the framework needed for the virtues to flourish in the city, until the *Statesman*, where he gives a detailed analysis of the virtue ethicists' attitude to the law and attempts to resolve it with an account which clearly anticipates Aristotle's concept of equity. So in this chapter I will outline Plato's first attempt at dealing with the incompatibility problem, but I will come back to the problem in Chapter 6, presenting Plato's mature and more definitive solution.

3. Unconditional obedience

To interpret the *Crito* as putting forward an authoritarian argument is to accept that Socrates agreed wholeheartedly with the Personified Laws' demand for unconditional obedience at 50c: 'Did you undertake to abide by whatever judgments the state pronounced?' According to some people[13], Socrates believes that it is just to obey the laws even when what they order is effectively unjust. It seems to them that we can only interpret Socrates' refusal to escape from his death sentence and his apparent agreement with the Laws of Athens' various claims at 54, if we suppose that he believed he owed the laws obedience, no matter what. This interpretation is highly dubious, at least in part because it leads to inconsistency between the *Crito* and the *Apology*, where Socrates twice defies the laws and threatens disobedience. Some writers on the *Crito* have inferred from this that Socrates cannot in fact be agreeing with the Laws' claims to obedience no matter what.[14] It seems to me that there are strong reasons to agree with the non-authoritarian interpretations over and above these inconsistencies. Socrates makes claims, before the Laws' speech even begins, from which it follows that he will only obey in certain circumstances. I will show how these claims should compel a non-authoritarian reading of the dialogue.

At least one[15] of Socrates' claims in the *Crito* is incompatible with his believing that he owes the laws obedience no matter what. It is his equation of justice with psychic health. I will explain how this claim entails that the Socrates of the *Crito* is not authoritarian, and consider an objection to my argument.

At 47e, Socrates suggests, through a series of rhetorical questions, that just actions are those actions, which promote psychic health:

> What about the part of us which is mutilated by wrong actions and benefited by right ones? Is life worth living with this part ruined? Or do we believe that this part of us, whatever it may be, in which right and wrong operate, is of less importance than the body?

This concept of psychic health is recurrent throughout the dialogues (see *Protagoras,* 313a–c; *Gorgias,* 464a, 480a–b; and *Republic,* 444c–e), where it serves to support an account of virtue. In the *Republic,* for example, Plato writes that justice and injustice

> are in the soul what the healthful and the diseaseful are in the body; there is no difference. [. . .]

> Virtue then would be a kind of health and beauty and good condition of the soul, and vice would be disease, ugliness and weakness. (444c–e)

The concept of psychic health is also central to the *Gorgias* in which Plato draws a double analogy at 466a between gymnastic and legislation on the one hand, and medicine and justice on the other. Those institutions, which promote justice and punish injustice, are, according to Plato, like those, which promote health and cure disease.[16]

The concept of psychic health is also inextricably linked to the function argument discussed in Chapter 1. Plato's concern with the health of the soul makes sense because he believes that there is a proper state for the soul to be in. His claim that a healthy soul is a just soul is explained by his belief that justice is the excellence of the soul, that without which the soul cannot attain its ideal condition. I will discuss the concept of psychic health and its relation to the virtuous life in Chapter 4. Here we simply need to focus on the claim that life with an unhealthy soul is not worth living.

Why does Socrates' adherence to a virtue ethics mean that he cannot believe he owes the laws unconditional obedience? As Socrates also believes that life with an unhealthy soul is not worth living (48b), he is unwilling to act in a manner that will harm his soul: 'Then in no circumstances one must do wrong' (49b). But because Socrates knows that laws will sometimes require him to act unjustly, as they did in the case of Leon and the Thirty (*Apology*, 32c–d), it follows that he cannot believe he should obey them no matter what. The passage at 48b–49b makes it apparent that Socrates' conception of justice is agent-based, it entails that actions are just, not because they accord with rules, but because they contribute to psychic health. Hence for Socrates, adherence to rules – and in this case laws – and justice are not necessarily co-extensive. He would not believe that his being just depended every time on his obeying the laws of Athens; as indeed he did not in the case of Leon and the Thirty, and would not in the hypothetical case of the jury ordering him to give up philosophy (*Apology*, 29c).

My argument so far relies on claims Socrates seems to make in the *Apology*, however, advocates of the authoritarian interpretation of the *Crito* may well question the validity of appealing to material outside that dialogue. One might defend the view that the *Crito* stands apart from the other early dialogues, it represents an ideological departure from the *Apology*. Kraut suggests such a view:

> It might be objected that the Crito's apparent authoritarianism is consistent with the authoritarianism of the Republic, and that the former

> work should therefore be considered a middle dialogue, or a least a transitional dialogue. According to the hypothesis, the *Crito* represents Plato's quarrel with Socrates, rather than the latter's quarrel with himself; and therefore there is no reason to try to interpret the speech of the laws in a way that makes it consistent with the Apology's tolerance for disobedience.[17]

Kraut replies to this potential objection that the *Republic* certainly does not advocate unconditional obedience. It only makes the claim that in the ideal state, the philosopher rulers must be obeyed. This is a far cry from the claim that rulers must be obeyed in any state. It depends on the presumption that the rulers of the ideal state will be as wise and just as it is possible for a human being to be. To demand from citizens total submission to rulers who are models of virtue may be authoritarianism of a kind, but of a very different kind from the demand that we submit to any authority we happen to live under.

There is another reason why the claim that the *Crito* is an authoritarian dialogue would not be an easy one to sustain. Although there might be reasons to believe that Plato changed his mind after writing the *Apology* about whether it is just to obey the law in any circumstances, the argument of 48b–49b means that he would have to change his mind about something more substantial. One must never act unjustly, Socrates says. But the laws have been known to request people to act unjustly – the episode of Leon and the Thirty is an example of such a request. So if Socrates now believed that it was always just to obey the law, it would have to be conjoined with his stated belief that one must never act unjustly, and thereby entail the unstated belief that the laws never request one to do something which is unjust.

Kraut again, notes this problem of internal inconsistency of Socrates in the *Crito.* He suggests that one way we could attempt to solve it would be by adopting the doctrine that law and virtue cannot conflict. He rightly recognizes this as Thrasymachus' relativist conception of virtue, i.e., virtue is whatever the rulers decide will best serve their interest. This association with the villain of the *Republic,* of course, makes it highly implausible that Plato could ever have adopted that doctrine.[18] (And note that in order to explain the inconsistencies both internal and with other dialogues, our objector would first have to liken the *Crito* to the *Republic,* and then distance it from it!)

Bostock, while arguing for the authoritarian interpretation, also remarks on the inconsistency issue.[19] He puts forward as a solution the claim that the Laws of the Crito are believed by Socrates to represent the expert he introduces at 47e. Many people will find this suggestion highly implausible. For one thing, it is hard to believe that a set of democratic laws, i.e. the laws of the majority, could represent an expert which is defined in an opposition to the opinions of the many. Socrates makes it very clear that the expert's pronouncements on justice have more value than the many's opinion. Could the many's opinions grow so drastically in value simply in virtue of becoming law? It does not seem that this could follow from what Socrates says at 47–48, nor does Bostock give any argument to show that it could. Bostock's main argument in support of his view that the laws are the expert referred to at 47e is that no other candidate seems suitable, the other candidates being Socrates, or 'the Truth itself'. I have no disagreement with the view that it is difficult to make either of these wear the hat. Indeed, it may be suggested that the invocation of an expert is an instance of Socratic irony. But contrary to what Bostock says, it is not just in the *Crito* that an expert is announced without appearing. The *Laches* does the same at 184e–185e. The question of moral expertise in general is much discussed amongst Plato scholars, and so far it remains an unanswered one.

What follows from the authoritarian interpretation of the *Crito* is a faith in the laws' unfailing capacity to know and to order what is just, basically the belief that a legal system (not just an ideal one, but for instance, the Athenian system) can never be corrupt and can never make mistakes. This is not compatible with anything Plato says in the *Crito* or in any other dialogue, early, middle or transitional. If the authoritarian reading entails that Plato believed at any point that the Laws represented the expert in virtue, then it seems we ought to reject that reading.

4. Agreement

One much discussed argument of the *Crito* is the one in which the laws tell Socrates that he cannot disobey them because he has come to an agreement with them. This is first introduced at 50c at the very beginning of the long speech on the analogy of laws with parents: 'Was this our agreement, Socrates?' It is then set out after the passage at 50c–51c:

> Then the laws will say: 'Consider, Socrates, if this is true, that in your present attempt you are going to do us wrong. For, after having brought you into the world, and nurtured and educated you, and given you and every other citizen a share in every good that we had to give, we further

> proclaim and give the right to every Athenian, that if he does not like us when he has come of age and has seen the ways of the city, and made our acquaintance, he may go where he pleases and take his goods with him; and none of us laws will forbid him or interfere with him. Any of you who does not like us and the city, and who wants to go to a colony or to any other city, may go where he likes, and take his goods with him. But he who has experience of the manner in which we order justice and administer the State, and still remains, has entered into an implied contract that he will do as we command him. And he who disobeys us is, as we maintain, thrice wrong: first, because in disobeying us he is disobeying his parents; secondly, because we are the authors of his education; thirdly, because he has made an agreement with us that he will duly obey our commands; and he neither obeys them nor convinces us that our commands are wrong; and we do not rudely impose them, but give him the alternative of obeying or convincing us; that is what we offer and he does neither.'

I shall be arguing, in what follows, that this argument is only significant as part of the law/parent analogy, in that if we do not accept that the laws' claim to obedience is, like our parents' were, a means for helping us flourish, then we have no reason to come to any agreement in the first place. The laws are telling Socrates that they have educated him, and that when he came of age, he was welcome to stay in the city provided he agreed to abide by their laws. But these laws include that the city should be able to put him to death if they decide that it is a good idea to do. They do offer the proviso that citizens are entitled to attempt to persuade the laws to change their mind, but how seriously should we take this claim? After all, Socrates, if not a sophist, is a very persuasive speaker (one of the reasons for his trial is that he has persuaded a bunch of wealthy youths to follow him around philosophizing instead of living properly aristocratic lives). Yet, he has failed to persuade the laws to let him live – so what chance would a normal citizen have had in those circumstances?

It does seem, that despite the persuade clause, the Laws are telling Socrates that should they decide to behave unreasonably at the cost of his life, he has agreed to let them do so. One might reply that this is not unusual in a contract theory. Hobbes, Locke and even Rousseau have such views on the nature of the contract: once we have joined the covenant, we have to obey no matter how unreasonable the order strikes us. But Locke and Rousseau do allow for disobedience in certain cases, and Hobbes certainly in cases where the state wants to put us to death.[20] Also, the contractarians of the modern period think that the state offers us rather more than a good education. We join the contract because the alternative is the state of nature in which we simply cannot live. But the Laws of Athens mention no such thing. In fact, they suggest that we do have alternatives to staying in Athens and obeying. Living under the law is not, on their account, inevitable, merely preferable.

The question is whether it really makes sense to say that we would prefer to stay in a city which had educated us even at the cost of being put to death. Imagine the following scenario. A girl has been educated for free in a good boarding school. Once she has all her diplomas, her teachers call her and say: 'You can now leave and try your luck elsewhere in the world, or you can stay in the school, use the facilities, and work as a teacher. But if you stay, you must agree to abide by our rules, and one of these rules is that we may put you to death if we see fit.'

The example seems quite reasonable, save for the last part. But the last part is simply outrageous, even someone who had no relative, and no wealthy friends to back them up in world would choose to leave under these conditions.

One may object that the city of Athens is offering rather more than what a school would offer. But that is not entirely clear. A boarding school can be like a small, enclosed world. And the laws, by their own account do offer mostly education and general upbringing. But if that is so, then it is strange that they in fact offer most of what they have to offer before exacting a promise to obey! It is as though they are offering the goods, and then suggesting that if we like them, we pay for them, but if not, we can keep them anyway. This makes it sound as though the laws are offering something more than just a good education. First, it is unclear that anyone would be willing to lay down their lives in exchange for good schooling, secondly, even if they were, in principle, they probably would not want to come to such an agreement once they had already received the schooling. This leads me to believe that what the laws are offering is rather more important than schooling, that it is important enough that an Athenian citizen would agree to die for it. If I am right, and the laws are indeed offering something more precious than life itself, then the agreement argument is not as powerful as may be supposed. The reason why Socrates may have come to an agreement is because he believes the laws are providing something more precious than life itself. But unless he has changed his mind, he would not need to be bound by agreement in order to protect that something, even at the cost of his life! This is why I argue, in the following section, that the most relevant one of the laws' arguments why Socrates should not escape is the parent/law analogy.

5. The role of the Laws: the parent analogy

At 50c–51c, in order to help him convince Crito that it would be wrong to escape, Socrates invokes the personified laws of Athens, and this is their first argument:

> Come now, what charge do you bring against us and the state, that you are trying to destroy us? Did we not give you life in the first place? Was it not through us that your father married your mother and begot you? Tell us, have you any complaints against those of us laws that deal with marriage?
>
> No, none, I should say.
>
> Well, have you any against the laws which deal with children's upbringing and education, such as you had yourself? Are you not grateful to those of us laws which were instituted for this end, for requiring your father to give you a cultural and physical education?
>
> Yes, I should say.
>
> Very good. Then since you have been born and brought up and educated, can you deny, in the first place, that you were our child and servant, both you and your ancestors? And if this is so, do you imagine that what is right for us is equally right for you, and that whatever we try to do to you, you are justified in retaliating? You did not have equality of rights with your father, or your employer – supposing that you had had one – to enable you to retaliate. You were not allowed to answer back when you were scolded or to hit back when you were beaten, or to do a great many other things of the same kind. Do you expect to have such license with your country and its laws that if we try to put you to death in the belief that it is right to do so, you on your part will try your hardest to destroy your country and us its laws in return? And will you, the true devotee of goodness, claim that you are justified in doing so? Are you so wise as to have forgotten that compared with your mother and father and all the rest of your ancestors your country is something far more precious, more venerable, more sacred, and held in greater honour both among gods and among reasonable men? Do you not realize that you are even more bound to respect and placate the anger of your country than your father's anger? That if you cannot persuade your country you must do whatever it orders, and patiently submit to any punishment that it imposes, whether it be flogging or imprisonment? [. . .] Both in war and in the law courts and everywhere you must do whatever your city and your country command, or else persuade them

> in accordance with universal justice, but violence is a sin even against your parents, and it is a far greater sin against your country.

In this long passage the laws lay out what seems like an authoritarian argument *par excellence*. Socrates owes his birth, nurture and his education to the city of Athens. The city and its laws therefore stand to Socrates as parents, but even more so. Just as a child has no right to stand up against her parents, Socrates then has no right to disobey the laws. Socrates expresses no disagreement with that part of the Law's speech and is thus in danger of being understood as accepting the Laws' claims to unconditional obedience.

This passage has traditionally been understood as unequivocally authoritarian. Nevertheless, there is no single interpretation of it available. Writers on the dialogue disagree as to what the Laws mean and in what way they are authoritarian. In this section I argue that a non-authoritarian interpretation yields a better explanation of what the Laws mean and why Socrates appears to agree with them.[21] First, I shall discuss the shortcomings of two different interpretations of the passage as authoritarian.

Kraut, when attempting to explain the passage appeals to an argument from gratitude:

> The Laws are relying on the assumption, widespread in Ancient Greece, that although there is no general objection to violence and killing, attacks upon one's parents are absolutely forbidden. They seek some rational basis for this ban on parricide and they find it in the extraordinary benefits conferred. Logically, anything that is no less responsible for these benefits is no less entitled to forbearance from attack; since Socrates owes his existence and upbringing not only to his parents but also to Athens, he must not, for his part, destroy its laws.[22]

Two points may be made in criticism of Kraut's reading of the passage. First, the Laws are not just putting a ban on violence done to them. They are referring to any kind of disobedience. Although they do regard the possibility of Socrates disobeying in this instance as an attempt to destroy them,[23] it is unlikely that they would interpret any kind of disobedience in such an extreme manner. Thus it may be that the ban on parricide can only shed light on some aspects of what the Laws say at 50c–51c.

Secondly, the argument from gratitude is difficult to extract from the passage for several reasons. As Weiss points out, if the Laws wanted Socrates to obey out of gratitude, they would not need the parent analogy, i.e. they would not need to invoke only the benefits of life and education which they give in common with parents.[24] They could mention shelter, safety from tyranny, food in plenty and comfort. The list would be greater and thus they would be in a better position to demand grateful feeling from Socrates.

The argument from gratitude also fails for the following reason. Children do not obey their parents out of gratitude. By the time offspring are able to understand what they do owe their parents (and some never do), they are no longer required to obey in the same way.[25] Gratitude is thus at least as likely to be expressed as love and respect than as straightforward obedience. I conclude that although the Laws may be appealing to gratitude, it would be surprising that Socrates does not spot the weaknesses of the argument, and expresses no disagreement with it.

The second authoritarian interpretation comes from Weiss.[26] Having rejected the argument from gratitude she goes on to propose an alternative reading:

> What the laws do instead is point to the laws concerning marriage, nurture, and education and assert that, because of these laws, they stand in a parental, hence hierarchical and unequal, relation to the citizen.[27]

According to Weiss, the Laws are arguing that Socrates must not disobey because he is on an inferior footing – his authority to decide what to do is overridden by the authority of the laws, just as the authority of a child is overridden by the authority of her parents. But where does the inequality come from? In the case of the child–parent relationship, it would seem that if there is a hierarchical difference it is derived, at least in ancient Greece, from the sacred.[28] Oedipus raises a curse from the Gods when he kills his father. This is in spite of the fact that he acted in self-defence and is ignorant of his lineage. Antigone defies the King, who represents her foster parent and her ruler, in order to bury her brother according to religious rites. In both cases, real blood matters more than parental or legal authority. Both Oedipus and Antigone have adopted parents who are in charge of their life and education. But in both cases, the real crime is to fail to respect what they owe to blood relatives. This sacred blood link is obviously absent from the relationship between a citizen and the law.[29] It is unclear what else we might appeal to in order to deduce that there is an unequal hierarchical relationship between citizens and the law.

There is another way to account for the Laws' puzzling paternalistic argument and Socrates' acceptance of it. What we need to do first is answer the question why we think children owe their parents obedience. Gratitude is clearly not the answer, as we saw, and the fact that they are blood relations and that the *miasma* will be raised if we harm them is a little fantastic and old-fashioned for a thinker, who, like Plato, is keen on psychological accuracy.[30]

The key to understanding the purpose of obedience lies in reflecting on the nature of the exchange that takes place, in particular, how it takes place in time. The Laws' speech makes it sound as though obedience is offered in return for a gift of life and education, after that gift has been offered. This is not, however, how this kind of exchange commonly works. Normally, a child must obey during the time she is being educated. She must refrain from playing with matches, she must spend time everyday doing her homework, she must answer questions politely, etc. If she did not do these things, her parents would not be able to teach her very much. By obeying she is transforming herself into a learner. Obedience is thus not primarily offered as payment or gratitude for education, after the benefits have been conferred, but it is a condition of being educated.

One problem with this interpretation is that it may seem that because Socrates is no longer receiving education from the city of Athens, he should no longer be required to obey. The point of obeying is to learn, but Socrates, as we know from the *Apology*, does not believe there is anyone wiser than him in Athens.[31] Consequently, there should be no need for him to obey. But this objection is spurious, and can be refuted in several ways. First, even if Socrates is the wisest person in Athens, this does not entail that he cannot learn from his interactions with other Athenians. Indeed, elenctic examination is just as much a means of clarifying one's own ideas as it is to clarify that of others. Let us not forget that by engaging in the elenchos, Socrates is, first and foremost, 'examining his life', in which case, he too is still a student. Is he a student in the relevant sense, i.e. in the sense that he depends on certain laws for the continuation of his studies? Certainly – he depends on the possibility of walking about safely within the city walls and being able to talk to other citizens freely and openly. He depends on other citizens having received the kind of formal education that encourages philosophical reflection. It is no coincidence that Socrates says at *Crito* 53d–e that he had rather die in Athens than live in Thessaly, the 'home of indiscipline and laxity', where no one will be interested in listening to him discuss goodness and justice.

Another way of refuting the objection that, as Socrates is no longer a child, he should not have to obey the laws, is to point out that the objection assumes that Socrates does not care about virtue, but only about his virtue.

But this is unthinkable given any sensible way of understanding what virtue is, and in any case not true, as we know that Socrates was deeply concerned about promoting virtue in Athens. Socrates may not need the laws to make him virtuous any more (although as we saw above, Aristotle believes the role of the laws is to promote virtue throughout life), but the Laws are asking him to recognize the role they play in maintaining the conditions necessary for virtue to flourish in all citizens. If Socrates cares about virtue, as opposed to his virtue, he should respect the laws.

This argument of 50c–51c can be expressed in virtue ethical terms. Parents give us what we need in order to flourish, i.e. in order to develop a virtuous character. They can only make that gift if children will lend themselves to a certain discipline: virtues are acquired through habit, and habit requires discipline, i.e. in order to become habituated to a certain kind of behaviour, one has to do it again and again. If we decide to acquire a certain habit, or if someone else decides that we should acquire it, then we need to discipline our behaviour in order that we behave in the required way regularly and frequently. For instance, in order to become a pianist, one has to habituate one's fingers to move effortlessly on the keyboard. This habit is acquired through practising playing scales at length. As most children are not self-disciplined enough to practise scales for an hour a day, the parents and the piano teacher impose that task and the child obeys.

In the same way that the parents' imposition of discipline can be seen as a prerequisite for the development of virtuous habits, and hence for flourishing, the law can be seen as providing the conditions needed for the nurture of virtuous citizens. Although Plato does not think that the relation between the law and the habituation of children to virtue is straightforward he believes that legislators should think very seriously indeed about the education of children but that they cannot simply legislate as far as early education is concerned:

> Now that we have our boys and girls born, the proper course will naturally be to deal with their nurture and education; this subject cannot possibly be passed over in silence, but our treatment will wear the guise rather of instruction and admonition than of legal enactment. The privacy of home life screens from the general observation many little incidents, too readily occasioned by a child's pains, pleasures, and passions, which are not in keeping with a legislator's recommendations, and tend to bring a medley of incongruities into the characters of our citizens. Now this is an evil for the public as a whole, for while the frequency and triviality of such faults make it both improper and undignified to penalize them by

> law, they are a real danger to such law as we do impose, since the habit of transgression is learned from repetition of these petty misdeeds. Hence, though we are at a loss to legislate on such points, silence about them is also impossible.[32]

Plato's subtle assessment takes in both the fact that education of the character is a matter of habituation (*Laws*, 792e and 653), and laws are a very good way of encouraging the formation of habit through repetition, and that certain things simply cannot be legislated over. This means that the legislators need to come up with 'recommendations' and 'guidelines' as well as laws.

Aristotle also comments on the importance of the role played by laws in becoming virtuous, but his view is less subtle in that he recommends that laws should dictate early education:

> But it is difficult to get from youth up to a right training for virtue if one has not been brought up under right laws; for to live temperately and hardily is not pleasant to most people, especially when they are young. For this reason their nurture and occupations should be fixed by law; for they will not be painful when they have become customary. But it is surely not enough that when they are young they should get the right nurture and attention; since they must, even when they are grown up, practice and be habituated to them, we shall need laws for this as well, and generally speaking, to cover the whole of life; for most people obey necessity rather than argument, and punishment rather than the sense of what is noble.[33]

Despite their differences, what these passages show is that according to Plato and Aristotle, the state is concerned with producing virtuous citizens. Both believe that moral education is a job parents alone are not best suited for, Plato because he believes that as the proper nurture of infants is a matter that may ultimately affect the entire city, then it has to be a public concern, and Aristotle because he believes paternal authority is just not strong enough to impose virtuous habit on offspring, and that moreover, children are more apt to resent impositions coming from an individual than from the law.[34] In other words, Aristotle believes that virtue requires an authority which on the one hand, cannot be easily questioned or challenged, and on the other, is impersonal and does not cause offence. For this reason, his view is unsatisfactory. There can be no real analogy between parental authority and state laws if one considers that parental authority is ineffective.

Plato's view is more persuasive, in that he believes that the authority of law is a continuation of, not a replacement for, parental authority. Moreover, Plato sees that the analogy can be given as a justification for the authority of law, and an argument for political obedience. Aristotle does not, it seems, consider that political obedience might be a problem – at least not in the arguments surrounding the passage quoted above.

In order to conclude, let us come back to the Very General Principle and show how in the *Crito*, it determines Socrates' decision not to escape.

> VGP A virtuous agent will obey the laws, provided they do not demand that she act in a way incompatible with remaining a virtuous agent, if their purpose is to guarantee the conditions needed for flourishing, in the same manner that a parent's claims to obedience is justified by the need to educate the children's character.

It is clear that the laws do not demand of Socrates that he act in any way unjustly. But if I am right, Socrates does perceive the laws as promoting the virtuous life in Athens, by making sure citizens are able to flourish in the way virtuous agents should, by guaranteeing the kind of protection from external threats and educational framework which are needed for a character to develop virtuously. It follows that Socrates does believe that the Athenian laws – even though they are far from perfect and may well have committed an injustice in condemning him in the first place – are worth defending.

I have argued that no part of the *Crito*, that is, neither Socrates' own argument nor the laws' speech should be read as in any way authoritarian, but that the dialogue in general, and 50c–51c in particular can be interpreted as an illuminating answer to the question 'why should a virtuous agent obey the law?' The *Crito* argues that laws have a claim on virtuous agent, even though virtue is not concerned with rules. This claim is grounded in an understanding that the development of a virtuous character requires habituation, and that habits are acquired through the authority of law. When the Personified Laws of Athens are asking that Socrates should obey them, they are not appealing to Socrates' respect for his older and better, but to his conviction that what matters is flourishing, i.e. living virtuously, as well as a recognition that in order to achieve this, people need laws. The Laws are not appealing to hierarchy, they are asking Socrates not to dismantle the system which is enabling him and his fellow Athenians to live the good life, i.e. the only life worth living. If, on the other hand, Socrates had good grounds to believe that the laws of Athens did not promote flourishing, or that they prevented it, then he would have no reason to obey. It seems that when Socrates accepts the Laws' argument, this is what he understands.

6. The *Crito*, the *Apology*, and civil disobedience

The previous section explained the rationale Plato offers in the Crito for obeying the laws. It also gives us good reasons to accept this rationale, namely, that obedience on the grounds is compatible with caring about the virtues. It is also a non-trivial rationale, in that it tells us why we should sometimes obey laws even when we know them to be unjust, i.e. when the overall legal system they are part of is one which promotes the virtues, and disobeying would threaten that legal system in some way. Of course, we cannot accept Plato's rationale until we know whether we accept his account of what it is for laws to protect and promote virtues (this is the problem I address in Chapter 3). But if we do decide to accept this account, then there is one more reason why we will find his explanation of why we should obey the law attractive.

One reason why we need to find a strong rationale for recognizing the authority of law is that we also need a way to decide when it is right not to recognize that authority. One question the *Crito* raises, is, given that we should respect laws that promote and protect virtue and flourishing, how do we know when the laws do this sufficiently well? How do we decide that they do not, and that we need to challenge them? If a state clearly fails to promote and protect virtue, then there is no difficulty in answering the question: we owe no obedience. The *Apology* explains what Socrates did when the Thirties took over Athens. They conducted a series of unjust actions, and tried to force Athenian citizens to participate in their injustice. This is definitely an instance of not promoting or protecting virtue! Socrates' response was not to recognize their authority. But what do we do in less clear cut cases, i.e. cases where the law seems to promote and protect virtue some of the time, but not in all cases? The Athenian law is a case in hand. It is not perfect, but it does mostly a good job, and this is why Socrates chooses to obey. But there is one very clear-cut condition under which, were it to obtain, Socrates would turn his back on the authority of the law. Were the laws to order him to stop philosophizing, then Socrates would disobey. What can we make of this as far as the more general problem of civil disobedience is concerned? Surely we cannot simply say that civil disobedience is justified only in cases where citizens are not allowed to do philosophy. Rosa Parks was most certainly never told she could not do philosophy. This does not make her right to disobey any less potent. She was denied other fundamental rights by law, and this is why she disobeyed. Rosa Parks wanted to sit on a bus, not philosophize in it.

This is too easy a dismissal of the proposal that the criterion for a set of laws to be generally acceptable is whether it allows citizens to conduct philosophical investigations. Certainly, it seems that a state that did not allow its citizens to question its laws and institutions would not command respect for its laws. It seems to be a minimum condition that citizens should be able to interact with the laws using their reason. They should understand the law, and they should be able to discuss among themselves and with those in positions of authority whether these laws are good or bad. This is, I believe, the true significance of the 'persuade or obey' clause of reference. The point of this comment is to highlight the importance of the philosophical dialogue that does (or could) go on between the laws of Athens and the Athenian citizens. Somebody who is unhappy about what the laws have decided or how they have decided it, has the right to use their reason to attempt to persuade the laws otherwise.

The right to persuade is possibly the most significant aspect of a set of laws that is 'good enough' as far as promoting and protecting virtue is concerned. The red flag has to be the absence of such a right. Let's go back to the example of Rosa Parks and the American Civil Rights movement. One might argue that despite their treatment of African Americans, the US laws in the 1960s were, on the whole, promoting and protecting virtues. Education was widespread and adequate, and most people lived in comparative safety from internal and external aggressions. People did have the option to 'persuade' the laws using their reasons. Indeed, this is exactly what Martin Luther King did through his speeches and the march to Washington. But the option to persuade was not open in the southern states under the Jim Crow laws. King was arrested in Birmingham Alabama for 'parading without a permit', so to march, was to disobey. In fact, in his letter from Birmingham Jail he notes the importance of this ability to dialogue with the laws in order to justify obedience: but in cases where it is impossible to do so, then citizens have a duty to disobey unjust laws.[35] In that sense it was not unjust for Rosa Parks to disobey. As a domestic worker in the South under the Jim Crow segregation laws, it simply was not open for her to protest peacefully without disobeying the law (whereas this was a possibility for Martin Luther King when he was in Washington).

There is no clear-cut, foolproof method for deciding which set of laws are 'good enough' and should be obeyed. Indeed, one should probably be suspicious of any method that did not demand that one think long and hard before engaging in an act of civil disobedience. But there is one telltale symptom that we should look out for: whether citizens are in a position to attempt to 'persuade' the state that the laws should be changed when they think they should. Where there is no mechanism in place that makes it straightforward for citizens to express their views when they disagree (i.e. no freedom of the press, no right to demonstrate) the duty to obey is diminished accordingly.

As Raz puts it:

> Given that the illiberal state violates its members' right to political participation, individuals whose rights are violated are entitled, other things being equal, to disregard the offending laws and exercise their moral right as if it were recognised by law. . . . [M]embers of the illiberal state do have a right to civil disobedience which is roughly that part of their moral right to political participation which is not recognised in law.[36]

Raz claims that it is 'illiberal states' that prevent citizens from participating and protesting without disobeying. For our purposes, this begs the question. But we can turn his thought around in the following way. An agent concerned with virtue and flourishing will only disobey the law if the law fails to protect and promote virtue *by preventing citizens from disagreeing with it by using their reason to attempt to persuade.* If they are not prevented from engaging with the law in a rational manner – i.e. citizens are able to put forward their arguments and the laws representatives engage with them at the appropriate level – then the agent will not disobey. This view makes sense of our general intuitions regarding the authority of law and civil disobedience, at least to the extent that it explains why it was appropriate and just for Rosa Parks, Martin Luther King and others involved in the civil rights movement to disobey.

The term 'civil disobedience' was coined by Henry Thoreau in his protest against war taxation, and it is not clear that he would have agreed with my characterization of what counts as justified civil disobedience, i.e. when one disobeys only in cases where we are confident the law does not promote or protect virtue and we have no way to try and persuade the authorities that they are wrong. But Thoreau's point is stronger than this, as he believes that allegiance to the law always comes second to following one's conscience:

> Must the citizen ever for a moment, or in the least degree, resign his conscience to the legislator? Why has every man a conscience, then? I think

> that we should be men first, and subjects afterward. It is not desirable to cultivate a respect for the law, so much as for the right. The only obligation which I have a right to assume is to do at any time what I think right.[37]

Thoreau is taking the Antigone line: moral/religious laws come before state law. This is not, however, the Plato line. Plato does think that to do what is just is the most important, but he also believes that we need the law to provide the necessary environment to be virtuous. So it is only in cases where the law fails rather spectacularly to provide this environment that one is justified in disobeying it. There is, however, another way to agree with Thoreau and those who evade war taxes: once the taxes are levied, there is little chance that the war will be stopped. So there is not really a chance to persuade. Hence, we may disobey. Similarly, there is not really time to persuade once we have been conscripted to go to war – so disobedience is justified then as well. So we may, if we follow Plato, agree with Thoreau's conclusion, but come to it via a different position.

Chapter 3

Promoting and Preserving Virtue in the *Menexenus*[1]

1. Introduction

In Chapter 2, I argued that following Plato, a virtue ethicist could explain both the authority of law and find grounds for civil disobedience by saying that we should obey a law if we believe that the system of laws it is part of sufficiently promotes and preserves virtue and flourishing. Mostly, that means that the laws should encourage, and at least not prevent, philosophical enquiry and debate as to what the good is. It follows that when laws do not allow this, they do not need to be obeyed. This sheds light on the significance of the 'persuade' clause of the Personified Laws of Athens' argument. As long as it is open to citizens to present their argument to the laws that condemn them, or force them to do what they think is wrong, then the laws still protect their capacity to be virtuous and to flourish.

We now need to look at that statement more closely, and ask whether virtue ethicists might adopt it as expressing the role of laws more generally. The dialogue I will focus on in order to do this is the *Menexenus*, in which Plato once again takes up the parent/law analogy and attempts to argue for it. I will show how we can begin to develop an account of the law as promoting and preserving virtue in the city following the *Menexenus*. I will also address an objection which is typically raised against such accounts: namely that laws which promote or protect virtue are paternalistic.

I will argue that Plato successfully uses the parent analogy in the *Menexenus* to answer the question 'what is it for a law to be a just law' from a virtue ethics perspective. This question is distinct from but as equally important as the question the *Crito* addresses, i.e. 'why should we obey the law?' As one argument of the *Crito* seems to suggest, it is at least conceivable that we should have good reasons to obey a law which was not a just law – because, for example, to disobey would endanger the authority of the state and we believe that this authority is on the whole legitimate.[2] This would be the case if, for instance, a state whose laws on the whole promoted and protected virtue decreed a new, unjust taxation law. Provided citizens were allowed to express their views regarding that new law, and were thus given a chance to persuade the state to change it, according to the argument given in Chapter 2, they would not be justified in disobeying it. Thus, an answer to the question 'why should we obey?' does not necessarily give us an answer to the question 'what makes a law a just law?', so what the *Menexenus* has to say about what makes a law a just law is crucial to the project of virtue politics.

Any argument that the law is to the citizen as the parent is to the child is very obviously open to charges of paternalism. Paternalism implies a claim that something is good for you even if you do not know it is, or you are persuaded it is not, as well as the intent to force that supposed good upon you. More straightforwardly, the worry is that by appealing to the parent analogy to explain the relationship between laws and citizens, we end up saying that laws should treat citizens as if they were children who did not know their own good and had to have decisions made on their behalf. If this is what the analogy is meant to convey then in a sense it must fail.[3] I will show that this is not the case.

Section 2 discusses the relevance of an account of laws as promoting and preserving virtue to current debates in political philosophy. In Section 3, I show why two alternative virtue ethical accounts of just laws – one account derived from the *Republic*, and one offered by Michael Slote (2001) in his 'War Crimes and Virtue Ethics'[4] – are unlikely to work. In Section 4 I argue that the *Menexenus* gives us a credible philosophical argument to the effect that laws are just only if they enable citizens to flourish. In Section 5, I argue that the resulting virtue ethical account of just laws is not overly paternalistic.

2. The relevance of Plato's proposal to contemporary debates

In the *Menexenus*, Plato argues that what makes laws just is whether they promote an environment that allows citizens to live virtuously. This Platonic argument is closely relevant to modern debate in virtue politics, not just as a pointer for future debate regarding the justice of laws, but as already present in some positions. In particular, it may be used as a defence of existing claims such as that from Martha Nussbaum (1992):

> The idea is that once we identify a group of especially important functions in human life, we are then in a position to ask what social and

> political institutions are doing about them. Are they giving people what they need in order to be capable of functioning in all these human ways? Are they making it possible for citizens to function well?[5]

Nussbaum derives this conclusion from what she calls Aristotelian essentialism: there is such a thing as human nature, and in order for human beings to flourish, to live good human lives, this nature must develop in the proper way. What Nussbaum claims is that laws and institutions must support and promote this development. In a more recent work, *Hiding from Humanity*, she backs up this claim with the psychological theory of Donald Winnicott, that moral development is in some way dependent on there being a 'facilitating environment', i.e. an environment which enables the maturation process and adapts to the changing needs of the infant.[6] Applying Winnicott's theory to the political domain, she says:

> By examining these aspects of the role of a legal system [shaming citizens and protecting them from shame] we are asking in effect how law can provide what Donald Winnicott called a 'facilitating environment' for lives of trust and reciprocity. We are thus investigating the psychological underpinnings of some cherished liberal norms. [. . .] One point should be emphasized from the start: the impact of institutions on child development goes deep. It is crucial not to think of children as if their development takes place in the 'private sphere' until they are adult citizens. At every stage it is affected for better or worse, by laws and institutions.[7]

The claim is that laws and institutions enable citizens to develop in the best way they can. The use of Winnicott is slightly misleading, as he is concerned mostly with child development. This could be taken to indicate that as far as Nussbaum is concerned laws are designed to benefit and protect children but not adults. But Nussbaum is not saying that laws are needed only to facilitate childhood development, but that, unlike what is sometimes held, children, like adults, are affected by the law. She emphasizes that the role of laws is not simply to enable growth and maturation, but to protect that which has grown in the facilitating environment. The aspect of the good human life she focuses on is 'human dignity', or a life which is free from shame and stigma.[8] But this is not simply determined by growth and maturation. A child can be nurtured in an environment in which she is not shamed and learns to live with dignity. But as an adult she may move to a different environment in which a stigma is attached to some aspect of her life or self and she is no longer able to live in dignity. The fact that she has grown without being ashamed of that aspect of her life will probably help her, but the lack of respect she encounters from others will still blight her life by preventing her from living in 'trust and reciprocity'. So I believe that Nussbaum is right to emphasize that the facilitating environment must be here throughout a human life in order for that life to be a good one.

She says of laws protecting citizens from shame and stigma that they: '. . . play a role in making society the sort of place that protects human dignity, creating a "facilitating environment" in which citizens can live free from shame and stigma' and that this should be 'a fundamental goal of any decent society'.

It is my belief that Nussbaum's position can be defended by appealing to Plato's various arguments on the role of the laws, starting from the ones he offers in the *Crito* and the *Menexenus*. But other contemporary accounts seem to cast some doubt as to whether the laws can truly promote and protect virtue in a community. One particular reason to doubt that they can is the suspicion that when communities are virtuous, it has nothing to do with the law. One such example is the community of Chambon-sur-Lignon, a Huguenot village in the south of France. In July 1942, after the round up and deportation of Parisian Jews, following a sermon of their Pastor, the entire community decided to harbour Jewish families, hide them, and help them escape to Switzerland. Lawrence Blum, in his 'Community and Virtue' uses le Chambon as an example of a truly virtuous community:

> Le Chambon is a clear case of a 'community of virtue'. The tremendous dangers involved plus the absence of mechanisms of direct social pressure imply that the individual decisions to help the rescue effort can plausibly be inferred to be virtuous ones.[9]

But Blum emphasizes that nothing structured or official was at play in le Chambon, that what helped the community be virtuous was a mode of life, a shared history of oppression, and maybe also a sense of moral isolation from catholic France, and therefore of self-sufficiency. Certainly, the laws did not encourage virtue. In harbouring refugees, the citizens of le Chambon were breaking the law.

What Blum could deduce from his discussion of le Chambon is that the law is simply irrelevant when it comes to virtue. In order to become virtuous the members of the community need to be nurtured by something that is both less rigid, and closer to them. Laws are simply too distant to have that effect. A sermon from a loved and respected pastor, one that is heard in the village church one goes to every week, is more likely to affect us than a set of laws which most of the time, we are only familiar with insofar as they interfere with what we want to do. Again, a neighbour or a parent's virtuous example is more likely to motivate us than the threat of a policeman.

This strikes me as powerful objection to the claim that laws can and should provide a nurturing environment for virtue, namely, that they are by far less well fitted to do so than other aspects of community life. Yet, I believe the objection is misguided for the following reasons. First, the example of Le Chambon takes place at a time when the law of the state was not of a kind that could ever promote virtue. Many of its dictates were in fact unjust and it did not provide citizens with the opportunity to 'persuade' the law when they opposed it. This means that even if the citizens of Le Chambon acted virtuously in spite of the law, it does not follow that a better set of laws would not have strengthened their ability to make virtuous decisions.

Secondly, it seems that if we think of Le Chambon as having come to a decision independently of the law, we are using an unnecessarily narrow understanding of law. Laws are not merely represented by written edicts, but they are also embodied in institutions, such as educational and religious institutions. Educational institutions represent the law of the state. But the adult population of le Chambon had not been educated under the Vichy laws, and their education would have been governed by more virtue-promoting values, such as laicity and equality. Both these values would have been highly relevant in coming to a decision to help those victimized for no other reason than their religious affiliation. The Huguenot, or French protestant church also promotes certain values, and promotes them in a law-like way (maybe in order to set itself apart from what it saw as the laxity of the catholic church). Possibly the fact that the community of Chambon's religion set it apart from the rest of France meant that they remained more closely influenced by their church than the average French catholic in the 1940s would have been. In a time when legal institutions could not be respected, a church that was untouched by nazi supporters would have retained a strong hold on the community.

In general, institutions and policies can influence the way a community thinks, is and acts more directly than simple laws can. Martha Nussbaum, this time talking of the way 'maleness' is perceived in certain societies, writes on this topic that

> There are many ways in which laws and institutions can affect these norms: for example, through public education, formal and informal, through policies that give men incentives to participate more fully in

> childcare; and through parental leave and incentives to employers to create more flexible work policies.[10]

So when we say that the law of a state can and should promote and preserve virtue, we are referring as much as anything else, to legal institutions and policies. Given that in ancient Greece the written law was not particularly well-known by citizens, it makes a lot of sense to suppose that this also what Plato had in mind when he argued that the law, like a parent, created an environment in which flourishing could take place.

Of course, it is not just Plato and Aristotle who believe that laws can and should influence the formation of good character. Machiavelli, in *The Discourses*, writes:

> It is said therefore that Hunger and Poverty make men industrious, and Laws make them good. And where something by itself works well without law, the law is not necessary: but when that good custom is lacking, the law immediately becomes necessary.[11]

But for Machiavelli, the law shapes character through strong emotions, such as fear, or patriotic feeling, rather than systematically encouraging all virtues. Machiavelli's idea of the good citizen, although not as dire as legend would have it, is still very far from the liberal ideal. My contention here is that Plato's is not, but that for him, the virtue promoted by the law benefit the citizens themselves as well as the city. This means that for Plato, the influence of law ought to be more pervasive, and not just touch on those aspects of citizens' character that directly affect the government of the city. Nussbaum's example of how laws and institutions can influence how something like maleness is perceived in a society shows how deep the influence of law on character can go. More particularly, it shows that the influence of law is not limited to the public domain, but goes deep in the private layers of citizens' life.

Plato's mention of the laws of marriage and education shows just this and is especially relevant to current applications of the principle that good laws are character forming. Marriage laws which do not represent men and women as equal, who give men rights over women's property, or career, or even life, not only support certain human rights violating practices, but also nurture them. Simply getting rid of those laws would not be enough to change a society's way of thinking about marital relationships, or at least, not for a long time. What is needed is a new set of laws encouraging the right kind of behaviour, and these almost certainly have to be institutional.

For example, in many parts of Turkey, women have gone, in less than a century, from being little more than slaves to their ottoman husbands and fathers, to an almost equal social status to men. This was due, not only to the reform of marriage laws, and the creation of new laws allowing women to vote and making their attendance to school compulsory, but by having these laws reinforced in institutions. The reform itself, and the importance of educating girls as much as and together with boys is taught in primary schools. Children are encouraged to reflect on this and to compare their educational opportunities with those of children in other times or places. As for parts of the country where the educational reforms were not so effective, and where girls still do not always go to school, special programs are developed, in part designed to raise awareness amongst better-off parts of the population, that their way of life is better, and that they should help promote the same for others. Here again, it is institutions, not just laws, which are able to reach far enough into the 'private' sphere, so that perceptions of what is good may change, and so as to improve the general well-being of the country.

3. Alternative accounts: Slote and the *Republic*

In this section, I want to consider whether there is not a virtue ethical account of what it is for a law to be a good law available in a more obvious source than Plato's *Menexenus.* One such source is Plato's conception of the good state in the *Republic,* and another is Michael Slote's writings on virtue ethics. I will show that neither of these sources gives us a satisfactory account of just laws.

The first, most obvious place to look for a virtue ethical account of a just law, it seems, would be the *Republic,* where Plato talks at great length of what it is for a state to be a just state, based on his definition of what it is for a character to be just. The focus of the *Republic* is the soul on the one hand and the organization of the form of the ideal state on the other. Although in the latter capacity it describes at length the political organization of the city and the rationale for distributing political responsibility what it says about laws is fairly limited. It is therefore not a source that we can obviously contrast with the *Crito* and the *Menexenus,* which are specifically about laws.

Moreover, we cannot simply say that a just law is a law passed by a just state, as it is not clear either that any law passed by a just state must be just, nor that an unjust state cannot pass just laws. There is nothing unjust about the French law which proclaims a certain day in May to be mothers' day, even though that law was passed by the Vichy government. On the other hand, the British law that London cabs must carry a bail of hay at all times is unjust despite having been passed by a government which was not obviously unjust. The point is that laws have to be assessed in the socio-political context in which they are applied, and this may be very different from the socio-political context in which they were created. So while a good legislator may be a good judge of his or her society's needs at a given time, he or she cannot guarantee that the law will remain just at all times. This is why we need to be able to say more about what makes a law a just law, and why the *Republic* cannot provide us with an account.

In a paper where he discusses the punishment of war crimes,[12] Michael Slote (2001) argues that a law is just if it is put forward by a law-maker whose intentions are just:

> Thus national legislators who pass a law may do so for many different possible reasons, but we might want to say that if they do so out of a desire for the public good, or the good of their country, then the law they pass is justly enacted and is a just law; whereas, if they act from greed or narrow sectarianism, then they don't act justly and the law they pass is tainted with that injustice.[13]

At first sight, Slote's argument looks like it is not going to work. Good intentions do not make good laws. At the very least the law maker has to be virtuous, i.e. he or she has to be able to judge what effects a law will have on citizens so that the good intention can be borne out by the effects.

But even with the above amendment, the account remains unsatisfactory. Slote is using the premise that in virtue ethics, an action is praiseworthy if it is performed by a virtuous agent, in other words, actions derive their value from the state of the character of their performer. As passing a law is an action, it derives value from the character of whoever passes it, i.e. the law maker. However, Slote fails to note that a law is distinct from the act of passing a law, and thus, a law maker may act justly in passing a law, and at the same time, that law may be unjust. This is clearest if we consider that laws age and that a law passed by a just law maker may come to be – rightly – regarded as unjust, simply because the circumstances in which it is applied have changed, or our perceptions of them have evolved. Once again we can quote the taxi and bail of hay example. It may have been a wise move at the time the law was passed to make sure the working horses of London were well fed. But clearly, the lawmakers did not envisage that a short time hence, the law would be redundant because taxis would no longer be horse driven. Equally clearly, it was not a failure of wisdom on their part they did not envisage this: the prediction of scientific innovations and their social and moral implications is not part of being virtuous.

Because it would not have been possible for the most virtuous of law makers to foresee that the law would one day become unjust (for a law which allows taxi drivers to be fined for not carrying a bail of hay is unjust), then it cannot be a sufficient condition of a law being just that it should be passed by a virtuous law maker.[14] Once again, we can conclude that the argument in the *Menexenus* remains the best source for an account of what makes a law a good law.

4. The argument in the *Menexenus*

In this section, I turn to the argument given in the *Menexenus* to the effect that a law is just if it is capable of producing virtuous citizens. The *Menexenus* can be divided into four parts. 234a–236c introduces the unusual theme: Socrates is about to make a speech, and he claims to be good at speech making despite all he says about rhetoric in the *Gorgias*.[15] The second part 236d–239a describes the origins of Athens and the Athenians. Plato argues that the earth and the city of Athens are the true parents of the Athenians, from which it follows that all Athenians are brethren and thus should have equal political status. The third part 239a–246a gives a curiously anachronistic and heavily revised history of Athens. If any part of the dialogue is meant to be taken as either parody or political commentary then surely this is it. At least one commentator has read this passage as a direct criticism of Athenian policy at the time it was written.[16] The last part, 246b–249c, on the other hand, is the most obviously philosophical part of the dialogue.[17] Socrates uses it to speak in the voice of the dead soldiers to pass on a message to surviving parents, children and to the state. Platonic themes such as the unity of the virtues (246e), and justice as temperance (248a–c) are prominent, and as I will try to show, there is an important philosophical argument in this passage.

Commentators who see some serious import in the *Menexenus* tend to think that it is of a political nature rather than philosophical. In particular, both Huby (1957) and Kahn (1963) read the dialogue as a political pamphlet, one which is meant to shame the current Athenian government into changing some of its recent policies. Their views are supported by a plausible historical analysis of the dialogue and I do not wish to argue against them. Nonetheless, I believe that the dialogue also contains a self-standing philosophical argument to the effect that laws are just only if they enable citizens to flourish.[18]

The argument presented in the *Menexenus*, like the argument in *Crito* 50c–51c, is an argument by analogy, and it draws a conclusion about what it is for a law to be a good law from a premise about what it is for a parent to be a good parent. The conclusion of the argument is that the measure of a good legal system is its success at producing virtuous citizens. This conclusion is presented both implicitly and explicitly in the dialogue. It is explicit at the end of the second part of the dialogue, where Socrates links virtuous men and good governments:

> For government is the nurture of men, and the government of good men is good, and of bad men is bad. And I must show that our ancestors were trained under a good government and for this reason they were good. (238c)[19]

At this point in the dialogue, the conclusion is not wholly supported, but the analogy is under way: Socrates has already argued that Athens is a mother to the Athenians and that a mother's function is to nourish and nurture. But he has not made it clear that the nurturing of citizens consists in making them virtuous. This he says at 249a when he states that the city will be responsible for turning war orphans into virtuous citizens:

> While they are children she [the city] is a parent to them, and when they have arrived at man's estate she sends them to their several duties, in full armor clad; and bringing freshly to their minds the ways of their fathers, she places in their hands the instruments of their fathers' virtues.

This is an implicit statement of the conclusion: if the laws of Athens are good, this is what they should do, care for the virtuous growth of citizens. The implied criticism, in the face of proposed reform, is that they are not doing this as they should, and therefore are no longer good laws.[20]

The argument Plato uses in order to support the conclusion that a good law is one which nurtures virtue starts off with premises about what it is to be a good parent. As for the conclusion, the premises can be found (explicitly) in the second and (implicitly) in the fourth parts of the dialogue. In the second part of the dialogue, Plato makes the offensive claim that a mother who does not feed her infant is no mother at all (237e). This is not, however, a random misogynistic comment, but an unfortunately worded claim about the function of parenthood leading to the conclusion that the measure of a good parent is his/her ability to bring up children who are successful human beings, i.e. healthy and virtuous. (Presumably prior to the existence of powdered milk, a mother who was unable or unwilling to feed her babies would not have had much success at keeping them alive). A second premise is implicit in the fourth part of the dialogue, the *prosopeia* (discourse of the dead) where Plato claims that the best reward for parents is not grief at their death, but that their children should live as well, i.e. as virtuously, as they can (247a). The grief must be played down (nothing in excess) and efforts at virtue must become greater if one is to honour one's dead fathers rightly. This implies that a successful parent is one whose children are virtuous and so supports the conclusion we got from 237e.

To go from the conclusion that a successful parent is one who brings up virtuous children to the conclusion that a good legal system is one which supports the virtuous life in the city Plato needs to say that laws are as parents to citizens, i.e. we need the parent analogy. The dialogue is rife with references to the analogy, most notably at 237b:

> And the country which brought them up is not like other countries, a stepmother to her children, but their own true mother; she bore them and nourished them and received them, and in her bosom they now repose.

This passage gives us the core of the analogy. Family relationships are rooted in nature and need: the mother is by nature best suited to provide for the infant's needs. In the same way, the land by nature provides for its inhabitants (237e–238a) and enables them to grow strong enough so that they may give themselves a government (238b–c). Thereafter the land and the city jointly provide for and nurture the citizens of Athens: the city educates them (238c) while the land carries on her task of feeding them and receives them when they die (237b). This echoes the passage in the *Crito* (50c–d) in which the Personified Laws of Athens point out to Socrates that they have held a function both similar to, and higher than, that of parents by enabling his progenitors to marry and start a family, and by providing for his education. In both dialogues, the City is presented as natural, that is, something that can be viewed and judged in terms of the functions it fulfils.

My reading of the analogy may be challenged as follows. When Plato talks of the city being as a parent to the children of the diseased soldiers, he may be appealing to a different argument altogether: the soldiers lost their lives for the city, and as a result their children are orphans. The city is therefore under an obligation to replace the lost parents as well as it can. Maybe even more strongly, an agreement is hinted at between the city and the soldiers it sends to war. The soldiers risk their lives on the understanding that the city will look after their children if they die. But this argument is not by itself sufficient to show that the city can be as a parent to the war orphans: it has to be the case that it is capable of being parent-like. I may promise a friend that if he dies I will look after his business. But if I am not a businesswoman, and if I have not the required qualities to make a good businesswoman, I will not be able to fulfil my promise. In the same way, if the law is to stand as a parent to the children of the dead, then it must be in some way parent-like, i.e. it must be capable of fulfilling the function of parenthood. This will clearly be the case if the city is as a parent to citizens anyway: when the soldiers die, it is only required to be more particular in its care of the orphans, but it fulfils some kind of parenting function for all citizens anyway.[21]

5. Why the virtue politics account is not overly paternalistic

A virtue theory of law will almost certainly bring with it a worry about paternalism. There are several things we might mean by paternalism and various objections we might hold against it. The particular kind of paternalism which seems to come with a virtue ethical theory of laws, a kind which presents a threat to our ability to choose for ourselves the best life we can. The anti-paternalistic position virtue ethicists are up against can be outlined as follows: Parents make choices for children because children are not capable of choosing the best for themselves, as they are not yet fully rational. But once they reach an age which is commonly agreed to be the age of rational maturity (be it 18, 21, or some other age), their parents are no longer entitled to choose for them.[22] In the same way, laws cannot rule over an adult's life choices – provided these choices do not harm others.[23] That is, they have to respect what Joseph Raz (1986) refers to as people's ability to 'shape their life and determine its course "and to be" creators of their own moral world'.[24]

Of course these abilities are already seriously limited by various uncontrollable aspects of our culture and environment. Being born in a certain part of the world, a certain social class, to a particular religion and at a particular time, and being born a man or a woman all affect the choices we are able to make. Nonetheless, if the law makes it very difficult for an individual to question her moral beliefs (such that very few individuals will in fact be able to do so) and to decide for herself whether she wants to renew her allegiance to them, then that law is threatening her autonomy in the way that her cultural background is not: in the modern world it is plausible that a cultural background should be partially rejected or modified to suit individual choices, without risking anything other than censure;[25] but to reject a law is to become a criminal, to put oneself in a position where society has a right to exact revenge and impose its conception of the good.[26] A good liberal can hold that the shackles of tradition are meant to be shaken or broken – not so those of the law.

The idea that there should be virtue-promoting laws is especially open to the kind of anti-paternalist objection I have described. If laws promote virtues, then there seems to be a very clear sense in which they do not allow individuals to create their own moral world. For example, they would not encourage an individual to flourish as a 'controlled intemperate', someone who allowed himself to drink, eat and take drugs to excess, while there was nobody around who might be harmed by his behaviour. This person would have been taught, at an early age, that intemperance was a vice, and that moral worth was not to be measured by the consequences of one's actions, but by the state of the agent's character. So, more generally speaking, people could not choose to shape their lives according to consequentialist or deontological theories. So people who lived under virtue-promoting laws would not be the 'creators of their moral world'.

Here it may be objected that the virtue-promoting laws need not be coercive laws: they do not put people in jail for behaving in ways which encourage the development of vices, or which do not encourage the development of virtues.[27] Living in an intemperate manner (if no one else was harmed) need not be a crime, and the person who chose to live in that manner would not necessarily be punished. But the point is not that somebody's attempt to live according to different values would be thwarted by the laws, but that nobody would even think of challenging the moral world in which they were born. This is not equivalent to saying that people are shaped by their cultural, social and family background, and is therefore not open to the reply that people are often challenging the values they were given as children. If moral education were directed by the state, then the usual pathways through which one comes to challenge one's values would be closed: one would simply not be able to discuss different value systems and different moral theories with people who had been brought up differently. The uniformity of moral formation would make it much harder for people to choose their own moral way of thinking.

Although it is easy to see how the problem, stated above, might threaten a contemporary virtue jurisprudence, it is not clear that this would have been a problem for Plato in the same way. One might just say that autonomy is too new a concept for Plato to have been concerned with it, and hence, that we shouldn't look for a solution to the problem of paternalism in his writings. This is true in that when we talk about autonomy in a philosophical context, we usually refer to the concept introduced by Rousseau and Kant, i.e. the moral and political importance of being ruled from within. But there is also a sense of autonomy which simply emphasizes the rule of reason: an agent is autonomous if he or she is able to determine what they should do by using their reason. Although this may fall short of Kant and Rousseau's concepts (for Kant, reason must also be the good will, and for Rousseau, what matters is that one is part of the decision making body – not necessarily that the decision-making body is rational) there is also a sense in which this more basic notion has to be at the root of modern concepts of autonomy – the rule of reason being after all the central concept of the enlightenment from where these modern concepts came.

A second reason why one might resist the thought that Plato has anything useful to say about how the virtue ethicist could respond to paternalism, is that in the *Republic*, he presents us with the ultimate example of paternalism brought on by a concern for the virtues. In the *Republic*, Plato certainly emphasizes the need to be ruled by reason. Unless one's rational part is in charge of the emotions and appetites one cannot be psychically healthy, or just, and unless society is ruled by its most rational members, it cannot flourish, or be just. Yet, by Plato's own admission, very few people are capable of being ruled by their own reason. Most of us do not have a rational part of the soul strong enough to do that. Yet, it is best for us that we should be ruled by reason, otherwise, we cannot flourish. So Plato's solution is that those who are not capable of being ruled by their own rational part shall be ruled by those whose reason is strong enough to handle themselves and others: the philosopher kings. So it turns out that on Plato's account in the *Republic*, not everybody is capable of being autonomous, and paternalism is justified.

The *Republic* is a prime example of the worry that virtue-focused laws may lead to unacceptable degrees of paternalism. But when we look at a later dialogue, the *Laws*, it seems clear that Plato is aware that paternalism is a problem and that he is concerned to solve it. One of the most important claims in the *Laws* is that each law proposed for the new colony should be prefaced by a preamble, the point of which is to persuade citizens, by appealing to their reason, that they should obey this law. This means that citizens are expected, helped and encouraged to decide for themselves that they want to obey the a particular law. Granted, there are many problems with Plato's solution, not the least of them being that many commentators simply do not believe in the sincerity or coherence of his proposal. It is not obvious how these problems can be overcome if at all. But at this point, the important discovery is that Plato does see paternalism as a worry, and that he does care enough at least to propose a way in which citizens can both be ruled by virtue-focused laws and by their own reason. In this last section, I will show how Plato, even if he does not directly deal with the paternalism problem in the *Menexenus*, the parent analogy presents us with one way of doing so. In order to do so, I need to refer to yet another use of the parent analogy, one presented much later, in the *Laws*. This does not anticipate the contents of Chapter 7, as the parent analogy discussed here is not central to the arguments I wish to focus on in that chapter. The use of the analogy in the *Laws* is nonetheless useful in order to show how the problem of paternalism arising in the *Menexenus* might be at least partially solved.

It seems that to legislate on the principle that the good life is the virtuous life endangers people's autonomy in that it prevents them from choosing for themselves a moral way of thinking. It is nonetheless true that autonomy requires the capacity to choose, that is, being informed about what choices are available, being able to reflect on the short and long term consequences they are likely to have, and on whether our several choices are compatible with each other. It follows that one virtue, wisdom, may be promoted without endangering autonomy: on the contrary, promoting wisdom is tantamount to helping people become more autonomous. If the virtue ethicist can limit her claim to the idea that laws should be wisdom-promoting, then the paternalism threat disappears.[28]

In order to show that the virtue ethicist can do just that, I turn once more to a parent analogy in Plato, but this time in the *Laws*. In Book III, 687d–e, the Athenian describes a father's attitude to his child's dreams as one of fear and worry that they should come true. This passage is suggestive. The parent often shudders at his child's ambitions, whether it be to become a soldier or a princess – equally frightening prospects. The parent does not necessarily see her role as removing these ambitions and replacing them with suitable ones. Nor does she encourage them or just wait and see whether they come to be realized and then bemoan the fact that they have. The parent's wish in Plato's *Laws* is this: that his child may acquire enough wisdom so that he may, come the time, make the best choices. Parental intervention thus takes the form of teacher of wisdom. In true Plato style, this example is then used as an analogy for the law/citizen relationship:

> I, for my part, urged that this is an injunction to legislate with a view to one single virtue out of four. He should keep them all in his view, I said, and in the first place that virtue which brings all the rest in its train, that is, judgement, intelligence, and right conviction attended by appropriate passionate desire.[29]

The *Laws'* proposal deflects paternalism without losing any ground for virtue ethics. Either Plato is right that the good life is the virtuous life or he is wrong. If he is wrong then the effect of wisdom-promoting laws will not be to impose the virtuous life as the best life, but merely to put people in a position to choose for themselves which life is the best life (as long as it is not harmful to others). So people will be able to 'create their own moral worlds' and live according to consequentialist, deontological or other moral norms. There is more in the *Laws* that is designed to solve the paternalism problem. The Laws' parent analogy is not central to Plato's solution of that problem, but it is useful in order to highlight how one might address the problem within the framework of the parent analogy. I will come back to Plato's solution to the paternalism problem in Chapter 7.

If Plato is right that the virtuous life is the best life, then wisdom-promoting laws will ensure that individuals flourish without endangering their autonomy. This is true whether or not we accept the unity of virtue thesis. If we do, then we believe that a wise person will necessarily be courageous, temperate and just. But if we don't we may still claim that someone who is wise will realize for herself that she needs virtue to flourish, and helped by her wisdom, will seek the virtues. Either way, the wisdom-promoting laws do not impose on the subject a conception of the good – but help her seek and achieve her own.

The claim that laws should be wisdom-promoting gives us a minimalist kind of paternalism. The laws do not make it their business to teach all citizens to be virtuous. On the assumption that wise people will know what is best for them and make the right choices, the laws only need to ensure that wisdom prevails. This leaves laws with two main tasks: to educate the young into wisdom, and to preserve a peaceful, stable and prosperous environment in which wisdom may be sustained. This covers laws on education, and laws which prevent harm to others, but it is not obvious that this virtue ethicist account will warrant other laws – it will be expected that citizens who have been properly educated will on the whole know how to make the right choices. If the system fails them and they make choices that threaten others, then they are faced with the laws designed to protect the environment – and these laws will therefore act as deterrent, or failing this, as protection. Thus the account I have described, according to which the function of laws is to promote wisdom in the community, gives us a very minimalist legal system – one which even Mill might find acceptable.

Of course, this is still paternalism of some kind, as the laws' role is not value free, and laws do impose some conception of the good upon citizens. At the same time, it must be very difficult to claim convincingly that one has no need to be wise, and that it is nobody's business but ours if we do not choose wisdom for our children. In other words, if the argument in the *Laws* suggests paternalism, it is not the kind of paternalism which we ought to reject. If we combine this reading of the *Laws* with the argument in the *Menexenus*, then we are left with a parent analogy which is not viciously paternalistic on account of imposing a conception of the good on citizens which leaves them no room for personal choice. The parent analogy, therefore, cannot be rejected on grounds that it is unduly paternalistic. I will take up this problem again when I discuss the *Republic* in Chapter 5, and finally in Chapter 7 on the *Laws*.

Chapter 4

Virtue as Mental Health in the *Gorgias* and Other Dialogues

If virtue jurisprudence is to be a viable option, it should depend on a plausible moral psychology that is capable of being translated into laws. Namely it has to be the case that

1. human beings have character traits which are capable of becoming virtues or vices,
2. human beings are better off if they are virtuous than if they're not,
3. there are mechanisms which enable the development of virtues,
4. these mechanisms can be embedded in laws.

In the first three chapters, I have begun to address the third and fourth points. I have suggested that character traits could become virtues through a process of habituation of the kind that is encouraged by parental rules, and that laws that are capable of reproducing this process thereby providing an environment in which it is possible for all citizens to flourish. I have argued, further, that this function of the law should be the basis for the duty to obey, i.e. that we obey if and because the laws promote and protect an environment in which it is possible for us to become virtuous.

In the preceding chapters it has also become apparent that the claim that the laws are virtue-promoting has two drawbacks. First it is not clear that laws can in fact reproduce the habituation mechanism since they are by nature general, and virtues, which focus on particular aspects of a person's character, and of the situations in which we are called to act, do not easily translate into a set of rules. Secondly, it appeared that a system of laws based on virtue would run the risk of being paternalistic, namely, that it would not grant citizens the freedom to decide for themselves what a good life for them would be.

I will return to these problems in Chapters 6 and 7. But the last one is reflected in virtue ethics itself: who is Plato to tell us what the good life is?

Is he appealing to an objective psychology that he can demonstrate is true or just imposing his personal ideals on us? It is in response to this worry that in this chapter and the next I will address the first two of the four points listed above, namely:

1. Is there such a thing as character traits that can become virtues?
2. Are human beings always better off when they are virtuous?

In the first two sections, I will discuss in some detail the moral psychology put forward by Plato in several dialogues but in particular in the *Gorgias* and the *Republic.* I call his theory the virtue/health analogy. I will show how in the *Gorgias* Plato uses a medical model to develop the virtue/health analogy, and how this model is a plausible one. A serious objection to Plato's model comes from social psychology's claim that character is a fiction, and the virtues or vices we believe we have do not in fact affect our actions. In Section 3, I will address this objection and show that it is grounded in certain misunderstandings of what virtue ethics suppositions are. Then, in order to link the discussion back to the third and fourth points, i.e. whether there is a mechanism for becoming virtuous and whether laws can appropriate this mechanism, I will look at the implication of the medical model of virtue for penology. In Chapter 5, I will turn more specifically to the paternalistic implications of the medical model with reference to the *Republic.*

1. The model of psychic health in Plato

For the project of virtue politics to work, we need to show that a character-based theory of ethical behaviour can be given content that is both coherent, and detailed enough to ground a moral psychology. What we need is a plausible theory in which character development is central and which holds that it is better for the agent if she is virtuous. This is a difficult task as the theory has to be detailed enough to be explanatory. We could just say that, generally speaking, human beings flourish when their characters develop in a certain way. But the only way for this kind of claim not to be dismissed as unacceptably vague is to turn to relativism, i.e. to say that we each flourish in our own way. This, however would lead to some very unpleasant moral claims, such as 'my character flourishes when I commit acts of violence, so for me, violence is a virtue'. For this reason, it is better if we can give a more detailed account of flourishing.

In the first part of this chapter, I will argue that Plato does offer a theory of human flourishing which uses the concept of health as central, and a medical model to explain how health of the soul can be promoted and maintained through just and unjust acts.[1] To begin with, I will try to establish that Plato does indeed claim that virtue or justice are some kind of healthy state of the soul.[2] However, this is subsidiary to my main claim which I shall defend in the next section, that the model does indeed deserve to be taken seriously and that the attractive feature of Plato's conception of health is that it does not rely on a narrow medical model of cure and disease, but appeals to a generally more satisfactory model in which development and prevention are central.

The key claim I wish to defend in this section is that Plato intended the analogy of virtue with health to be taken seriously. This does not necessarily mean that it should be taken literally, but that there should be a significantly large number of points of comparison between health and virtue so that we could be justified in using the term mental health to refer to virtue.[3] The difference between taking the analogy literally and merely taking it very seriously is cashed out in the following problematic. Do we have a concept of health which is the same in bodily health and mental health, or do we have a concept of bodily health from which we derive a concept of mental health because there are many and obvious points of comparison between the good functioning of the mind and that of the body? Whatever the answer, we still end up, it seems, with a pretty solid concept of mental health, one which legitimizes the psychiatric classification and treatment of mental illness. For this reason, I propose that we consider only the question whether Plato meant us to take the analogy seriously, without asking further whether he meant us to take it literally.

Plato's early and middle dialogues are ripe with evidence that he took the health analogy very seriously indeed. In the *Republic*, for example, he writes that justice and injustice

> are in the soul what the healthful and the diseaseful are in the body; there is no difference. [. . .]
>
> Virtue then would be a kind of health and beauty and good condition of the soul, and vice would be disease, ugliness and weakness.[4]

There are also many such references to it in earlier dialogues. In the *Crito* (47e–49a) it is central to the argument for the conclusion that Socrates should not escape: if unjust actions harm the soul as unhealthy ones harm the body, then Socrates must avoid injustice at all costs, even that of his life. According to the *Protagoras* (313a–c) going to consult a sophist is to expose one's soul to a treatment or cure which may turn out to be harmful. At *Gorgias* 464a, Socrates explicitly says that there is a healthy condition (euexia) for the soul as for the body, as well as an apparent but false health for both. At 480a–b, he recommends that one who does wrong go to a judge as to a doctor in order to prevent the sickness of injustice from festering in the soul and becoming incurable:

> But if he is guilty of wrongdoing, either himself or anyone else he may care for, he must go of his own freewill where he may soonest pay the penalty, to the judge as if to the doctor, with the earnest intent that the disease of his injustice may not become chronic and cause a deep incurable ulcer in his soul.

In the *Republic* Plato elaborates on what psychic health actually consists in. In Book IV he tells us that for someone to be psychically healthy, he must have

> attained to self-mastery and beautiful order within himself, and [. . .] harmonised these three principles [the three parts of the soul: reason, the emotions or high spirit, and the appetites], the notes or intervals of these three terms quite literally the lowest, the highest, and the mean, and all the others there may be between them, and [. . .] linked and bound all three together and made himself a unit, one man instead of many, self-controlled and in unison.[5]

Although the analogy here appears to be musical, rather than medical, Plato does maintain, a few lines further at 444c that a soul which has not reached this harmony is sick in some way. Thus there seems to be a three way analogy going on, between justice, health and music.

Harmony is attained when each part fulfils its proper role, which means that the rational part of the soul, aided by the *thumos*, must rule over the entire soul 'being wise and exercising forethought in behalf' of it (441d–e). That this is what psychic health consists in is deduced by Plato from a consideration that health in general depends on the establishment in something of 'natural relations' amongst its parts. Just as a body becomes diseased if its parts behave 'contrary to nature' (444d), the soul will not be healthy if the rational part does not rule over the appetites and the thumos. Because of this we should understand the analysis of the soul as tripartite in Book IV as an attempt to describe the mechanics of psychic health in the same way that a treatise on anatomy can serve to explain what it is to have a healthy body. Only by understanding how the parts relate to each other can we hope to understand how the whole functions.

From the picture of justice as psychic health, it follows that we can apply a medical model to our understanding of vice and virtue.[6] A soul which is dominated by either the appetites or the thumos is, according to Plato, diseased or in some way not functioning at its full strength. In Books VIII and IX Plato explains the different ways in which a soul may be diseased. For example, the type Plato refers to as tyrannical, which applies to those who are ruled by their appetites, will inevitably 'always be needy and suffer from unfulfilled desire', 'be full of terrors and alarms', and be 'maddened by [. . .] desires and passions' (578a). These descriptions leave open the possibility that failures of psychic health manifest themselves over a wide range of disorders, from mere neediness to actual madness. We must bear this in mind when replying to critics who argue that Plato believes all non-virtuous agents are mad (I will introduce these objections briefly in the following section and discuss these in the next chapter as they apply principally to the problem of paternalism in the *Republic*).

2. How the model works: elenchos as therapy

A critique of Plato's analogy of virtue and health, Anthony Kenny[7] has claimed that the analogy is unacceptable because it entails that vice is a defect and therefore that criminals are all mad. Kenny's objection could be summarized thus. If we say that virtue is health, then vice is sickness, i.e. mental illness. But the mentally ill are very vulnerable to the control of psychiatric doctors. They often have no choice as to whether and how they should be treated. Also, Kenny claims that according to Plato the mentally ill have no property rights and no right to the truth. Moreover, as Plato appears to believe that only the philosopher kings are virtuous, it follows that he must believe most of us are insane. He can therefore recommend a totalitarian regime in which we are all under the control of philosophers/psychiatrists.[8]

In Chapter 5, I will address this objection in some detail, paying particular attention to the allegations of paternalism. In this section I will simply show that the conception of health Plato worked with is not the narrow one his critiques have in mind, i.e. something that can go wrong only with sickness and be redressed by cures only. On the contrary for Plato, health is something that must be attained, and maintained, and things can go wrong at any time in the process without requiring medical intervention in the form of cure. It follows from this wider conception that only in very few cases does failure of mental health equate with madness.

The implications of the analogy for the medical understanding and treatment of vice, however, are clearest, not in the *Republic,* but in earlier dialogues, especially the *Gorgias.* There Plato presents an argument which pertains to the ways and means in which mental health can be achieved, and its conclusion is that in order to be mentally healthy we must practice the elenchos, i.e. the Socratic method of inquiry.

Without suggesting that criminals should be forced to enrol in Phil. 101 courses, Plato's linking of philosophy and health is useful because it shows both how his model of mental health corresponds to a medical model we are familiar with (one in which health is pursued as well as rescued) and at the same time different from a medical model we would find objectionable were it to be applied to the mental domain (i.e. that which is concerned only with cure).

A medical model which most of us would be comfortable with would regard cure as a last resort only. It would emphasize preventive actions, negative (do not smoke, do not eat too much fat or sugar) and positive (exercise regularly, eat plenty of fruit and vegetable). And rather than listing the things we can and can't do, it would aim to develop 'health consciousness', i.e. a disposition to think about what may or may not be good for one's health, an acquired disposition to prefer healthy foods and activities to unhealthy ones, and a certain familiarity with our body's reactions leading to a knowledge of what is in fact harmful or beneficial for us. This would take care of development: people who are health conscious, or whose carers are health conscious, are more likely to grow strong and healthy, and less likely to contract diseases.

Health consciousness, however, is unfortunately not sufficient to ward off all ills. Luck and genes play a part in how long we can stay healthy, or even whether we are able to become healthy at all (congenital diseases may have nothing to do with how healthy the parents of the sick baby are). So cure, it seems, will be the most important part of any medical model after all. Whatever we do, we may become ill, and we will have to see a doctor for a cure. But this does not quite follow. A disease may be detected before it has properly developed, and actions can be taken to prevent it from developing without requiring a major intervention on the patient's body. For instance, a wound will be disinfected, so as to prevent gangrene, and the necessity of amputation; a mole will be removed, to stop cancer from developing, thus preventing future invasive treatment. This, however, the dealing with a minute symptom in order to prevent grave illness from developing, requires early detection of symptoms which may be invisible to all but a medical doctor. So what it requires, is that we submit ourselves to regular check ups so that anything unusual may be detected and dealt with before it becomes a problem. If that works, then we put one more step between us and serious medical intervention or cure.

Of course, this system of development and prevention may fail, the symptoms may be too minute even for a doctor to detect, or they may develop in between two check ups (although not if the check ups are close enough together), or worse, there may be no known way of stopping them from developing. In this case, we need to turn to medicine for the purpose of curing illness, or if that is not possible, for palliative purposes. This, however, comes last in our expectations of what medicine should do for us. First we expect that it should help us grow strong and healthy, second that it should detect anything which is likely to develop into a disease or illness before it does. Cure should be, as far as most of us are concerned, a last resort only. In what follows I will argue that the medical model Plato uses when drawing the virtue/health analogy is similar to the one I have just described, i.e. that in order to be psychically healthy one must follow the same three steps: first developing a healthy soul, second, checking regularly for symptoms of diseases, and third, cure as a last resort.

To become 'health conscious' means becoming aware of what will benefit or harm the body and acquiring a set of healthy habits, including diet and exercise. If the body/soul analogy is to hold, then the same must be true of psychic health. In order to acquire a healthy soul, we must first become aware of what contributes to its health, and actively seek it. In the case of bodily health, a doctor will tell us what it is we need to do in order to become healthy, and – if we're lucky – a trainer, or maybe some health institution will help us to stick to it. According to Plato, there is a mental equivalent to this kind of preventive therapy in the elenchos. The philosopher, like the physician, and the trainer, pursues citizens and urges them to 'set their thoughts on goodness', to stop worrying about secondary goods, such as wealth and get their souls into shape. Thus, Socrates sees his role in Athens in this way: he has to engage the Athenians into philosophical debate about the nature of virtue, the dialectical nature of the elenchos meaning that it will encourage debate and make the citizens take an active part in the well-being of their souls.[9]

By discussing philosophical questions about virtue, the Athenians become virtue-conscious, i.e. not only do they come closer to understanding what virtue is, but they become habituated to thinking that virtue and virtuous behaviour matter, and thus are more likely to behave virtuously themselves.

According to the medical model we described, the second function of the elenchos has to be to test the soul in the same way that a doctor will carry out routine checks on the body to detect any illness. This will enable the person whose soul or body it is to prevent defects from developing, and to acquire peace of mind if she is healthy. This must be what Socrates has in mind when at 487d, he compares Callicles to a touchstone, one which will tell him of the state of his soul, if he engages in an elenctic dialogue with him.

Although this passage is obscured by poetic licence and rather strong irony,[10] it none the less sheds some light on one of the purposes of the elenchos. If it turned out that an ideal interlocutor agreed with what Socrates believes about virtue, then not only would Socrates' beliefs be true, but his soul would be cared for and in good condition. Conversely, if the interlocutors disagree, then the beliefs held by them have to be further examined, for they might be false, and the soul which hosts these beliefs is unhealthy.

It is in this spirit that Socrates enjoins Polus at 475d to submit himself to the elenchos:

> Don't shrink from answering, Polus – you won't be harmed at all; but present yourself nobly to the argument (logos) as to a doctor; answer, and say either yes or no to what I'm asking you.

In this passage (473a–475d) the argument is presented as a doctor, and the elenchos as the cure. This confirms our hypothesis as to the second function of the elenchos: to test the patient's soul as a doctor would carry out a check on a patient's body. If the test shows that the soul is sound, 'well cared for', then there is nothing to worry about. If it does not, then the elenchos must perform its third function, i.e. cure the soul.

Just how the elenchos achieves this is probably what Socrates is alluding to at 458ab when he remarks to Gorgias:

> For I think that being refuted (elenchesthai) is a greater good, insofar as it is a greater good for a man to get rid of the greatest evil himself than to rid someone else of it – for I think there is no evil for a man as great as a false belief about the things which our discussion is about now.

Plato's view of how the elenchos affects mental health forces us to question the model of medical care as cure only, and its implication that the only way in which one can fail to be healthy is by being ill or diseased. Plato encourages us to focus on what we know already, namely that physical development and maturation are necessary before we can stop worrying about bodily health, and that diet and exercise need attention in order for health not to deteriorate. Thus it would be a mistake to assume that the only way in which someone may fail to be mentally healthy is by being mentally ill – questions must be asked about the maturation and development of the subject's mind. This implies that it would also be a mistake to believe that any failure of mental health must be 'cured'. We do not 'cure' a child who is not growing enough, we control her diet and make sure she gets all the right nutrients, and we do not 'cure' an adult who is unhealthy due to being overweight until he has tried to modify his exercise regime.

Plato's model of mental health, therefore, does not imply that all criminals should be cured. It implies, however that everyone should pay greater attention to their psychic development so as to mature in such a way that we will not be likely to develop vicious character traits. So far, we are able to draw the following conclusion. Plato's use of the medical model does not imply that all who are not virtuous are mad and should be subjected to psychiatric treatment,[11] or give up their autonomy to those who are not mad. What it does imply is that psychic health is not a given, but something which must be developed through careful maturation, and which must be watched over throughout one's life – as it is true of physical health. Absence of virtue is thus more likely to mean incomplete development than disease, and thus the adequate response is education rather than psychiatric treatment or confinement.

3. Virtue and the situationists

In the late 1990s, philosophers who had read and been impressed by the findings of social psychologists 20 years earlier started to challenge the view that any character-based ethical theory was viable. Specifically targeted was virtue ethics. The central claim of virtue ethics is that good and bad should be judged not by looking at actions and how they accord with rules or not, but at the character of the agent, whether she is courageous, just, temperate and wise (These are specifically the ancient's virtues, but we could add to the list generous, honest and many others).

Underlying the claim that ethical praise belongs to character, not actions is the belief that human beings have character traits which are capable of becoming virtues, given the right kind of training. But social psychologists had apparently been saying that there was no such thing as stable character traits that would reliably determine what a particular agent would do on any occasion. Instead, the main causal factor was the situation itself, i.e. given a particular situation, most agents will react to it in the same way, regardless of the virtues or vices they believe themselves, (or are believed by others) to have.

There are several experiments which philosophers who believe that situationism can undermine virtue ethics commonly refer to. I will concentrate on two of these experiments which the philosophical literature discusses the most.[12] The first is the 'Dime helping' experiment, conducted by Isen and Levin in 1972. Forty-two subjects were observed leaving a phone booth. For some of those subjects, a coin was left in the return slot for them to find, but not for the others (the control group). As they were leaving they were confronted with an actor dropping their papers on the floor. Isen and Levin found that the subjects who had found a coin in the return slot were more likely to help pick up the files than those who did not.

The second experiment which has been discussed in the philosophical literature on situationism is the infamous Milgram experiment, in which 'teacher' subjects are told that they will participate in a study on the effects of punishment on learning. They are asked to inflict electroshocks on a 'learner' subject (in fact an actor) when he fails to give the right answers to questions. The buttons for dispensing the electric shocks were labelled from 'very strong' to 'XXX', and despite the screams of the 'learner', most subjects carried on inflicting shocks as long as they were told to do so by the men in the white coats.

In response to the situationists' findings, one might be tempted simply to cave in. Maybe Plato and Aristotle just got it wrong. Maybe we should be grateful to the social psychologists for correcting our antiquated 'folk' theories of character, in pretty much the same way as their predecessors freed us from our false beliefs about phrenology. However we should be cautious before embracing theories which claim to make fundamental enduring beliefs redundant, especially when these beliefs happen to be shared by Plato, Aristotle and others. So before accepting what philosophers tell us social psychologists have to say, there are two questions we should ask. First, do the experiments actually show what philosophers who take them up believe they show? Secondly, whether they do that or not, is what they purport to show actually inconsistent with virtue ethics? I will address both questions in turn.

(i) Do the experiments show what philosophers think they do?

The first question is whether the experiments conducted by social psychologists have been interpreted in the right light by the philosophers who discuss them, and whether they do in fact show what these philosophers take them to show. A certain amount of scepticism is warranted here: the experiments referred to in the philosophical literature are old, conducted in the 1960s and the 1970s.[13] They are also taken somewhat out of context and the impression is given that social psychologists conducted these experiments with the explicit purpose of defeating virtue ethics, which, given the fairly recent renewal of interest in the virtues, is anachronistic. At any rate, these experiments are interpreted as attempts to revolutionize our way of thinking about ethics, and agency.

More recent takes on the experiments by psychologists tell a slightly different story. According to one psychology textbook, it is highly doubtful whether anyone took the social psychology experiments to entail that character traits did not exist at all. The view expressed in that textbook is that the experiments were simply intended as a corrective to what might be termed the 'naïve and extreme trait attribution theory', the view that all human behaviour can be explained in terms of character traits which are easily and immediately identifiable.[14] The naïve and extreme trait theory would warrant the following inferences. Imagine that a person walks past someone in obvious need of help. The naïve and extreme trait theory will have us believe that a helpful person will almost certainly help, and that if the person does not help, it is a sure sign that he or she is not helpful. In other words, whatever we do or not do is an expression of our inner character and has nothing to do with the situation. Clearly such a view needs moderating and if the purpose of the social psychologists experiments was to do that, then the experiments must have been welcome indeed.

However, it is important that we distinguish at an early stage between this 'naïve and extreme trait attribution theory' and virtue ethics. 'Traits' as understood by the naïve theory are not the same thing as virtues. Virtues are usually defined as stable character traits, and are differentiated from mere dispositions. One may have a tendency or disposition to be helpful, but, as Kant remarked long before social psychology came along, a bad day can weigh against this disposition and nullify its effects. A virtue on the other hand is anchored in the character. It is a disposition that has been trained, consciously, that has been recognized, accepted as good, and worked on. A virtuous person knows how to be helpful even in cases when it is hardest to be so. In fact, a virtuous person will have practised being helpful on a bad day.

Some psychologists reacted to the situationist experiments by remarking that if we are really interested in testing character, then we need to conduct longitudinal studies rather than cross-situational ones, i.e. studies that show character development and consistency over a life-span.[15] It certainly seems that this would be a better way of testing for the growth and presence of virtues in an individual than any of the situationist experiments. In what follows, I would like to focus on certain aspects of two of the experiments referred to in the philosophical literature, aspects which show that the experiments are not really suited to help us draw conclusions as to the existence of virtues.[16]

The dime helping experiment conducted by Isen and Levin in the early 1970s follows subjects as they leave a phone booth. A confederate walking ahead of them suddenly drops a folder and the files fall on the floor at the subject's feet. The question is 'does the subject help pick up the files?' For a random group of these subjects, it was arranged that they would find a dime in the return slot. The other group had no dime. The first experiment, conducted by Isen and Levin in 1972 found that out of 42 subjects, most of those who found the dime helped pick up the files, but most of those who did not find a dime did not help. If the experiment does in fact work, it is a very significant one as far as the theory that character determines behaviour is concerned. It shows that a trivial difference in the situation appears to cause a significant difference in the subjects' behaviour. The triviality of the situational variable means that it is not possible to respond to the experiment that the situational factors put such pressure on the agents that even very virtuous agents would have failed to respond appropriately. It shows that if our behaviour can be swayed by something so small, then character, if it has any effect at all, is mostly very weak indeed. Whereas this does not entail that there cannot be some people who have character traits strong enough to be termed virtues, it makes it unlikely that virtue ethics should be the best way of explaining what it is for human beings to be good. It would make it unrealistic for most of us to succeed in attaining anything resembling excellence.

This explains why the experiment has been taken to be such a strong objection against virtue ethics. But a closer look at what happened on the psychologists' side tells a different story. Two years after the original experiment, it was reproduced in the same conditions by Blevins and Murphy, but this time the findings were quite different. Most of the subjects, whether or not they had a dime, failed to help, in the same proportions. The experimenters concluded that there was in fact no relationship between finding a dime and helping. That the experiment failed to repeat once does not show, of course that its results are worthless, but it is enough to cast serious doubt as to their implications for moral philosophy. Isen and Levin repeated their own experiment with more success in 1975, but further experiments by other groups were also inconclusive.

If the dime helping experiment fails to show what philosophers who use it to undermine virtue ethics think it shows, this is even more true of the Milgram experiment. The Milgram experiment has 40 subjects told that they are going to take part in a 'teaching' experiment, not as subjects, but as 'teachers'. They are placed in a room separated by a glass partition from a pretend 'learner' subject. The teachers ask questions which the learners must answer. If the learner gets the answer wrong, the 'teacher' is told by a man in a white coat standing next to them to press a button dispensing increasingly high electric shocks to the 'learner'. There are several buttons each labelled with voltage and danger (e.g. 300 volts, extremely intense), so that the 'teachers' know what they are doing. They can also observe the results of their actions on the 'learners' who's job it is to 'act' in accordance with the shock the 'teachers' think they are administrating, i.e. begging for the experiment to stop, screaming, then passing out.

The results of the experiment were alarming. All 40 subjects went past 150 volts (labelled 'very strong'). Only 5 of them (just over 10 per cent) stopped at 300 ('extremely intense'), and 65 per cent continued till the end even though the 'learner' had apparently stopped responding. What this seems to show, is that out of 40, otherwise 'normal' people, nearly all of them are capable of behaving like dangerous sadists if they are told to do so by a figure of authority. This is indeed an appalling conclusion, but maybe not entirely surprising. After all, the human characters' tendency to be swayed by authority and the need to obey over virtues such as compassion has been well documented by Hannah Arendt's observations on the Eichmann trial. Obedience may be a virtue, but it is one that has a sad propensity to turn to a vice of excess and take away all other virtues.

However, discussions of whether obedience is a virtue and whether most of us are capable of behaviour worse than we'd care to imagine is besides the point that Harman, at least, is trying to make. The Milgram experiment does not show that situation alone determines behaviour. If that were the case, then given an identical situation, all subjects would behave in an identical manner. But they certainly did not. More than 10 per cent stopped at 300 volts, and 65 per cent continued to the end. That leaves 25 per cent stopping somewhere between the two. This means there is in fact significant variation in the subjects' responses. Maybe we tend not to notice this because their behaviour is, to our eyes, equally horrifying. However, this is not what Harman wants the results of the experiment to show. In order to pause a real threat to the concept of character, it would have to show that behaviour is entirely determined by the situation. It does not.

(ii) Do the experiments pose a threat to virtue ethics?

The second question with which I chose to approach the situationist challenge was whether the results of the experiment, whether or not they are true, are of a nature to pose a threat to virtue ethics. I think they are not, mostly because the challenge rests on certain misconceptions as to what virtue ethics entails. Once these misconceptions are cleared, it becomes clear that virtue ethics can survive the situationist challenge even if the experiments did show what they purported (or were understood) to show. Possibly the most convincing of the philosophers defending situationism, J. M. Doris sets up the contradiction between the claims of virtue ethics and the findings of social psychology in this way.[17] Virtues are supposed to be 'robust' character traits which are 'substantially resistant to contrary situational pressures in their behavioral manifestations' (1998, 506). In other words, a virtuous agent will act virtuously in a consistent manner, across a wide range of situations in which her character is being tested. By contrast, experiments in social psychology show that most people tend to react to the same situations in the same way, regardless of what character traits they are supposed to have: 'systematic observation typically reveals failures of cross-situational consistency; behavior is often surprisingly unreliable. We have good reason to consider an alternative, more empirically adequate, conception of moral personality' (1998, 507).

Without questioning either Doris's description of a virtuous agent, or the findings of the experiments (although, as we saw, these are far from reliable), I want to suggest that nonetheless the experiments do not necessarily undermine virtue-based ethical theories. This is because, according to the kind of virtue ethics that can be derived from Plato, for instance, there is no reason to expect 'cross-situational consistency' of character traits on a large scale, such as would be noticeable in the results of an experiment. This for two reasons: first, the virtue ethicist shares Doris's claim that the situation matters morally, and will try to avoid certain situations which they deem to be bad for their character development. Secondly, although virtue ethicists do believe that virtues are robust character traits, they do not, by any means, have to believe that there are many full-blown virtuous agents. Most of us will have flailing virtues, growing stronger maybe, but not yet robust enough to withstand the tricks of the social psychologists.

A corollary of this claim, which I will defend alongside it, is that as far as virtue ethicists are concerned, character traits which are not virtues tend not to be robust. I will argue for each of those claims in turn.

A good way to understand how a normal agent is likely to weigh the relative dangers of situation vs character is to take a real life example, rather than an artificial one created for the sake of an experiment. This is what Doris does when he gives the following example. Imagine your partner is away, and a colleague who is clearly interested in you invites you to dinner. The situation, should you choose to accept the invitation, clearly presents risks. After a few glasses of wine, given the right atmosphere, you might let yourself be seduced. According to Doris, then, the right thing to do is to refuse the invitation:

> you might think that there is little cause for concern; you are, after all, a morally upright person, and a spot of claret never did anyone a bit of harm. On the other hand, if you take the lessons of situationism to heart, you avoid dinner like the plague, because you know that you may not be able to predict your behavior in a problematic situation on the basis of your antecedent values.

The plausibility of his example serves to support his view that character traits, and virtues are redundant when we try to understand moral problems. For in this case, if we rely on character, rather than situation, we will get it wrong. Someone who goes to dinner thinking that their upright character will see them through a pleasant evening out with no personal risk is fooling herself. But is that to say that such a person is one we would call virtuous? It seems to me that a person who uses their character as an excuse to indulge in slightly dubious going-ons is not virtuous. It seems on the contrary that this person is suffering from a severe case of self-deception. I am faithful, she says, so there is no harm in my going out with X who is trying to seduce me, because I will not be seduced. So I can enjoy a pleasant evening in X's company at no personal risk. But we have to suspect that the most pleasant prospect of the evening is the possibility that she might succumb to X's attempts, and that she is using her virtue as an excuse to go ahead in spite of the risk!

In order to see why a truly virtuous agent who thought that their character had an effect on their actions would not behave in the way Doris describes, let us take another example. Imagine that there is a building in your area which is known to be dangerous. It is either old and liable to collapse, inhabited by bears, or haunted. There is a clear sign on the building saying 'enter this building at your own risk'. Would a courageous person, seeing this sign, decide that her courage will protect her from any dangers (or enable them to deal with them well), disregard the sign and go in? No, she won't. Not, at least, unless she has a very good reason to do so (for instance rescuing some mindless idiot who went in earlier and is now buried under the ceiling/eaten by bears/scared to death by ghosts). A courageous person does not go into danger simply because it is there. What might motivate someone to do something like this is the need to prove to themselves or others that they are indeed courageous, curiosity, boredom or a death-wish, but not the confidence that one will be able to deal well with any dangers that come our way.

What I am trying to show by this example is that a virtuous person does not regard their virtue as a reason to go into a situation that will test that virtue unless they have other, very good reasons to do it. So what will a virtuous agent really do in Doris's example? She will weigh the situation carefully. She will understand that by accepting the invitation, she is at least acknowledging the attempt at seducing her. She might think that even this might be harmful for her partner, and for the seducer (if he is a friend, she does not want him to have false hopes). There might be other considerations, for instance she might feel obliged to attend the event, for social or professional reasons, or she might think it is a good occasion to make it clear, once and for all, that she is not interested. In any case, there will be far more deliberation going on than Doris lets on. It is not the case that an agent in that situation will have to think either 'I am virtuous and cannot be swayed by the situation' or 'I am aware that this is a dangerous situation so I won't go'.

We come now to the second response to situationism. Doris says, rightly, that virtues are 'robust' character traits, and that they are 'substantially resistant to contrary situational pressures in their behavioral manifestations.' So if virtue ethicists believe that a lot of people are virtuous, then the experiment showing that situations cause us to act viciously are problematic indeed. However, it is far from clear whether virtue ethicists should in fact believe that enough of us are virtuous for it to show up in the experiments described by the situationists. Certainly Plato did not. In both the Socratic and other dialogues, it seems, on the contrary, that Plato is quite confident that most people are not, in fact, virtuous.

This is not to say that he thinks most people are vicious – simply that they are indifferent, that their character traits have not yet become virtues. So what evidence do we have that Plato thinks we are not virtuous. On the one hand there is the constant search for the expert in virtue in the

Socratic dialogues. The expert is never found. All those claiming expertise are shown to be incapable of giving a good account either of what virtue in general is, or of a particular virtue. Given that for Plato virtue is wisdom, not knowing what virtue is, for him amounts to not being virtuous.

On the other hand, we have the political dialogues, *Republic*, *Statesman* and the *Laws*, which all insist in some way or other that perfect virtue is exceptional, or even inexistent. In the *Republic*, the only fully virtuous individuals are the philosopher kings, i.e. the smallest of the three groups into which Plato divides his society. Whether there could in fact be philosopher kings is put into question. In the *Statesman*, the ideal ruler is virtuous. But, and Plato is quite clear on this, he is not coming any time soon. In the *Laws*, most citizens of the new city are 'ordinary people' who will receive the best possible education, thereby rendering them as virtuous as they are capable of being. But whereas all will benefit from such an education, it is not expected that many or indeed any of them will achieve perfect virtue.

There are two immediate problems with the view I have defended. First, even if virtue ethicists (at least those of the Platonic persuasion) believe that there are very few virtuous agents, don't they believe that some traits which are not virtues can be robust? Secondly, what is the point, one might ask, of a perfectionist ethical theory that can give no examples of perfection? Do we have any reason to take such a theory seriously, let alone try to apply it to jurisprudence?

The first problem can be stated in this way. Even if we were to accept the virtue ethicist's claim that completely virtuous agents are rare or non-existent, we may still think that there are plenty of non-virtuous, but robust character traits around. For instance a person may be habitually lazy, bad-tempered or weak-willed. Why shouldn't these character traits be as robust as those of someone who is hard-working, sweet-tempered, and self-controlled? They are certainly more prevalent. Even if we concede that truly virtuous individuals are rare or non-existent, we could not deny that traits such as laziness were quite common, and at the same time maintain that character is not a myth!

Here we probably need to revert to a distinction I made earlier on, between dispositions on the one hand, and robust character traits on the other. The virtue ethicist will not deny, I think, the existence of character traits which are not robust, i.e. traits which are not merely natural dispositions, but which are in some way the product of habituation, but at the same time, are not yet robust. Such a category is absolutely crucial if we want to make sense of the idea of character development in virtue ethics.

An agent becomes more virtuous by consciously habituating himself or herself to respond in certain ways to certain situations. Correspondingly a person becomes vicious by failing to break bad habits imposed on them in their childhood environment (Note that there is a difference here, in that it is hard to imagine that a person would consciously habituate himself or herself to vice, and hence one might actually expect to see even less truly vicious agents than truly virtuous ones).

To talk of character traits in the process of becoming robust is not to minimize their potential effect on agency. Maybe it's true that, given a random group of people and a controlled situation, their actions may not provide evidence of robust character traits. Yet, it is equally plausible that although these agents seem to be responding in the same manner to the situation, thereby precluding differences due to character, their responses are in fact very different. Take the following situation: one person offers three different people a cigarette one after the other. Each accepts. Person A accepts because they are a smoker, and they fancy a cigarette. Person B accepts in spite of the fact that she has given up smoking three weeks previously, because she simply cannot help herself (although she doesn't really understand why she is suddenly so weak-willed, as she has been resisting temptation for three weeks now). Person C is an undercover agent, and although she doesn't smoke, she is keen to gain the trust of the person who is offering her a cigarette so as to break a heroin smuggling operation. So A, B and C, despite their characters' different takes on smoking all end up accepting the cigarette. But in this case (where we know more about what's going on) it is clearly not the case that their character doesn't affect how they respond. If smoking is a vice, then A accepts the cigarette out of vice. B is clearly on the way to become more virtuous, but she is still suffering from instability of the character trait that enables her to resist this particular temptation. C is accepting the cigarette because she is courageous, and because she is prepared to sacrifice her health to protect others.

An experiment which puts a number of agent in a particular situation misses out on the deliberation which leads the agent to act as they do. However, these deliberations are a very strong indicator of how the agent is doing in terms of character development and virtue. A longitudinal study, on the other hand, would be better suited to study the growth of a character, and an agent's success or failure at becoming more virtuous. In fact, when longitudinal studies were conducted as a response to the situationist experiments, the results were in favour of the existence of character traits.

In order to answer the second problem, the example of health may (again) prove useful. We all know that being healthy is good, and we all think that doing things that improve or maintain our health is good, whereas doing things that endanger it is bad. Yet we know of no example of a perfectly healthy individual. Some come close enough, but even for those, one small flaw may prove fatal. A healthy individual in their prime may contract a disease that will kill them. When that happens, it is discouraging. We ask what the point of trying to be healthy might be if even someone who is really good at it can be struck down. But then we look around and notice that there are still plenty of people healthier than we are, who are as a result of their health, enjoying life more.

So the perfectionist model is not based on the supposition that after trying, we attain perfection. Rather, we have an image of perfection, an image made vivid perhaps by putting together the few examples of near perfection we come across, and, under the influence of this image, we strive to become better. How does this affect our reading of the experiments cited by the situationists? Someone who is trying to become virtuous, as opposed to someone who is already so, will be more likely to do to the right thing in some situations than in others. This does not, however, mean that situationism is right and that character is just swept along with the situation. The person who is trying to become virtuous will also spend a lot of time choosing situations in which they are likely to do the right thing. If they are younger, their parents will create situations for them. If they are older, and they belong in a state in which laws are focused on virtue, they will be helped by laws and institutions in making the right choice. This is not all that different from what Doris believes we should in fact do:

> We should try, so far as we are able, to avoid 'near occasions for sin' – ethically dangerous circumstances. At the same time, we should seek near occasions for happier behavior – situations conducive to ethically desirable conduct. (2002, 147)

But there is an important difference between Doris' recommendations and what the virtue ethicist believes, namely that as far as the virtue ethicist is concerned, choosing your situations carefully is part of a learning process, but not what being virtuous entails. And this makes sense: it would not do for a so-called virtuous agent to refuse to try and do the right thing because they felt the situation presented a risk that they might not be up to it. Consider the protagonist of Stephen Crane's novel, *The Red Badge of*

Courage, who is worrying that in his first battle, he will flee. A fellow recruit tells him that it's quite common for new recruits to run when they're first faced with the Confederate troops.

> 'Think any of the boys'll run?' persisted the youth.
>
> 'Oh, there may be a few of 'em run, but there's them kind in every regiment, 'specially when they first goes under fire,' said the other in a tolerant way. 'Of course it might happen that the hull kit-and-boodle might start and run, if some big fighting came first off, and then again they might stay and fight like fun. But you can't bet on nothing.'[18]

The hero becomes shamefully aware that he might well be one of these 'fresh fish' who run the first time they're in battle. But should he avoid the situation that will make act in a cowardly manner and leave the army to return home? Should he not face up to his fears and take the chance that he, like many others, might get it wrong the first time? Such a policy of risk avoidance sounds very little like anything we might call morally good behaviour, and if this is what Doris is recommending, then I suggest he fails in his mission which is to make moral theory fit real life (2002, 1).

Although virtue ethicists do believe that awareness of situations matter, and that in order to become virtuous, we should pick and choose situations in which it will be easier to do the right thing, what really matters is the agent's ability to understand what the morally relevant features of the situation are. Given a situation in which she is called upon to act, a virtuous agent is able to tell which aspects of the situation require her intervention and which do not. Taking the example of a mother faced with her teenage son misbehaving. If she is virtuous, she will be able to judge whether her son's behaviour is simply a case of growing pains, a symptom of existential angst, or a desperate call for help. As a result she will know whether the right thing to do is to let it pass, offer advice, or to put her foot down. Typically, the kind of deliberation which goes on in the virtuous agent's mind depends on a deep understanding of the situation. But what do the situationist experiments do? They control the situation, unbeknownst to the agent. Thus a large part of the agent's agency is taken away from her, and she has much less of a chance to act virtuously. The subjects of the Milgram experiment are in no position to make accurate or deep judgments about the situation they are in, as the situation is deliberately made to look different from what it is. Of course, we might reply that what is being tested, is how they would do in the situation which is being (falsely) presented to them. But a made up situation does not present the same opportunity for deep and accurate judgment as a real one. Hence the possibility of acting virtuously is undermined from the outset.

4. Community service for offenders as elenctic therapy: a case study

In this last section of this chapter, I will show how the conclusions reached so far may be applied successfully to a particular criminal justice problem: how community service should be used in sentencing. I will argue that the elenctic model supports the view that its use as a rehabilitative punishment should be more widespread.

Community service as punishment in Britain is at the same time well-established and under-developed. Introduced in the Criminal Justice Act in 1972, it has significantly failed to reduce prison population, due to sentencers' reluctance to use it instead of custodial sentences, this despite several revisions which emphasized the punitive aspect of community service.[19]

Community service orders are typically issued by Sheriff courts, that is courts dealing with minor property rights offences, instead of short prison sentences or fines. It is sometimes, but not always, issued together with a probation sentence. Most of the offenders who receive community service sentences are white and male. In the light of these facts, it is hard to see whether community service is effective in reducing offending and promoting offenders' reintegration in society: those who receive community court orders being 'low-risk' subjects when it comes to re-offending, and generally having stable home and work environment to support them during their sentence.[20] Nonetheless, the results so far are positive,[21] and thus, there is every reason to hope that if the use of community service orders was more widespread, re-offending would become less widespread.

Community service, when it conceived as a primarily rehabilitative punishment, one which reduces re-offending and facilitates the offender's reintegration into the community, follows almost precisely the elenctic model set out in Section 3 of this paper.[22] This particular type of community service, which is currently being evaluated in Pathfinder Projects,[23] has two main features. The first feature could come under the general heading of character rehabilitation, it comprises of the development of pro-social behaviour, and problem-solving, which can take the form of developing employability skills, or addressing problems underlying offending.[24] The second feature is the presence of a supervisor, or even in some cases, probation officer, who on the one hand 'models' pro-social behaviour and encourages its development in the offender, and on the other, offers assistance for problem-solving, both with the tasks presented by the community service itself, and with the offenders' 'crime-related needs', i.e. the problems that led the offender to commit a crime in the first place.

There is a striking correspondence between these two features of community service and the first two features of the elenctic method. In the first instance, the subject of the elenchos is asked to become 'virtue-conscious', i.e. to habituate his or her mind to think about the things that matter (i.e. virtue) and to ignore to some extent those that don't (for Plato: money, bodily comfort, reputation).[25] Whereas we might have doubt as to whether just any physical activity is really suited to assist the growth of virtue, it is undeniable that the right kind of activity has just that effect. When community service is used in its rehabilitative capacity, the activities chosen focus on working with members of the community who most need help (e.g. in soup kitchens), and places the offenders in contact with the beneficiaries of their work. This inevitably has a positive effect on the offenders' character: they acquire increased self-knowledge, confidence, a concern for others, and a sense of belonging that they previously lacked.[26]

In the second instance, the subject must bring his or her mind to an elenctic 'doctor' or a 'touchstone' for testing through debate, in order to detect problems that need solving, and at the same time to receive assistance in 'training' one's mind and emotions to focus on pro-social virtues. Community service programmes include in all cases supervision, and in some, probation. Their role, in modelling pro-social behaviour and problem solving is highly reminiscent of the Socratic elenctic interlocutor. They direct the offender's inquiry into his or her search for virtue and his or her understanding of what motivates him or her.

Given its past successes, and the overwhelming plausibility of community service sentencing, it is, to say the least, surprising that it is not more widely used. As Richard Brandt has argued there is something 'manifestly immoral' about a system which imprisons predominantly young people, from predominantly poor backgrounds, in such a way that they become hardened criminals by the time they finish their sentence.[27] There are of course, some objections as to why its use should be restrained. But these objections are hardly convincing.

For example, one might ask why offenders should receive benefits (for example accredited training) that people from similar backgrounds or worse who refrain from criminal acts, don't get? To this objection there are at least two (conclusive) answers. First, community service is, and is perceived as a form of punishment. It is a 'fine' on the offenders' time, time that he is not free to use otherwise. This loss of freedom, and imposition of an activity which is often physically tiring would certainly not be welcome by everyone. Secondly, there are voluntary community service programs targeted at 'at risk' people, people from deprived backgrounds whose situation is such that crime may seem to them a viable option. These programs are significant from our point of view, i.e. from the point of view of Platonic ethics, as the point of the elenctic model is that it should be applied primarily to those who have not yet shown signs of ill health, i.e. that it is preventive rather than curative.

A second objection to the more widespread use of community service sentencing is that by letting criminals out in the community instead of locking them up, we put the community at risk! But is this worry justified? Certainly it is not in the case of offenders who are sentenced to less than life and who therefore will come back to the community, hardened by prison life, as soon as their sentence is over. Possibly, long sentences, and life sentences should not be converted to community service sentences in order to protect the community. It is also true, no doubt, that the issuing of such sentences is an important deterrent for grave crimes, i.e. murder, and possibly rape.[28] However, these are not the majority of sentences, and murderers or rapists are possibly not the offenders we are keenest to rehabilitate.

What is distinctive about community service, is that it can be reformative, without any appeal to psychiatry. Those involved in the projects are not doctors, but police officers, probation officers, or simply members of the community. This, as I have argued in this paper, is the kind of moral reform which is mainly recommended by the Platonic medical model, i.e. one which depends on emotional and intellectual development rather than on the use of drugs or medical intervention.

Chapter 5

Paternalism in the *Republic*

1. A problem and a solution?

Mill's harm principle states that

> The only purpose for which power can be rightfully exercised over any member of a civilized community, against his will, is to prevent harm to others. His own good, either physical or moral, is not a sufficient warrant. He cannot rightfully be compelled to do or forbear because it will be better for him to do so, because it will make him happier, because in the opinion of others to do so would be wise or even right.[1]

Paternalism, the exercise of power over citizens for their own good, beyond what is needed in order to prevent citizens harming others, is thus first and foremost a restriction of citizens' freedom. Moreover, it is a restriction that seems to us unjustified and intrusive. The idea that the state should use laws to force us to do what it believes is good for us is in many ways frightening and repulsive. If any one is going to force us to promote our own good, that had better be ourselves. Anyone else attempting to do so would be crossing an important boundary. As adults, we believe that we are in the best position to judge what our own good consists in, and that even if on occasion someone sees it more clearly than we do, they should do no more than advise us.

As we saw in the preceding chapters the attempt to use virtue ethics to come up with an account of the role and place of laws in a just society brings up some serious worries about paternalism. If we are told by the laws not just what we should do, but also what we should be, we somehow loose control of a fundamental freedom, the freedom to create our own ethical world, to decide for ourselves what the good life might be, and to take certain attitudes towards the laws, such as obeying in spite of the fact that we disagree with certain fundamental assumptions which appear to be behind it. In other words, by inculcating virtues, the laws ensure that we become docile citizens who do not question the lives that are made for us, and the acts we are told to do.

In Chapter 3, we saw that there was a way in which a Platonic account of laws as promoting virtue could avoid the paternalistic threat, or at least its most worrying aspects. This way out is for the laws to promote only one virtue, namely wisdom. A legal system that is wisdom-promoting does little more than to enable citizens to decide for themselves what the good life is. It puts them in a position where they are able to make that choice because they can see the merits and demerits of available alternatives. It ensures that they have the mental tools to understand what it is they need, and what the best way to achieve it is.

It might be argued that this falls short of what Plato intends: he does not believe that each should choose for himself or herself just any 'good life'. For instance, Plato would not condone my saying that, as I see it, the best overall thing for me to do is to become a criminal, even if I have benefited from the best possible education and consider myself wise. But what we also saw in Chapter 3, was that this proposal, that only one virtue should be promoted by the laws, wisdom, is to be taken in conjunction with Plato's unity of the virtue thesis. Because he holds this thesis, Plato believes it would be in fact impossible for any one to be wise, and not also develop the other virtues. In other words, if I had benefited from the kind of education that makes people wise, I would not desire to become a criminal.

That the unity of virtue thesis is contentious does not weaken our tentative solution to the problem of paternalism. If Plato is wrong and it is possible to be wise without becoming courageous, temperate and just, then so be it, and at the very least citizens will benefit from wisdom-promoting laws. They will benefit even though they are not virtuous in other respects because they will know themselves, they will understand the society they live in, and be able to regulate their actions so that they maximize benefit for themselves without endangering the social framework that supports them. Possibly very few will choose to become criminals.

If Plato is right, and by developing wisdom we automatically develop the other virtues, then all the better, and we cannot say that the laws, by promoting wisdom, are forcing us to accept a set of values that we would not necessarily choose for ourselves. If those values come to us naturally when we are wise, then they are values we choose for ourselves.

There is one important objection to this thought. Do we and Plato mean the same thing when we talk of wisdom, that is, the ability to think about our lives, consider our options, and choose the best one in the most efficient way? Or does Plato mean something very different, namely knowing the truth such as he conceives it? It is hard not to see Plato as dogmatic here. As far as he is concerned, being wise does mean knowing the Forms, and those who know the Forms must agree with him that, for instance, justice is always more beneficial than injustice.

On the other hand, we saw in Chapter 4 that what it means to try and become wise is very different from seeking knowledge about the forms from those who know. What is 'needful' is not obtaining this knowledge by whatever means, but conducting philosophical inquiry, examining one's beliefs through the elenchos, until one is satisfied that one has no inconsistent beliefs. To become wise, for Plato, is first and foremost to ask questions, of others, but also of oneself. Socrates in the *Apology* is not wise, he tells us. But because he knows that he is fundamentally ignorant, he is closer to wisdom than any one in Athens: he does not take any of his beliefs for granted, does not mistake them for knowledge, and forever inquires.

If the aim of wisdom-promoting laws is to encourage citizens to question their beliefs, seek to understand others, and not be too confident that one's own beliefs are closer to the truth than someone else's, then in a sense it does not matter that Plato also believes that those who have achieved wisdom will all share the same beliefs.

Another important point I made in Chapter 3, and which is relevant here, is that wisdom-promoting laws will be concerned mostly with education which reduces the extent to which they are paternalistic. The best way to promote wisdom is surely to educate the young. Thus a state that is concerned with promoting wisdom will concentrate its legislating efforts on schooling.

So children, not adults will be the target of laws concerned with the good. Although this is paternalism, it is far less objectionable. Children are not on the whole deemed capable of deciding for themselves what the good life is before they have completed at least part of their education. Parents might feel that they, not the state, should be in charge of deciding on behalf of their children, but this is a very different claim than that we should be in charge of creating our own moral universe. A different claim might come from communities within states who feel they are entitled to make decisions concerning the upbringing of their youngest members, for instance, bring them up according to certain religious rules. But this is a case of paternalism against paternalism, and the question is which of these two, the community, or the state, should be entitled to shape a child's future, not whether the child should shape his or her own future.

The *Crito* presents strong evidence that Plato believes that state laws should focus primarily on the young. The laws brought forward by the Personified Laws of Athens in order to remind Socrates of his debt are the laws concerning marriage and education (50d). These are the laws that enabled Socrates to be born and brought up in such a way that he was able to become a virtuous citizen. Yet, clearly, no state can confine its legislation to education. But what should also be clear, is that once education is legislated for in such a way that the young citizens will be able to develop wisdom, any remaining laws need not concern themselves with promoting virtue, but merely with making possible for citizens to live according to the virtues they have developed. These would mostly be laws protecting the environment, i.e. making a safe place in which to live virtuously, but also laws regulating public institutions so that it is possible for citizens to interact with these institutions in a way that is compatible with living a virtuous life.

The first point is fairly obvious: there is little use in promoting wisdom in the young if they are living in an environment in which their prime concern is for their survival and safety. It is important to realize that what Socrates owed to Athens was not simply a good education – if that was the case, he would have been happy to accept exile to some other city. But also, Athens provided him with the freedom to walk around the Agora, talking to his fellow citizens, in comparative safety. He was not rejected as an outcast and was able, despite apparent lack of paid work, to ensure that his family did not starve. This might have been the result of friendship with aristocrats, rather than the direct influence of the laws of Athens, but that he was not marginalized by the laws for his unconventional activities is itself non-negligible.

The second point, that public institutions should not discourage virtue is equally important and is also a matter of protecting the environment so that it is possible for citizens to flourish. A young citizen who has spent his childhood learning to be wise will not find it easy to continue developing wisdom if she finds herself having to bribe state officials, or dealing with other unjust practices, such as racial or sexual discrimination when she interacts with the state. There is little point in educating children into wisdom to teach them that virtue doesn't pay as soon as they enter the adult world.

My central claim is that if we want laws that promote virtue, it is enough to concentrate on educational laws that promote wisdom, as long as we also use laws to promote the environment in which we expect citizens to flourish. But the laws protecting the environment are in no way paternalistic: in fact, they are perfectly compatible with Mill's harm principle.

In the following sections of this chapter, I want to test this claim in various ways. First, I want to ask whether Plato is himself able to sustain this proposal in one of his dialogues that has the most to say on the question of virtue-promoting education, the *Republic*.[2] I shall argue that even though Plato seems to have the tools for building the kind of theory of education we might accept, in the *Republic*, he fails to do so quite spectacularly. I will show several of the overly paternalistic aspects of the proposal of the *Republic*, and ask why and where Plato was not able, in that dialogue, to develop a more acceptable version of virtue-promoting education. In the last chapter, it will become apparent that Plato does in fact find a way of using the tools he has given us, and that he does in the end offer a system that is less objectionably paternalistic.

Secondly, I want to ask what place, if any, paternalism has in education nowadays, and whether it is possible to conceive of a modern day educational system that is virtue-promoting.

2. Paternalism in the *Republic*

The *Republic* raises some very obvious worries that Plato does not believe virtue can play a part in politics without a hefty dose of paternalism. Even if we think, as I do, that this is not a sign that Plato does not try to avoid paternalism generally, it is good to mention some of these worries outright, so they do not hover in the background of further discussion of what the *Republic* might teach us about how to avoid paternalism.

In this section I, will touch on two different problems. First, Plato's attitude to lie and censorship, secondly his apparent belief that only a minority of the population of his ideal city would be capable of ruling themselves wisely. I will argue that although the first clearly shows that Plato does not wish to avoid paternalism, the second is in fact a highly disputable interpretation of what he says, and moreover, one that gets Plato's analogy of virtue and health (discussed in Chapter 4) wrong.

The clearest sign that Plato does not believe the non-philosophers are able to look after themselves is that he recommends that the information they receive from an early age should be vetted by the philosophers, i.e. some should be constructed from scratch, lies,[3] whereas the rest should be modified in order to have the required effect.

The latter, censorship, appears to be an absolutely crucial step in promoting virtue: the citizens of the ideal city simply cannot be relied on to become temperate and courageous if they are allowed to hear Homer in the original. For Plato, poetry gives a direct access to the character, shapes it, unbeknownst to the agent and those around him or her, and the only way to control its effects is to control its contents. He does not see that there might be any interference from the rest of the agent's life. Someone who hears of Achilles' vices will think they must be virtues, or that heroes are vicious. There is no viewpoint that enables the public to stand back and reflect on what Homer is trying to do – everything goes straight into character shaping, and the public is little more than a sponge.

We might have some sympathy for Plato, in that we might think that some films or television programs, for instance, do nothing but reinforce bad habits of character and moral prejudice among uneducated people. But we see the problem somewhat differently: we do not think these films or programs should be censored and edited so as to have a different effect. Take a random violent movie in which men fight with machine guns and women have blond hair and large breasts. Would editing out the guns and the plastic surgery make the movie more likely to promote virtue? No: it would just make it more boring. The problem with such movies is that they are simply bad – they do not present a picture of life that is worth any one thinking about.

What we do object to, when we are considering a modern application of Plato's thoughts on censorship, is not that such movies exist, but that they seem to represent all that's available culture-wise for a percentage of the population. So there is a chance that whatever makes its way to the character-forming mechanism of the viewer will not be fought back by anything. First, someone brought up on bad television may not have had the chance to develop much of a critical sense (although thankfully, many people seem to be born with one!). Secondly, the media itself does not provide any opportunity for reflection or criticism. Like fast food, it is designed for immediate consumption and approximate digestion.

Is there any chance that Plato could have thought of Homer in the same way? Leaving aside any historical interpretations of how Homer may have been perceived during Plato's lifetime, this strikes me as unlikely. Plato himself often refers to Homer and other poets to illustrate a point, and when he does this, he is often very critical indeed. So he could not have considered Homer as any less than thought provoking. Given this, whatever sympathy we might have with censorship based on the omnipresence of cheap media culture does not in any way apply to Plato's proposal. He seems less worried by the potential harm to be caused by the poets, than he seems interested in the potential character shaping powers of censorship. For this, I think, we need show no sympathy.

Even if we were to forgive Plato for his abuse of censorship, there are other ways in which the *Republic* has been perceived not only as paternalistic, but dangerously so. In particular, Plato's emphasis in the *Republic* on very rigid class distinctions is problematic, to say the least. Are only the philosophers capable of being wise? Are the others fundamentally incapable of becoming wise because they were born with an undersized rational part? Does this mean that all apart from the philosophers are in some way mentally deficient, sick, and unable to care for themselves? Philosophers have often argued that these were ways in which the *Republic* was not only paternalistic, but dangerously so, totalitarian even.

But unlike in the case of censorship, I believe that here the objection is wrong-headed. This is because it lies in a misunderstanding of what Plato's analogy of virtue and mental health consists in. For the sake of balance, I spend the end of this section showing why the objection, as presented by one philosopher, Anthony Kenny, fails.

Kenny's objection could be summarized thus.[4] If we say that virtue is health, then vice is sickness, mental illness. But the mentally ill are very vulnerable to the control of psychiatric doctors. They often have no choice as to whether and how they should be treated. Also, Kenny claims that according to Plato the mentally ill have no property rights and no right to the truth. Moreover, as Plato appears to believe that only the philosopher kings are virtuous, it follows that he must believe most of us are insane. He can therefore recommend a totalitarian regime in which we are all under the control of philosophers/psychiatrists.[5]

To understand Plato as Kenny does, we need to make two disputable assumptions. First we have to believe that all failures or insufficiencies in psychic health equate to madness, which is tantamount to believing that a head cold or a stomach upset is some form of cancer. I made it clear in the previous chapter that Plato does not make this assumption, but that he believes that one can fail to be perfectly healthy in many ways without justifying medical intervention in the form of treatment – not all mental insufficiencies are diseases. Secondly, in order to agree with Kenny, we also need to believe that psychiatric medicine is necessarily a coercive practice, i.e. that doctors do not recommend treatments, diets, exercise, etc., but force them upon patients.

Kenny's interpretation relies on claims about the nature of mental health and medicine that we have no reason to believe Plato shared. Neither of these two assumptions are assumptions that one would readily make, and there is certainly no evidence that Plato made them. Thus, prima facie, we have no reason to take Kenny's reading of Plato seriously. His interpretation relies on claims about the nature of mental health and medicine that we have no reason to believe Plato shared.

In order to read all that Kenny does in Plato's health analogy, it seems that we need to misinterpret radically several passages from the *Republic*. The one reference Kenny gives to support his claim that Plato equates vice with madness 329b–d:

> How about your service of Aphrodites, Sophocles – is your natural force still unabated? And he replied, Hush, man, most gladly have I escaped this thing you talk of, as if I had run away from a raging and savage beast of a master. I thought it a good answer then and now I think so still more. For in very truth there comes to old age a great tranquillity in such matters, and a blessed release. When the fierce tensions of the passions and desires relax, then is the word of Sophocles approved, and we are rid of many and mad masters.

But this passage is in fact a reading of Sophocles by Cephalus on sex and youth. There is no reason to think that Cephalus is speaking for Plato, nor does his reading of Sophocles obviously suggest an equation of vice and madness, merely that some of the impulses of youth are hard to master with reason.

The second reference Kenny offers is the passage in which Socrates claims that it would be wrong to return a weapon one has borrowed to a friend gone mad (331c):

> If one took over weapons from a friend who was in his right mind and then the lender should go mad and demand them back, that we ought not to return them in that case and that he who did so return them would not be acting justly – nor yet would he who chose to speak nothing but the truth to one who was in that state.

From this he infers that Plato believes that the mentally ill have no property rights. But there are two obvious replies here. First, it is clear that there is nothing legalistic about Plato's claim: Socrates is talking about friendship, not rights. The leap from how one should behave towards a friend and legal rights is a big one: in many cases, what I owe to a friend and what they have a right to expect from me legally are very different, and nowhere does Plato talk of the legal treatment of madmen. Secondly, surely the type of property referred to in the example is relevant. Even if Plato was making a point about rights and mental illness, the relevant right is not property right, but the right to own weapons. It is unclear whether there should be such a right in the first place, but if there was such a right, it would not be especially controversial to suggest that it should not apply to the insane.

Kenny's supporting arguments are therefore based, at least in part, on clear misreadings of the *Republic*. More importantly, his thesis, and the underlying belief that Plato's moral philosophy is motivated by totalitarian ambitions, rests on a misunderstanding of how the health analogy works, and of the medical model it implies. Kenny believes that if virtue is a matter of health, then all vice must be madness, and that the proper treatment of madness is coercive. However, this medical model is a very poor one compared with the ones Plato would have been familiar with.[6] In the previous chapter I argued that Plato's own development of the health analogy implied a much richer, and thereby not morally objectionable, medical model.

3. Educating the philosopher kings and the rest

In the previous section, we saw that there is no doubt but that the proposal for educating citizens in the *Republic* remains highly paternalistic, at least in some respects. In this section we shall explore the reasons why this is so. We shall see how despite some promising appearances, Plato's educational program does not satisfy the requirement that insofar as they are to be virtue-promoting, laws should be wisdom-promoting only.

The *Republic* might seem like a strange place to look for virtue-promoting laws. After all, Plato says that virtuous citizens do not need laws, indeed, that it would be wrong to prescribe to them when they are capable of working out what the right thing to do in any situation for themselves:

> It would not be fitting, he said, to dictate to good and honourable men. For most of the enactments that are needed about these things [contracts, declarations, juries, policing, etc.] they will easily, I presume, discover.[7]

But this claim has a context: it follows a discussion of the education of the children of the polis. If the youth are educated in the right manner, then they will become lawful citizens, such that they will not need laws to tell them what to do: 'our youth must join in a more law-abiding play, since, if play grows lawless and the children likewise, it is impossible that they should grow up to be men of serious temper and lawful spirit' (424e–425a).

It seems that in the *Republic,* there are laws – indeed, the guardians are described as 'Guardians of law and of the city' (421a) – but these laws seem to be concerned mostly with 'education and nurture' (424a). The principle seems to be that provided children are well educated, they will grow to become lawful citizens who have no need for the imposition of penalties to regulate their behaviour, as they are regulated from the inside (591a).

Accordingly, the role of the rulers, the philosopher kings, is to legislate for the education of all, and that of the guardians, to ensure that these laws are respected. The first point is made at 590c–591a:

> And it is plain that this is the purpose of the law, which the ally of all classes in the state, and this is the aim of our control of children, our not leaving them free before we have established, so to speak, a constitutional government within them and, by fostering the best element in them with the aid of the like in ourselves, have set up in its place a similar guardian and ruler in the child, and then, and then only we leave it free.

Thus the law, rather than control the behaviour of citizens, determines what that behaviour is most likely to be by controlling the education of young citizens. But once the citizens have grown up, they are no longer subject to legislation regarding their every day or business transactions with each other. They are deemed capable of doing the right thing without fear of retaliation from the state.

The second point, that the task of the guardian is mostly the control of education is made at 423d–424b:

> These are not, my good Adeimantus, as one might suppose, numerous and difficult injunctions that we are imposing upon [the guardians], but they are all easy providing they guard, as the saying is, the one great thing, or instead of great let us call it sufficient.
>
> What is that? He said.
>
> Their education and nurture, I replied. For if a right education makes of them reasonable men they will easily discover everything of this kind and other principles that we pass over now.

The key point of the passage is the appeal to sufficiency: Plato does appear to believe that if the children of the state are brought up in the right manner, they will be lawful citizens and require none of the squabbling legal threats and disputes that he sees democratic states as suffering from. This ties in nicely with the proposal we first aired in Chapter 3, and that I reiterated in the introduction to this chapter, namely, that a platonic virtue-jurisprudence might limit its reach to wisdom, and that this would entail that virtue-promoting laws would be focused on education of the young citizens, i.e. both on the curriculum and on the safety of the infrastructure which makes this education possible.

In the *Republic*, Plato does spend some time dealing with the minutiae of a suitable curriculum for the citizens of the just city. This is because he believes firmly that what they are taught will determine whether children can become just citizens:

> And so we may reason that when children in their earliest play are imbued with the spirit of law and order through their music, the opposite of the former supposition happens – this spirit waits upon them in all times and fosters their growth, and restores and sets up again whatever was overthrown in the other type of state. (425a)

Before we examine whether what Plato suggests in the *Republic* does indeed fail to avoid the pitfalls of paternalism, we need to ask whether his intention matches his practical proposals, i.e. whether he does indeed believe that all children can receive an education such that they will not need to be ruled by laws in the detail of their adult lives. There are two points in particular which might lead us to question Plato's intentions. First, is it the case that all citizens will receive sufficient education for his intentions to be realized? And secondly, should we assume that simply because the laws concern education, they are wisdom-promoting rather than generally virtue-promoting?

It is fairly clear that Plato does not believe all citizens can be educated to the point where they may rule themselves. At 590d he writes that

> It is better for everyone to be governed by the divine and the intelligent, preferably indwelling, and his own, but in default of that imposed from without, in order that we all so far as possible may be akin and friendly because our governance and guidance are the same.

This means that for some citizens, their education will not suffice to render them wise enough that they can do without laws. Therefore we need to investigate Plato's educational system, and in particular, the differences between the types of education offered to each of the three classes.

In spite of the fact that Plato does deal with the education of the citizens in great details (even to the extent of going through some of the texts they may or may not be taught) he is not clear on who will benefit from what education. For instance, although there are sections of the text dealing with the education of the guardians and of the philosophers, there is none to deal with the education of the third and the largest class. Are we to assume that they receive none, and that they will therefore, throughout their lives, be guided by laws that they cannot anticipate and that regulate their behaviour down to the last detail? Plato does not tell us that specifically. Indeed, some of what he says in his discussion of the education of the guardian may lead us to believe that he intends at least part of this education to apply to the third class as well.

At 389d–e while discussing the censoring of texts depicting the gods as intemperate, he says that this type of censorship is especially important because of the effect it will have on the multitude. The role of the third and the largest class is first and foremost to obey: they must obey their rulers, and to do this they must develop the kind of gentleness that is present in the temperate agent, so it is crucial that they should be taught self-control. Thus it does seem as though the third class will benefit from some kind of education. But it is clear that this education will concern itself first and foremost with promoting temperance, not wisdom.

What is also not clear is the extent to which the education of the guardians and that of the philosophers is separate. Although they are detailed in different parts of the book (that of the guardians at 376e–412b and of the philosophers at 521c–541b), it seems they must be connected. At 521e Plato describes the early part of the philosophers' education as music and gymnastic, and implies that he is referring to that which has already been described in the earlier discussion of the education of the guardians.

What one might conclude from all this is that all the citizens follow one educational program and that they stop, earlier or later, depending on their class or ability (as Plato does recommend that a member of one class who shows abilities that are characteristic of another should move up or down in the system at 423d). But this would not entail, presumably, that the classes are educated together, as Plato seems to believe that it is important that members of different classes do not mix (459a–460b).

It does seem that the educational program proposed in the *Republic* is largely unequal, with only the smallest portion of the society receiving a complete education, and the possibility that the largest part receives none at all. In that sense, whatever Plato's beliefs about the role of education in promoting virtue, what he has to offer in the *Republic* will certainly not be enough to render all citizens virtuous and to make laws outside of the domain of education redundant. But another way in which Plato's proposal in the *Republic* fails to implement the solution to the paternalism problem we discussed in Chapter 3 and the introduction to the present chapter is that the education proposed here is not merely wisdom-promoting, but is concerned at least as much, and in some cases exclusively with promoting temperance and courage.

The later stage of the philosophers' education is indeed wisdom-promoting in that it is concerned with pulling the soul away from 'the world of becoming' and towards 'the world of being' (521d). But the first part of their education, and therefore the entire education of the guardians, is concerned with something different, namely the promotion of temperance and courage. It follows that the educational system promoted by the *Republic* is not, for the most part, the kind that we would expect to solve the paternalism problem. We shall see, in Chapter 7, that the *Laws* comes a lot closer to a solution, in part because it emphasizes the importance of promoting wisdom amongst the citizens, and also because its educational program is intended to apply to all the citizens.

4. Paternalism in education

A paternalistic state build on the line of a virtue ethics theory not only tells us what to think, but it moulds our minds in such a way that we will think what it wants us spontaneously. Of course we do not object systematically to the state shaping children's minds according to certain values. In many countries the national curriculum is consciously value-orientated at least to some extent. Sometimes the values pushed are worthwhile – children are taught to be open-minded, not to be racist, and to be accepting of differences generally, sometimes they are more questionable – nationalistic or religious values are in the foreground. What makes us regard some value-orientated educational laws as worthwhile and others as dangerous? It seems that the main difference is that some values require the use of reason in order to be developed, while others preclude the use of reason.

The UK national curriculum for primary years emphasizes that schools should put forward a common core of values, and that it should emphasize respect for difference in values.[8] The rationale behind this is that children can learn better if they are able to manage emotional and social situations well. Emotions such as anger and depression which are common in situations such as bullying, inhibit learning skills. The view being defended is that if children are able to deal with their own emotions, and relate well to others they will be in a better position to learn what the curriculum has to offer.

On the other hand, the French ministry of education opposes, in the name of secularism, the display of religion in schools. Secularism, it is argued, encourages respect for the diversity of religious belief. This is derived from a meeting point of its republican origins, and human rights. A human being is owed respect independently of his or her religious, linguistic, ethnic or cultural affiliations. Schools should therefore encourage students to respect each other, no matter what their background is. However, the ministry emphasizes, this is not an excuse for allowing religious displays in schools. In particular, female Muslim students should not be allowed to wear a headscarf in school. This would, according to the ministry, render students captive of a religious or cultural 'pseudo community' and therefore negate the principles of secularism.[9]

It is unclear which side is right, whether respect for differences is better achieved through an open display of these differences together with a system of core values and regular dialogue about how the differences and the values meet, or whether it is better to encourage students not to display differences but to shed their cultural differences before they come to school. In both cases there seems to be a conflict between wanting to teach values and wanting to keep them out of the classroom. In other words, some values are deemed beneficial, and some harmful, as far as educational purposes are concerned.

However different the policies of the two states on education, it seems that both are concerned with the same thing, i.e. that schools should promote the ability to think for oneself. One common argument for secularism in schools is that children should be in a position to make up their own minds what to believe once they are in a position to do so, i.e. once they understand enough about what religious belief entails and once they can reason independently of their parents. In the meantime, they are supposed to learn to be accepting of various beliefs and customs, to see the sameness rather than the differences between people.

The British system, on the other hand, recognizes that the ability to accept different ways of life and belief system helps one overcome emotional barriers that may stilt learning. It does so in great part by lessening conflict between children born out of prejudice, and frees the child's emotions to develop in more productive ways.

In other words, both secularism, and the teaching of tolerance (recognizing and accepting difference) are seen as the basis for an opening of the mind to learning, and a fostering of the capacity to think for oneself, outside the framework provided by one's immediate environment. What is interesting about this is that although promoting wisdom seems to be the ultimate goal, there has to be some promotion of other virtues before it can be achieved. Children have to be taught to respect and care for others; they have to be taught to deal with their emotions appropriately, in order to be in a position where they can learn to think independently. So although wisdom is not the only virtue that is being promoted, it is because they enhance wisdom that the others are promoted. This, it seems, still fits in the spirit of the solution we presented in Chapter 3.

5. Conclusion

Plato fails in the *Republic* to implement the solution we presented in Chapter 3 for two main reasons. First, he believes that there should be a strict separation of the citizens in three classes, and that only the smallest class can successfully be educated into virtue. Secondly, the education he proposes seems to promote equally temperance, courage and wisdom, whereas we saw that in order to avoid paternalism, virtue-based education should focus on wisdom.

However, it seems out of place to demand that education should promote only wisdom. The British system is a good example of how promoting other virtues and generally educating children's emotions is a necessary part of promoting the abilities to learn and to think for oneself. In Chapter 3, we saw that wisdom-promoting laws should not only focus on education, but should ensure that the environment in which this education takes place (and the environment in which we live after the education is completed) should be one in which wisdom can be achieved (and later in which it can be maintained). Thus, if the best way to promote children's learning abilities is to lessen emotional tensions and struggles, then a wisdom-promoting education will, first and foremost, teach students to accept themselves and others, and not to respond to differences they perceive between others and themselves with hostility.

So even though in the *Republic*, Plato fails to implement the solution to paternalism we proposed in Chapter 3, studying how he fails gives us a clearer insight into what that solution might be. In Chapter 7, we will see how Plato comes closer to the solution in the *Laws*.

Chapter 6

The *Statesman* and Equity

1. Introduction

One important premise of virtue ethics is that human goodness is first of all personal growth, and character change. Through confrontation with new situations, and a process of conscious habituation, a person's character traits slowly develop to become virtues. This means that human life is never at rest, but always changing – from person to person, and from time to time. What a young agent does the first time she is confronted with a certain type of moral difficulty is bound to be different than what she does when she has achieved a greater maturity. Her capacity to judge what the relevant features of the problem are will to extent determine what she should do, and how one should respond to her action. So in order to find the virtuous solution to a problem, one must exercise wisdom by judging the problem on its own merits.

From the point of view of virtue ethics, however, laws are too rigid to be able to deal satisfactory with particular cases. Laws are meant to be universal and stable. We rely on laws to deal with different individuals in the same way, and to remain the same for substantial periods of time. As the Eleatic Stranger puts it in the *Statesman*:

> Law can never issue an injunction binding on all that really embodies what is best for each; it cannot prescribe what is good and right for each member of the community at any one time. The differences of human personality, the variety of men's activities, and the inevitable unsettlement attending all human experience make it impossible for any art whatsoever to issue unqualified rules holding good on all questions at all times.[1]

Before I start, I would like to draw two caveats. First, it may seem from the passage just quoted that far from presenting a solution to the incompatibility problem, the *Statesman* merely charts the problem.[2] If so, it is of little use to those who hope to construct a philosophical account of laws based on virtue ethics. However, I believe that this reading, with the emphasis on the passage quoted above is mistaken. Plato is aware of the apparent incompatibility between laws and virtue, but in the *Statesman*, he offers some tools for resolving it.

Secondly, in order to present a clearer account of what Plato's solution in the *Statesman* might be, I have found it useful to refer to Aristotle's writings on laws, and in particular on equity. Although Aristotle's views on that subject are almost certainly derived from his acquaintance with Plato's *Statesman*, and although he presents less detailed argument than Plato does on this particular point, his formulation of the principle of equity helps us make sense of what Plato is trying to do in the *Statesman*. I shall therefore spend some time, in Section 4, discussing some relevant Aristotelian texts.

2. Two attitudes to the laws in the *Statesman*

In order to understand the *Statesman's* discussion, I shall begin by giving a brief summary of the plot.[3] The *Statesman* is generally understood to have three main parts – the division, the myth, the paradigm – in which the Stranger from Eleas and Socrates the Young attempt to define the role of the Statesman or more generally of political science.[4] The first part of the dialogue (258b–268d) attempts to define the role of the statesman as shepherding. It is proposed that a statesman is a king who has pastoral duties and responsibilities towards herds of 'free bipeds', that is, human beings. However, this king has to fight for his title against several competitors who also pretend to the function of 'caring' for human beings, that is, feeding, doctoring, teaching, etc. Because it cannot distinguish the statesman from these other professionals, The Stranger from Eleas and his interlocutor, Young Socrates, decide that there is something amiss with the definition.

They hope that what is amiss will become apparent and be resolved with their second attempt at definition, the Myth of the second part (268d–277c). The Eleatic Stranger tells a creation myth according to which the cosmos was first ruled by Kronos and his demiurges in a very pastoral manner. Everything, even reproduction, is organized for the free bipeds so that they have nothing to worry or think about. By contrast, when Zeus takes over the ruling of the Cosmos, he learns to delegate. First, human beings are put in charge of their own reproduction; second, they are given the *technai*, or the arts, so that they may care for themselves in everyway. The second part of the myth, the rule of Zeus, is then shown to be a better model for political rule, as unlike shepherding, it depends on there being a more active involvement on the part of those who are being ruled.

This version of the creation myth recalls Protagoras's version in the dialogue of the same name (320d–323a). Zeus, finding that humans are equipped to take care of themselves in every respect but cannot live together in peace, and fearing that the race will self-destruct, offers them the gift of political wisdom, in the form of respect for others and a sense of justice, so that they are able to come together in cities. This gift he bestows on every single member of the race, because he believes that unless all have it, co-operation will not be possible. Although in the *Statesman,* Plato does not reiterate Protagoras's story (and indeed there are other versions of the myth elsewhere in the dialogues[5]), it is clear that the central message is the same.[6] Under Kronos, there were no political constitutions (272a) Zeus decides that this is essential if the universe as a whole, and the human race in particular, are to take care of themselves.

The weaving paradigm of the third and last definition (277d–311c) completes this thought by arguing that ruling is nothing but the harmonizing of the strengths and weaknesses of citizens, binding them together so they can rule themselves. Several writers have commented that this conclusion was somehow at odds with most interpretations of the *Statesman* as offering a paternalistic view of the rule of law.[7] I agree with them that the *Statesman's* picture of ruling and laws is in fact neither absolutist nor authoritarian. However, in order to defend this interpretation, one first has to make sense of the several apparently contradictory claims that Plato makes about the role of laws in the dialogue. I shall argue that when these contradictions are resolved what we get is a plausible and attractive account of the role of laws, in particular in judging, from a virtue ethical perspective.

The two controversial and apparently contradictory claims about laws are made in the third part of the dialogue. The Stranger from Eleas argues the following:

1. That a true king will not rely on laws except as convenient shorthand to avoid having to review each individual case, and as guidelines for his people on occasions when he has to go away.[8]
2. That in the absence of a true king, states must do their best to imitate the rule of the true king and that to do so, they must stick to their written laws, whatever they are, and not attempt to change them or write new ones.[9]

These two claims are each problematic in themselves – neither is prima facie wholly acceptable for reasons I will discuss below and in the following section. But also, there appears to be a stark contradiction between these two views, the first promoting a virtue ethical understanding of laws as rigid and unlikely to lead to just rule, the second claiming that only rigid obedience to laws *qua* laws (i.e. regardless of whether they are good laws) is likely to yield justice.

This leads to the following paradox. If we believe that just rule is virtuous rule, i.e. that it depends on the correct appraisal of and appropriate response to each situation, and moreover, we do not believe that there are likely to be perfectly virtuous rulers, then, according to the *Statesman*, we should come to the conclusion that the exercise of the virtues, and of the ability of the virtuous person to judge what the right thing to do is for each situation, should be kept entirely separate from just rule. In other words, the paradox states first the desirability and then the impossibility of a virtue-led understanding of the role of laws.

The first claim, although apparently outrageous, is a natural implication of the kind of virtue ethical thinking we have been discussing. A virtue ethicist believes that to be a good person is to have certain character traits which enable us to perceive or decide (depending on whether we are proponents of agent-focused or agent-based virtue ethics) for each situation what the proper thing to do is without having to rely on moral rules, because reliance on moral rules prevent us from perceiving special, morally relevant features of a situation. These features, again depending on whether we account for them from the perspective of agent-focused or agent-based virtue ethics, either determine, or help us decide what the proper course of action is. In my introduction I used the example of King Solomon's judgment of two women both claiming to be mothers of the same baby. What may Solomon have noticed, when confronted with the true and the fake mothers? That at least one of the women seemed genuinely distressed at the possibility of losing the baby, and was not acting.

Recognizing human emotions, thus, is one of the skills that a virtuous person will have. But had Solomon relied on a more 'legal' judgment, he would not have been able to act on this perception of the emotions at play. He would have had to say that, in the absence of conclusive evidence, the baby had to be either taken into care, or given to the woman best able to bring it up, or whatever the local laws might have said on such issues.

It seems a natural progression from this to the thought that reliance on written laws cannot yield justice in all cases as 'justice is blind' and laws fail to take into consideration aspects of situation which may be relevant to its justice or injustice. As Aristotle famously put it, reflecting the statement of the Eleatic Stranger quoted earlier:

> And this is the nature of the equitable, a correction of law where it is defective owing to its universality. In fact this is the reason why all things are not determined by law, *viz.* that about some things it is impossible to lay down a law, so that a decree is needed. For when the thing is indefinite, the rule also is indefinite, like the leaden rule used in making the Lesbian moulding; the rule adapts itself to the shape of the stone and is not rigid, and so too the decree is adapted to the facts.[10]

So Aristotle describes the perspective that virtue ethics, whether agent-based or agent-focused, will almost inevitably take on laws, and at the same time outlines a possible solution to the problem which faces the virtue ethical account. Laws, because they are universal and do not pay heed to the particular, cannot ensure that justice will be done. Therefore they must be supplemented with decrees or judgments that will adapt themselves to the particulars of a situation just as the Lesbian rule adapts itself to the shape of the stone.[11]

I will return to Aristotle's short account of equity (in Book 5 of the *Nicomachean Ethics* and Book I of the *Rhetoric*) in Section 4. First, I shall look at some responses to the Stranger's two claims that, I shall argue, are unsatisfactory, because they fail to make sense of the apparent paradox.

3. The anti-democratic reading of the second claim

The first one of the Stranger's suggestion – that the true king should rule without laws – is hard to stomach. If that were to be realized we would have to take a serious gamble with the character of the king and hope that he was both capable and willing to rule us fairly.[12] In Section 4, we will return to this claim and see how this prima facie reading falls short of what the Stranger from Eleas is in fact proposing, and that it is rather less threatening on the whole than what we might think at first.

In this section, we will concentrate on the Stranger's second claim, that in the absence of the true king we should never attempt to change existing laws in anyway. Constitutions which do not benefit from the rule of the true king 'owe their very preservation to their following a code of laws enacted for this true state and to a strict adherence to a rule which we admit to be desirable though it falls short of the ideal' (297d). In order to live just lives, citizens should then do nothing 'contrary to the laws and [. . .] if any of them ventures to do such act, the penalty is to be death or the utmost rigour of punishment' (297e).

In brief, what the Stranger appears to be proposing is that we should hang our hopes on a system of laws that was written in another era, by a king who ruled through laws only as a last resort, and that we should neither attempt to reform these laws, nor forgive those who disobey them. This proposal is absurd in the sense that it relies on an unbounded trust in a largely mythical past, and that practically, it is bound to lead to the collapse of any society attempting to follow it.

The Stranger is suggesting that we abide by a system of ancestral laws, and to assume both that these laws were originally created by a true king, an unfailing legislator, and that they have not been meddled with at all since they were put in place by that individual.[13]

But legal systems do become outdated in a way that makes it at best futile and at worst dangerous not to recognize that this is the case. They can become outdated in at least three ways. A good case study for how a legal system can become outdated is the Napoleonic code of 1804.[14] This code is still largely in place, although it has been subjected to many revisions. First, individual laws will have been designed to deal with situations that no longer arise. The Napoleonic code does have such laws, some of which have yet to be repealed, as for instance, the law forbidding anyone from naming their pig Napoleon, or (more worryingly) the law requiring a woman who wants to wear trousers to obtain a signed authorization from the police prefecture. This latter law was revised in 1909, so that it no longer applies to women riding a bicycle or a horse. No one is however prosecuted under these laws, and, one hopes, if it were to arise, the laws would be repealed.[15]

The second way in which a legal system can become outdated, is if it is unable to deal with new situations, such as would have been inconceivable at the time the laws were created. Sections 16-10 to 16-13 of the Napoleonic code deal with the question of DNA – under what circumstances it should be allowed to examine a person's DNA, or to attempt to identify a person by their DNA. These sections of the code were introduced in 1994. In 1804, when the code was originally imposed, there was of course no question of DNA identification. But the advent of DNA research has led to the need for new laws regarding consent, etc. A code that did not make any provision for dealing with these questions would be inadequate.

It is hard to see how the Stranger from Eleas could have objected to the two points I have just made. If he had, it would have been because he considered a static society in which there would be no scientific or technological advancement. The third way in which I consider a legal system to be outdated, however, he might regard as more controversial, since it regards moral advancement, how we come to see certain situations in a very different light as our society evolves. Our perceptions of these situations may change to such an extent that we feel existing laws no longer deal with them appropriately. One good example for this are the part of the Napoleonic Code that deals with marriage laws. In 1804, Article 213 of the code stated that a husband owes protection to his wife, and that a wife owes obedience to her husband. In 1970, this law was amended to the following: married persons are together responsible for the moral and material well-being of their family. The reform reflects our changing attitude to women and marriage. Whereas at the beginning of the nineteenth century fathers were considered the heads of their families, and had full powers over their spouses and children, and women were deemed 'impotent' and had only very limited ownership rights, by the second half of the twentieth century, things were very different, and a code granting more rights to men and less to women would have been deemed unacceptable. At the beginning of the twenty-first century, it would be inconceivable for the laws on marriage to have remained as they were in 1804.

The idea that moral progress matters, however, may not be as easily accepted by the Stranger from Eleas as the thought that we should change laws to account for technological progress. His main concern is that, unlike the True King, we are not fit to decide which laws would best serve justice. So to say that we think a law is outdated because we are now capable of better moral judgments regarding certain issues might strike him as presumptuous. Who are we to decide which ones of our moral judgments are good and which are bad? The ancestral laws are, after all, our only guides to what is right and wrong. Without these laws, we are not in a position to form good judgments.

Various commentators have attempted to make sense of the Stranger's proposition so that it seems less absurd. Christopher Gill sees the Stranger's second claim as a 'theoretical reconstitution' of the constitutionalist position apparently held by the Young Socrates and refuted by the Stranger at 291–299.[16] Laws should be respected, but not for the reasons that apparently led the Young Socrates to express reservations about lawless rule.[17]

However Gill's response to the Stranger's second claim is unsatisfactory for two reasons. First, there is little evidence in the text that the Young Socrates holds any particular view about why we should respect the laws. All he does is to express reservations about lawless rule, in one short sentence at 293e![18] Secondly it is not clear how Gill's view accounts for the more extreme claims that the Stranger makes – he does not, after all, simply say that we should respect the law. Gill's explanation of the Stranger's claim that it is better that we should not be allowed to change our laws is simply a reiteration of what the stranger himself argues: we do not have 'true' knowledge, therefore our understanding of what would constitute a 'better' law is necessarily flawed and unreliable. This, however, in no way mitigates what the Stranger says, nor does it render it more acceptable.

Melissa Lane offers an explanation of the Stranger's authoritarian claim that is *prima facie* more satisfactory than Gill's, but still leaves some questions unanswered. She argues that the state in which laws remain unchanged imitates the rule of the true king in that laws are not to be changed when the true king is absent, with the proviso that members of imperfect states should be prepared to welcome the true king, were he to appear, and accept that any changes he would make as being for the better.[19] This has at least the advantage that we are not relinquishing the very possibility of virtuous rule, and that we are keeping in mind the fact that such rule would be better than what we are presently forced to accept.

But Lane also emphasizes that human government imitates the rule of Zeus, rather than the rule of Kronos, as they are presented in the Myth.[20] Kronos ruled the universe as a shepherd, providing everything for its herds, so that they did not have to be autonomous in anyway. The rule of Zeus introduced autonomy, first in self-generation, human beings were no longer born from the earth and were responsible for finding a mate and producing children, and self-rule – Zeus gave human beings the arts and left them to organize their own lives. The art of Statesmanship imitates the rule of Zeus, rather than the rule of Kronos, in that its ultimate aim is to hand over the administration of the city to the people: 'When he has woven his web smooth and "close-woven", as the phrase goes, out of men of these different types, he must entrust the various offices of state to them to be shared in all cases between them' (311a). Because of this, we should expect that if the actual states imitate the rule of the true king, they also imitate the rule of Zeus, and there must be a certain amount of autonomy in the way they are ruled. This autonomy is absent from the scenario proposed as 'second best' by the stranger, and also from the interpretation Lane gives of it.

At least one recent commentator, Rosen, has argued that the Stranger's proposition is in fact absurd and insulting – that it is not a logical consequence of the Stranger's discussion of the true king and the role of law, but of Plato's anti-democratic tendencies that are reflected in the Stranger's views on what we should do in the absence of the true king.

According to Rosen, a significant aspect of the Stranger's second claim is that he emphasizes that existing laws are the result of long experience and that this is one good reason for not changing them. The Stranger gives no reason why we should believe this to be the case, and, moreover, he had earlier attributed the laws to the many and ignorance.[21] The Stranger is therefore playing fast and loose with his argument, modifying premises without giving reasons so as to get to the conclusion that we should respect laws. However, Rosen points out, the conclusion itself is strongly linked with the Stranger's criticism of democracy and self-rule by the many, thereby helping to fulfil an anti-democratic agenda not unlike that of the *Republic*.[22] The many are not capable of ruling themselves, therefore, we should limit the extent to which they are allowed to do so in states such as Athens by forcing them to respect tradition.

Rosen's interpretation makes sense of the apparent contradiction between the Stranger's two claims by retaining it. The second claim is not a logical implication of the first; it contradicts it in order to fulfil a political agenda. Rosen's position is attractive for its honesty, and for its refusal to try just anything in order to erase some apparent absurdity in Plato.

It seems that if we take Rosen's proposition seriously, it might lead us to recognize the following implication. We need not take seriously what the Stranger says about laws when there is no true king and we can go ahead and apply the model he suggests earlier for virtue jurisprudence, i.e. judge each case according to its particular merit.[23] This would enable us to make sense of Plato's claims, as noted by Lane, that human rule must be self-rule. But before we jump to this solution, I want to express two strong reservations.

First, it is not clear that this model is in fact a good idea. We do not want anyone who is not perfect (or even someone perfect) to rule without laws – this is an even scarier prospect than the authoritarian view suggested by the Stranger. The possibility that this might lead to abuse, or the thought that we have to trust implicitly decisions concerning our lives without being able to predict what they will be, or even maybe without understanding them can only bring on terror on the part of citizens subject to this kind of rule. Indeed, when the Stranger brings up the question of whether the true king should govern without laws, Young Socrates is quick to reply 'All the rest, sir, I believe to have been spoken in due measure – but the saying about ruling without laws is a hard saying for us to hear.'[24]

Secondly, although the Stranger does put forward strongly anti-democratic views, it is also the case that there is a great emphasis on self-rule in both the myth and later, the weaving paradigm.[25] So it is not clear that we have enough evidence to read the conclusion of the dialogue as authoritarian and anti-democratic reliance on laws.

4. Equity

In Section 3, I suggested first that it would be no victory for virtue jurisprudence if the *Statesman* concluded that rule by law was harmful, and secondly that it is not the case that the *Statesman* draws a conclusion that is *a priori* incompatible with virtue ethical views (i.e. as an authoritarian anti-democratic claim that we should rely solely on laws and not change them would be). So is there a third way, something that avoids rejection of virtue ethical perspective but does not adopt a naive one either? The only conclusion that we can draw with confidence is that Plato thought there must be, as he rejected the other two answers. The 'true king' is declared non-existent and unlikely ever to come forth,[26] and the dialogue concludes with the necessity of giving over the running of the city to the citizens in common, thus supposing that the citizens rule themselves in a non-negligible way, and not that they are slaves to sacred and unchanging laws.[27]

It is not clear that the Stranger from Eleas is claiming that the perfect king should govern without laws. Young Socrates worries that governing without laws is something that the Stranger is indeed considering, but his intervention at 293e makes it sound as though the Stranger is proposing that the perfect king should systematically do without laws (except as reminder and shorthand). Not only does this not fit what the Stranger actually says before Young Socrates' intervention (he gives a list of ways in which a king might rule without laws is simply one of these possible ways), but it is also contradicted by the final definition of the statesman as 'kingly lawgiver' at 305b.[28]

If the Stranger is not defending the view that the perfect king should govern without laws – he says that at least, he should use them as shorthands and reminders – then his view is better interpreted less dramatically as claiming that laws may be insufficient as far as justice is concerned, but they are not dispensable. The king must attempt, whenever possible, to judge individual cases on their own merits, but he cannot possibly sit by every citizen and teach them what life would be fitted to their character and situation[29] – so he must use laws as 'shorthand', and 'reminder'.[30]

This is only possible because laws are general enough that they benefit a large majority of citizens. This being the case, it makes more sense to rule everyone by laws, and then deal with exceptions, or problem cases separately.[31] This resolves the practical impossibility to deal with each citizen on an *ad hoc* basis, without sacrificing the benefit they receive from the rule of the perfect king.

If the Stranger does indeed believe that the true king will rule partly through laws, then the role of laws in the perfect constitution and the role of law in actual constitutions need not be that different, i.e., the Stranger does not contradict himself when he says that in order to imitate the perfect king, actual rulers should respect existing laws. The true king also has to rule according to laws that he cannot, presumably, change at the drop of a hat – for if he did, they would not have the authority of laws.

Nonetheless, it remains that in the absence of a true king, the Stranger recommends that we do not attempt to modify existing laws, whatever they are, and whoever made them even if we truly believe we can improve them. Undeniably, there is something unpleasantly paternalistic about this view. But we should note, that from a virtue ethical perspective, the alternative is that those who are not fully virtuous should be able to create laws, the purpose of which is to produce virtue and eradicate vice in society. This is what liberals fear about virtue jurisprudence, and Solum, for example, only wishes to apply virtue ethics to judging, and not legislating. For a virtue ethicist, there is no escape from the fact that law-making is a value-laden process, so to restrict it to those who are sufficiently virtuous, may be an important way of limiting the damage, rather than a paternalistic imposition.

But even if we accept that the ban on legislating makes sense, how can we possibly find of way to imitate the wise king and to rule ourselves in a virtuous manner if we cannot use our reason to do so, but must in all cases refer to pre-existing laws over which we have no control whatsoever?[32]

I suggest that there is more to be learnt about what the Stranger has in mind for actual, imperfect constitutions by studying the rule of the wise king. In particular, a certain feature of what the wise king does strikes me as highly relevant to an understanding of what the Stranger has in mind for actual constitutions, namely that there is no evidence that the wise king sees that justice is done simply by changing laws. On the contrary, the Stranger emphasizes that what is specific to the wise king is that he promotes justice sometimes by decrees that go against existing laws.[33] He is capable of dealing with particular cases without appealing to laws. In other words, he exercises equity.[34]

Lawrence Solum, notes the centrality of the concept of equity in a virtue-centred theory of law, and claims that this concept is rooted in Aristotle's *Ethics*, quoting 1137b9–24.[35] According to Solum, the two significant characteristics of equity are first, a departure from the rules, with the intention of correcting the generality of the rule by allowing exception in cases where the rule leads to unjust results; secondly, particularism, i.e. the tailoring of the law to the demands of particular cases.[36] But because the wise king does not rule entirely without laws, and at the same time, what is specific about his ability to promote justice is to act according to the demands of the particular case, then it is fair to say that the wise king practises equity, and that the concept is rooted in Plato's *Statesman*, rather than in Aristotle's *Ethics*.[37] As such, it is capable of yielding an agent-based account of virtue jurisprudence, which is what Solum seems to need, and not merely an agent-focused one, which, according to Slote, is all that Aristotle would offer.

Although Aristotle does not offer a complete account of equity – he talks about it briefly in Book 5 of the *Nicomachean Ethics* and in Book I of the *Rhetoric* – as is often the case, what he has to say is useful in order to understand Plato's own views.[38] First, as we saw in the passage quoted in Section 1 from the *Ethics*, Aristotle regards the laws as necessarily failing to deal fairly with each and every particular case. The laws are by nature general, and generality by nature is blind to particularity. That the laws are general and not particular is a good thing, as it prevents judgment from being arbitrary and clouded by private likes or dislikes, and for this reason it is better to rule by law than by decree.[39] Moreover, the law commands justice. By doing what the law bids us do, we act in a virtuous manner, i.e. temperately, courageously, justly.[40] Aristotle is firm on this point: 'all lawful acts are in a sense just acts'.[41] Yet, because of the general character of the law, it can also be just to go beyond the law: 'For the equitable is held to be right, and equity is right going beyond the written law.'[42]

Given that the law is just and by nature incapable of dealing justly with all particular cases, it follows for Aristotle that equity is also just, not as a 'moral supplement' to a morally neutral law, but rather as a way of supporting the law in the spirit in which it was originally conceived. For Aristotle, the equitable judge seeks to act in the spirit in which the legislator created the law that is seen to fail in a particular case.[43] This may be for one of two reasons. First, the legislator may have overlooked some possible cases that the law would have to deal with. Secondly, he may have realized that the law would not be able to deal with all cases, even be aware of what some of the cases in which it would fail would be, but nonetheless wished to create a general law that would deal justly with most cases.[44] In the second case, the legislator is explicitly relying on the practice of equity, in the first, implicitly.

Short of a theory of equity, we can certainly attribute the following conclusions to Aristotle. First, laws are valuable because they are general, and consequently, the exercise of equity in no way presupposes that we are justified in violating laws on grounds that they fail to cover certain cases. Secondly, even though equity goes beyond the written law, it is not a way of compensating from an external moral point of view for the failings of a morally neutral law, but a way of supporting the legal system in the spirit in which it was created.[45] These conclusions, I believe can equally be applied to the apparent paradox of the *Statesman*, and clarify Plato's views.

The true king, if he relies both on a legal system (305b) and goes beyond it when he perceives that the law is unable to deal with the particular, exercises equity in the sense in which Aristotle understood it. That is, equitable judgments are judgments that depend on their being a system of just laws that necessarily are incapable of dealing fairly with each and every case. If actual rulers are to imitate the wise king, and they are to rule according to whatever laws they happen to have, then it is reasonable to suppose that they should also exercise equity in that sense.

That this is what Plato thinks is strongly compatible with the claim, suggested in the myth and the weaving paradigm that actual rulers should rely on their own judgment as to what the just way to rule might be. The practice of equity, as understood here, enables us to exercise a certain independence of judgment *vis a vis* the laws, while at the same time having full respect for the authority of those laws. The practice is rooted in the belief that laws both ought to be general in order to be just and that because they are general, they will necessarily fall short in certain particular cases and will have to be supplemented by equity.

If Plato in the *Statesman* is not as explicit as Aristotle is in telling us why the law should be general, he does give something like an argument at 294e. The legislator's concern for generality is similar to that of the trainer. General instructions can reach and benefit a larger number of people and are therefore superior to decrees directed at a small group of individuals. Thus, the true king, even if he will rely on decrees to correct the shortcomings of general laws, will nonetheless start off with a system of general laws. Thus, for an actual ruler to imitate the true king as far as possible, that is, short of legislation, he or she must rule both according to a legal system and allow for the practice of equity to take place.

There is an apparent contradiction between the claim that rulers should rely on their own judgment and the claim that they should not attempt to modify laws even when those appear to be bad, and when they have a clear idea of what would constitute an improvement. But if they are expected to exercise equity, then the contradiction disappears, as equity requires a reliance on one's own judgment at least equal to that required by legislation. The equitable judge must be capable of perceiving the features of a case which prevent it from being dealt with justly by the law, and she must be able to judge what a good solution in that case would be.

But doesn't this 'perceiving' of the morally relevant features of the case mean that the equitable judge perceives, rather than produces the right judgment? This makes it sound as though virtue-jurisprudence would be agent-focused rather than agent-based – following Slote's distinction – which we saw would be less advantageous. But in fact it does not follow that this would be the case, as the morally relevant features perceived by the judge, when put together, are unlikely to yield the judgment. Solomon's perception that one of the two women appeared to display genuine concern for the baby she was claiming as hers did not entail that the right course of action was to offer to split the child in two halves. Had he made his perception known to a friend, the friend would not have been in a position to use it in order to come up with a similar judgment. The judgment had to come from Solomon, because he alone was virtuous enough to come up with it.

An interesting analogy to this can be found in crime literature. Often, a good, intuitive detective will perceive certain aspects of the crime which he or she will use to produce an answer. The detective may point out those features to their subordinate. They may even attempt to explain why to their mind these are relevant features. But although the subordinate will spend time puzzling over those 'pieces of evidence' he or she will never come up with the solution before the detective does. The evidence simply has to be processed in the mind of the more experienced and gifted detective in order to produce an answer.

There is also a strong disanalogy here, for although I am claiming that the equitable judge produces, rather than perceives the right judgment, it is always the case that the detective finds out a truth that was always there for all to see. But there is a sense, nonetheless, in which the detective 'produces' rather than simply 'perceives' the solution, a creative aspect to their work. This is no doubt why, in some kinds of crime fiction, the detective never simply comes up with the truth, but, at the same time, with a decision as to whether to disclose the truth, when, how and to whom. The detective is portrayed as a judge, and this is because the process of detection, in analogy to equitable judgment, is portrayed as 'agent-based'.

Of course, it would not do to interpret Plato as saying that it is fine to disregard the laws, and that the only reason why we should not change them is that they are ineffective when it comes to practice anyway. If Plato thinks that legislation in the wrong hands is dangerous, then he must also think that lawless judgment in the wrong hands is a bad thing. So we must make sure that by equity, here, we do not understand licence to act in any way proscribed by our laws whenever we feel that the laws are inappropriate. In other words, the laws must remain binding, and there must be very strong limits to the exercise of equity.

5. An objection

One potential problem with understanding equitable judging as in part the ability to perceive the morally relevant features of a case and to process them in a virtuous character is that the equitable judge may turn out to be as much a fictional creature as the true king. Solum himself claims that since equity requires fine judgment about what is required to bring about justice in a complicated particular situation, judging at the same time that the available laws are incapable of bringing it about in this case, equity should only be practised by a *phronimos*.[46] But if this is right, then why expect that actual, imperfect rulers will be able to exercise equity anymore than they would be competent law-makers and reformers?

Solum is right to say that in order to practise equity, a judge should be virtuous. One would be suspicious of a judge who was known to be sexually promiscuous deciding to exercise equity on behalf of a young and handsome accused! Or we would be weary of letting a judge use his or her discretion when he or she was suspected of taking bribes. But we do not generally regard it as a good thing that a judge should have such defects! A judge may be prey to the same vices as the average citizens, but we would regard it as a breach of their professionalism if they were to give in to these vices immoderately. This does not amount to saying the judge should be a *phronimos*, in the sense of a perfectly virtuous individual, but simply a person of good character, well-versed in the law, and with a superior ability to understand people's motivations.

This, I think, fits with Plato's idea of what is needed in order to exercise equity. Although Plato thinks only a perfect ruler could both legislate and exercise equity, he can say that as long as we can rely on our laws being basucakkt good, we don't have to be perfect to be equitable.

In a situation in which we had to do both, i.e. legislate and practise equity, there would indeed be no reason to expect us to perform well in either. Equity requires skills that are as uncommon as legislation, and that arguably, only a *phronimos* would master perfectly. But this is not the situation under scrutiny here. Plato's actual rulers are not required to practise equity *and* legislate. Indeed, they are required not to legislate and to stick closely to the laws that have been transmitted to them. In other words, they are not practising equity from scratch, having to work out what justice is, and how to recognize it in each particular situation. They can assume that their laws are for the most part just, and that in most cases, they bring about justice.

Here it is helpful to refer back to what we identified as Aristotle's view of equity. The very possibility of equitable judgment as Aristotle understands it relies on the assumption that the laws are just, and that when they fall short in a particular case, to exercise equity is to recommend an action that the original legislator would have understood as just.

So, to come back to the *Statesman*, it is not the case that an actual ruler who is an equitable judge ought to be such a rare animal as a true king, or a good legislator. What the equitable judge needs to do is to observe what it is that the existing laws generally bring about, identify it as justice, and to learn to recognize cases in which the laws fail to bring about justice. In these cases only, should they practise equity.

This thought also enables us to confirm the following suspicion. Yes, there must be strong limits to the practice of equity, and these limits must be set by a general respect of the laws, and the belief that in many cases, there is no need to practise equity as the laws bring about justice. Under these circumstances, it is possible and desirable for an actual ruler who is not perfectly virtuous to practise equity.

6. Making way for the *Laws*

I have tried to show in this chapter that Plato does not argue that the particularity of the wise king is that he rules without laws, but that his laws are supplemented by equity, judgments tailored to the needs of particular situations. It follows that the ban on legislation imposed by the Stranger on actual rulers does not preclude their imitating the wise king. Like him, they can supplement the existing laws with the exercise of equity, within certain, very strict, limits. This seems, on the whole a reasonably satisfactory resolution of the paradox outlined in Section 2, and at the same time, a plausible proposal for a virtue ethical account of the role of laws in government.

One conclusion we might feel tempted to draw from the *Statesman* is that virtue jurisprudence should limit itself to judging and not be applied to legislating. Plato seems to feel that virtue legislation is dangerous work, and that unless one happens to be a 'perfect king', one had better steer clear of it. This does in some ways reflect liberal concerns about virtue and the laws: we cannot trust ourselves to 'moralize' the laws and do it well, without damaging personal freedom and diversity. Of course Plato is in no sense a liberal. His solution in the *Statesman* is not that we should be legislators without the virtues, but that we should not legislate at all, that we should keep whatever laws have been passed down to us by our ancestors.

The concern that we should not use our conceptions of virtue to legislate, as this would be too dangerous, is one that I will address in the next chapter. It seems that in his last work, the *Laws*, Plato does believe it is possible to draw laws according to the dictates of virtue, and in such a way that they will, indeed, be virtuous laws, i.e. laws that promote and protect an environment in which it is possible for citizens to lead virtuous lives. It also seems that in the *Laws*, Plato changes his mind about the deeply unsatisfying ban on revising old laws and creating new ones. With this next chapter I therefore hope to complete my project of showing how Plato's dialogues teach us how we may develop a virtue jurisprudence which avoids the pitfalls of paternalism as much as possible.

Chapter 7

The *Laws*: Persuading the Citizens

1. Introduction

In *Pride and Prejudice,* Elisabeth Bennet confronts Mr Darcy about some accusations that have been levelled against him. Darcy refuses to defend himself. He believes that a gentleman should expect to be trusted to do the right thing and not have to account for himself. Elisabeth is unimpressed and puts his reply down to excessive pride. Later on in the novel, when Darcy's slanderer, Wickham, has eloped with Elisabeth's younger sister, Darcy regrets his silence. By speaking out against the accusations, he would have warned Elisabeth, and whomsoever cared to listen, that Wickham was dangerous. Darcy comes to recognize, that if he is to function in a world where not everyone is a gentleman, he too must account for himself; he must not only expect to be trusted to do the right thing, but he must also be seen to do it publicly. When Darcy rescues Elisabeth's sister, he comes down from his moral isolation, and agrees to the terms of the world of ordinary people.

It may seem that Plato once experienced a similar change of heart, for in the *Republic,* he suggests that a city in which virtue prevails will not need laws. 'It would not be fitting' he said, 'to dictate to good and honorable men', as they should be in a position to discover by themselves what should and should not be done in all cases (425d–e). But later in the *Laws,* he offers a very different position. Even though the citizens of the *Laws,* like those of the *Republic,* are to be educated into virtue – Books II and III give a detailed account of what that education would consist of – every aspect of their lives will be regulated by a great number of very detailed laws.

Did Plato, like Darcy, abandon the world of the pure and the virtuous to ask how things should be done in the world of ordinary people?[1] And if so, why did he? If we believe he did change his mind, and if we assume, that, as in Darcy's case, it was because his previous attitude got him into trouble, in other words, if one looks for a psychological explanation, rather than a philosophical one, then the Sicilian debacle is a good candidate for explaining Plato's supposed change of heart. Having tried, and spectacularly failed to set up the tyrant of Syracuse as a philosopher king, Plato decided to place his trust in laws rather than men (*Seventh Letter*, 334c). The *Laws* is said to reflect this change.[2] Plato started with unrealistic expectations as to what human beings were capable of in the political domain – namely that they were capable simply of acting virtuously without having to be checked by laws. He was brought up against harsh reality when his Sicilian project failed with disastrous consequences to his friends. Like Darcy, he decided that ordinary people could not function in accordance to the ideals he had set out. Coming down to the real world, he wrote new ideals that provided guidance for these ordinary people, in the forms of laws regulating every aspect of their lives.

This view of what happened is attractive to Plato's detractors because it shows Plato as having been mistaken, unable to understand the real world; and when he finally does understand, he is, much too harsh with it. On the other hand, it does place undue reliance on an incident in Plato's life for which we have very little historical evidence, and it mostly ignores some relevant aspects of the texts we know he did write. At no point in the *Republic* does Plato express confidence that the state he is describing could be realized. Even if it could be realized (and it is not clear that he thinks this as it would depend on the philosophers' willingness to quit philosophy and become kings – see 473 and 499b) it is not the point which Plato wants to make. What is important he says at 472c is that we can picture an ideal in order to understand what justice is and then apply it to ourselves as best we can. Whether the ideal city can be actualized, Socrates tells Glaucon, is neither here nor there.

The *Republic* is concerned with drawing up an ideal which is used to define justice, not to realize it. Therefore its practical value is little more than offering guidance regarding the effects of education, some insight into the workings of the human soul and the corresponding forms of government. Even the *Seventh Letter* tells us that Plato did not himself come up with the idea of applying the ideas of the *Republic* in Sicily: he did it at the urgent bequest of his friend Dion (327b–330d).

If the *Laws* is not a consequence of Plato's failure to apply the theories of the *Republic*, how then may we explain the Darcy-like change of heart that we witness between the *Republic* and the *Laws*? The simplest answer is that whereas the *Republic* describes an ideal city, the *Laws* is concerned with what can be done with a real city and real citizens who have only their elders to guide them; and these elders fall very short of the philosopher kings. Plato is working on two different projects, with different purposes, and there is no 'coming down to earth' on his part. As far as he is concerned, the *Republic* serves theoretical purposes, but does not pretend to be a guide to politics. The *Laws*, on the other hand, does. The *Laws* is a treatise that is meant to be applicable to the world of ordinary people.

2. Preambles

In Chapter 6, I argued that the *Statesman* could be understood as an attempt to infuse the way citizens are ruled by laws with certain virtue ethical conceptions. The laws themselves should not be meddled with, but those citizens who are gifted with a greater amount of political wisdom can exercise equity in the way they apply the law, i.e. they can try and understand the spirit of the law and find ways of judging particular cases for which the letter of the law does not offer a satisfactory solution.

This compromise falls short of what we might expect from a virtue jurisprudence in two ways. First, it does not allow citizens to use virtue in order to legislate: they have to make do with whatever laws they happen to have. Plato's claim that these laws will be just laws, because they will have been created by some ancestral true king is simply not convincing. And we saw that even if that were to be the case, even good legal systems can become outdated and call for substantial revisions.

Secondly, one central aspect of a virtue-centred legal system, we saw in Chapters 2 and 3, is that citizens should be able to 'persuade' the laws if they feel that the laws do not promote virtue, and that this was a precondition of obedience: we do not have a duty to obey a law unless we know that we could try to persuade the state that that law is wrong. This clearly is not going to be possible if citizens are not allowed to create, or modify their laws, but merely to reflect on the best way of applying them through equity if needs be. So in this last chapter, we shall have to see whether Plato's last dialogue allows citizens to modify existing laws, or create new ones. I shall argue that it does because in the *Laws*, Plato insists that there has to be a dialogue between the laws and the citizens, not a static relationship. The emphasis is on the laws persuading citizens, but this, I shall argue, is only really possible if citizens are in turn able to persuade the laws.

The main innovation of the *Laws* is the concern that laws should not just be given, but explained and made convincing to the citizens–a practical touch that distinguishes it from Plato's other project the *Republic*, and indeed, from any actual or theoretical legislation before the *Laws* (722b–c).

Preambles should be given for each individual law – except maybe the least significant ones (723c) – and for the legislative system itself (722d).

The preambles should persuade in such a way as to produce in the subjects 'a spirit of friendliness and consequent docility' (723a) towards the law; this makes it more likely that the law will be obeyed, and less likely that its 'dictatorial' aspect, i.e. the law itself with its specification of penalties, will have to be applied (772e, 887a).

The model for the preambles is given by a contrast between the free doctor and the slave doctor who used to treat the servants of the free doctor's patient. The slave doctor ministers to servants 'in the brusque fashion of a dictator' simply issuing prescriptions without bothering to explain what is wrong with the patient (720c). The free doctor, on the other hand, spends time talking with the patient, both to find out what is wrong with him or her, and to educate the patient into understanding their own body and their ailment. The free doctor can then *persuade* the patient to accept a particular cure. The slave doctor is the model for the kind of legislators who do not employ persuasion but just tell 'us curtly what we are to do or not do, add the threat of a penalty, and then turn to the next enactment, without one word of exhortation or advice to the recipients' (720a). This kind of legislator, according to the Athenian and his friend, is clearly inferior, just as the slave doctor is not as good a doctor as his free counterpart. Instead, we should have laws which attempt to persuade, before they decree, and especially before they threaten. The persuasion should be as like that of the doctor to the patient as possible: it should educate the citizens and insofar as it is possible, engage them in dialogue.

The model of the free doctor highlights Plato's concern for something akin to citizens' autonomy[3] in choosing to obey the law. Just as it matters to the effectiveness of the doctor's treatment that the patient understands and agrees with his choice of cure, Plato appears to believe that laws will be better if citizens reflect on them and understand that they are good laws.[4]

By Plato's own admission, the preamble's means of persuasion are in part rhetorical (723a). This is borne out by his doctor analogy, as a free doctor would sometime employ a rhetor to talk a patient into an amputation (a practice described in *Gorgias,* 456b). Yet the persuasion is also philosophical. The doctor talks to his patient 'almost like a philosopher' (857d).[5] This view of preambles is illustrated by the preamble for the law against atheism, the longest preamble to a law offered in the text: (Book X). This preamble takes the form of an elenctic debate between an imagined atheist and the three legislators,[6] or at times between Clinias and the Athenian (891c). The task the legislators set themselves is to 'furnish the undevoutly disposed with adequate proofs on the points which they said we were bound to treat' (887a). This is more than a rhetor would do; a rhetor is not so much concerned with imparting justified belief as with imparting belief (*Gorgias*, 454d). Yet, the truths are only adequate, and may thus fall short of what is required to count fully as knowledge.

Despite this, there is a tendency to see the preambles of the *Laws* as purely rhetorical devices whose entire purpose is to persuade citizens to obey without putting up a fight. So Popper for example sees the preambles as a piece of 'lying propaganda'.[7] Of course, Popper's angry rejection of Plato's politics is not widely shared among Plato scholars; however there are certainly other writers who agree that on the whole, when Plato talks of persuasion, he is not to be trusted. Both Glen Morrow (552–57) and Richard Stalley have argued that the preambles Plato describes, instead of giving citizens a greater autonomy in forming their moral beliefs, represent a threat to autonomy.[8] Citizens are being psychologically manipulated to accept as their own certain moral truths that Plato has found for them. Even if these 'truths' are dictated by reason, Morrow and Stalley believe that ordinary citizens do not access them through reason. The preambles do not persuade 'rationally' in the right manner and they cannot be said, in that case, to encourage citizens to decide for themselves that the laws they are told to obey are good laws.

The problem as Stalley sees it, is not whether the preambles appeal to the citizens' reason: they do.[9] The question is rather whether the appeal to reason is pitched at a sufficiently high level to be enough, by itself, to convince, so that recourse to rhetorical trickery will be unnecessary. To return to Plato's analogy of the doctor – it may be true that in most cases, the doctor can explain the reasons for certain tests or cures so clearly and convincingly that the patient is able to conclude that he had better go through with the cure. But when the doctor brings a rhetor along to visit a patient, one has to wonder what the purpose might be. Is the argument for the need for an amputation much more complicated than the argument for taking a herbal remedy? It seems a lot simpler: if the leg stays on, it will rot. If it rots, the rot will spread to your vital organs and you will die. And however painful it will be to have your leg sawn off without proper anaesthesia, death from gangrene will be worse! The thought behind the rhetor's presence must be that very few people would find it in themselves to listen to the voice of reason in such circumstances: we are just not rational enough! In fact, we would not be surprised to see, standing behind the rhetor, a strong slave holding a big stick, waiting until the rhetor is finished to knock the patient out!

In Stalley's account, the natural conclusion to draw from Plato's insistence that the preambles will in part be rhetorical is this: Plato thinks we are not rational enough to be swayed by the voice of reason alone. For the preambles to be fully rationally persuasive, according to Stalley, they would need to resemble the elenctic way of talking about justice which, in the *Gorgias*, Plato refers to as the proper way of doing politics (527c–d). The true politician of the *Gorgias*, as opposed to the rhetor, seeks the 'unforced agreement of individuals in free discussion'.[10] By contrast, the statesmen of the *Republic* have rational insight into what is good for citizens and are concerned that the citizens should hold the right opinions but not that they should comprehend them.

There is indeed evidence for Stalley's claim that the preambles may not quite be meant as the tools of philosophical persuasion that they purport to be. For one thing, many of them are altogether devoid of argumentation. What is characteristic of these preambles, he says, is a 'tendency to rely on un-argued assertions and appeals to conventional morality'.[11] Where argument is present, it is not of the kind that would actually convince any reasonable person. A paradigm example of this, is the preamble to the law on marriage (773a–774a), of which Stalley says 'There is undoubtedly an argument here, but it is an embarrassingly bad one'.[12] It would be difficult to disagree with Stalley's judgment on this particular preamble. The preamble is meant to persuade us that it is in everyman's interest to find a wife, and that he should be penalized if he fails to marry by a certain age. The argument holds that it is a man's religious duty to marry, for he must 'cleave to everlastingness' (774a) which means producing children who will serve God when he is gone. It is also his civic duty to marry humbly, if he can, for it will bring 'balance and proportion' to the city, and avoid 'extremes'. This preamble is very short, and patronizing in tone. The argumentation is poor – it is only there in form (barely) in that Plato offers a rationale for each of his exhortations. But the rationale is in each case unconvincing, and apparently in need of much explanation if it is to make any sense.

One worry about the preambles is that although they do appeal to reason, it is not at a level that we humans pride ourselves on mastering.[13] Argument used in this way is a kind of pacifier, something that will help the rhetor's project of 'taming' the citizens, making sure that they are in a 'gentle and passive' frame of mind when the laws are delivered to them. But not all preambles offered in the law represent an insult to human intelligence, as Stalley does acknowledge. Indeed, he refers to one of them, the preamble of atheism, as 'one of the most sustained piece of argumentation in the whole of the Platonic corpus', and he generously adds that 'although it is probably fallacious, it is not obviously so'.[14]

In contrast to Morrow and Stalley, Christopher Bobonich, has argued that when Plato talks of 'rational persuasion' we should try taking him at his word.[15] The preambles of the *Laws*, he says, truly appeal to reason; they do not attempt to manipulate emotions, and they do not try to inculcate false beliefs in order to encourage people to act in certain ways. If Bobonich is right, then the *Laws* differs greatly from the *Republic*. For in the *Republic*, although it is better for everyone to be ruled by reason (590d), the rule of reason need not come from within, but may be imposed by an appeal to the emotions (such as is the case for the auxiliary guardians) or by the inculcation of false but useful beliefs (such as the myth of the three metals).[16] Bobonich believes that the purpose of the preambles is 'to provide all citizens of Magnesia with an explanation of the basic ethical principles which underline the legal and social structure of the city'.[17] Thus the preambles provide, if not quite the knowledge of the forms possessed by the kings of the *Republic*, 'true beliefs and reasoned explanations of why these beliefs are true'.[18] This is definitely an improvement over the calming or taming influence of 'unargued assertions and appeals to conventional morality' which, Stalley claimed, are characteristic of the preambles.

Bobonich focuses on the preamble for the law on atheism; this means that he is able to show that the Athenian's claim that the law-maker, like the free doctor is 'nearly doing philosophy' is not an empty one. The long preamble is a dialogue, and it takes seriously the claims which the atheist might make, refuting them very much as Socrates might have in an earlier dialogue. This preamble does not 'give' assertions, nor does it suggest that there are certain things we had better believe. It compels us to examine our beliefs rigorously by applying philosophical method to them. It demands that we should provide a justification for what we believe; if we fail, we should abandon the beliefs we cannot justify. In other words, the atheists are made to use their judgment: 'A certain kind of activity is required of them: they are to learn'.[19]

Of course, Plato does not envisage that the atheist might be capable of refuting the Athenian's arguments, and in turn convince him not to believe. This is disturbing in the way that philosophy always is when it is dogmatic. But if Stalley's worry is that the preambles do not require that the citizens of the new colony engage in elenctic examination of the principles behind the laws they must obey, then Bobonich's analysis of the atheism preamble proves him wrong. There might be something wrong-headed about Plato's confidence that no one will succeed in challenging his arguments, but this does not make them any less of an appeal to reason.

Despite his conviction that the preambles really are rationally persuasive, Bobonich is still profoundly dissatisfied with them. Like Stalley, he finds the majority of them wooden and unpersuasive, and for some of them, the argumentation they display insultingly poor. He also notes a certain 'rigidity and fixity' of the laws themselves, which sits uncomfortably with the idea that citizens will want to obey once they understand the rationale for the laws. Bobonich suggests that this gap between the stated intention of persuading rationally and this reluctance to do so can be accounted for by the fact that Plato, despite his good intentions, is persuaded that citizens, if left to their own rational devices, are bound to misunderstand the preambles and make terrible mistakes. Plato is, in principle, convinced that citizens need to understand the laws they are to obey, but at the same time, he is incapable of the necessary trust in human beings' ability to use their reason well. Is this enough of a reason for discounting the atheism prelude's attempt at engaging with citizens philosophically, and agreeing with Stalley that Plato is merely offering a palliative? No, for there are two strong reasons, besides the existence of that preamble, for believing that Plato's stated intention is genuine.

The first of these reasons is his convincing case for the need for rational persuasion. The analogy with the free doctor at 857 is sufficiently developed to be taken seriously. Also, the claim at 722d that all that preceded the actual law giving in the dialogue was a preamble, and that this is what was needed before any laws could be decided on lends support to my claim that we should take Plato seriously here. Plato is making the point that laws need to be understood in order to be effective, not just by the law-makers, but also by the subjects who will obey them.

Secondly, although the atheism preamble is by far the most philosophical, it is not the only one which uses the dialogue form, that reflects the need for the subject to be engaged in elenctic deliberation in order to understand the law. For example, the laws on sacrilege, theft and injuries, are preceded by an elenctic examination of Clinias and Megillus in lieu of a prelude (858a–864c). Here the preambles are not speeches which immediately precede the law, but instead, a conversation with the Athenian as to what the purpose of these laws should be.

These two points, taken together with the preamble for the law on atheism should be sufficient to support Plato's claim that the preambles persuade rationally. However there is still a strong need to explain why so many of these preambles are so little persuasive. I shall attempt to do so in the following section.

3. The two audiences for the preambles

The negative attitude to the preambles outlined in the previous section reflects badly on the possibility of a non-paternalistic virtue jurisprudence. I would like to suggest a different view of why the preambles of the *Laws* are not as persuasive as they might be – namely that the preambles given in the *Laws* are not identical to the preambles that the Athenian would expect to give to the citizens of the new colony. What the preambles can and should be is determined by the education received by those to whom they are addressed. This places two limitations on the Athenian's ability to formulate appropriate preambles for the citizens of the colony. First, the preambles must be understood by Clinias and Megillus who will have the job of writing them; these two have received an education which the Athenian regards as insufficient. Secondly, the Athenian is at the same time writing for an audience which does not yet exist, and so he cannot fully predict what will and will not be appropriate for that audience. This last point relies on the assumption that the preambles given in the *Laws* are somewhat provisional. In Section 5, I will present some evidence that Plato thought the laws and the preambles were up for revisions.

The Athenian stranger is engaging his two elderly friends – Clinias from Crete and Megillus from Sparta – in a project to create a constitution and laws for a new Cretan colony, which Clinias has been asked to work on.[20] That the Athenian's two friends are old,[21] and that they have grown old in Crete and Sparta suggest that no matter how well intentioned, and educated they might be, they do not have the quick intellect that younger protagonists of Plato's dialogues sometimes have, and their education has been, as far as Plato is concerned, far from ideal. They might be the best of the Spartan and the Cretan, but they are not, in any way, the kind of citizens which a model city such as the one they and the Athenian are trying to create, would hope to foster.

Plato makes sure that right from the opening, we are aware that the education Clinias and Megillus received was not the kind he regards as good for they are concerned with military values, rather than human virtue as a whole (666e–667a). This is preceded by the Athenian's attempt to define education:

> I call 'education' the initial acquisition of virtue by the child, when the feelings of pleasure and affection, pain and hatred, that well up in his soul are channeled in the right courses before he can understand the reason why. Then when he does understand, his reason and his emotions

> agree in telling him that he has been properly trained by the inculcation of appropriate habits. Virtue is this general concord of reason and emotion. But there is one element you could isolate in any account you give, and this is the correct formation of our feelings of pleasure and pain, which makes us hate what we ought to hate from first to last, and love what we ought to love. Call this 'education', and I, at any rate, think you would be giving it its proper name. (Book II, 653)

Later, in Books III and IV of the *Laws*, Plato takes great care to outline a theory of education, which will serve to determine what kind of education the citizens of the new colony should receive. Two things must be noted. First, in Book II, Plato defines education in terms of acquisition of virtue through the correct habituation of emotions, and feelings of pleasure and pain. The passage quoted above, which is clearly the source for Aristotle's own account of how one may become virtuous, tells us that an 'educated' citizen will be more receptive to appeals to virtue than someone whose education has been merely factual.[22]

Secondly, although it has been said that the citizens of Plato's Cretan colony receive a more limited education than the philosopher kings of the *Republic*, (for instance, see Aristotle, *Politics* Book II), this education is universal. What is at stake is the education of ordinary citizens, not just the ruling class – and in that context, it is less problematic that the education proposed in the *Laws* is slightly less highbrow than that offered to the philosopher kings.

The citizens of the new colony, if they have been habituated into virtue, will find it a lot easier to understand certain claims being made in the preambles, claims which appeal to a well-balanced character, such as the appeal to 'balance and proportion' in the marriage preamble (773a–774a). It would be futile to claim that any appeal to reason, however, 'universal' is ever free of assumptions as to the educational background of the audience. Certainly, if we know that a certain audience has been educated in a certain way, then it is much more effective to take this education into account when deciding how to 'pitch' an educational speech.

To come back to Plato's medical analogy, explaining the benefits of a particular kind of exercise will be a very different matter if the audience is already 'health-conscious' and aware of the benefits of exercise in general, than if the audience does not regard exercise as a way of staying healthy. The latter, would require a much lengthier exposition of the benefits of exercising regularly on the body's ability to cope with stress, ageing and disease. To an audience already conscious of the benefits of exercise, we need only stress what the effects of this particular type of exercise will be. In the same manner, if the preambles are addressed to an audience who has received an education such as the one defined in Book II and outlined in Books III and IV, we should expect them to be received somewhat differently than by an audience who has not received such an education.

Because the Athenian is proposing a general education program which he claims to be superior to that received by his two interlocutors,[23] it follows that ordinary citizens of the new colony, when they reach the age of Clinias the Cretan and Megillus the Spartan, will either need less persuasion in order to obey a law, or else be able to understand, and be persuaded by far more complex and deep preambles. In other words, if the preambles in the *Laws* are pitched at the level of ordinary citizens who have not yet benefited from the educational system of the new colony, then it is to be expected that the level they will be pitched at will be somewhat lower. If any one should feel insulted by the simplicity and the patronizing tone of the preambles, then it is Clinias and Megillus.

This is somewhat paradoxical, as the simplicity of some of the preambles seems to be explained in two contrary manners. On the one hand they may be simple because they are addressed to an audience who is pre-conditioned to respond to certain pieces of reasoning through the education they have received. On the other hand, they may be simple because they must be understood by men who have not received the kind of education necessary for understanding preambles of this sort.

It is not difficult to understand how such a situation would arise. The Athenian is after all dealing with two different audiences, and in so far as the preludes educate, they have to educate two groups of people with very different educational backgrounds.[24] Not only that, but one of these groups of people is largely unknown – the Athenian can only imagine what the future residents of the new colony will be like as a result of the laws he is helping to make for them. Clinias and Megillus, while they are not as well-educated as the future colonists will be, must nonetheless be capable of framing laws for them. So the preludes must also be designed to educate them, put them in a position where they will be capable of framing laws that will educate the citizens of the new colony.

Two important conclusions can be drawn so far about the manner in which the preambles should be interpreted. The first conclusion is that persuasion in the *Laws* is not done simply through preambles, but through education. The major difference between the intended and the actual audience of the preambles is the manner in which they have been educated. The citizens of the new colony will have gone through a program of education by habituation. They will have learnt that vice is a form of ignorance (689a), and they will have grown more virtuous. The preambles are expected to persuade the kind of people who have benefited from this form of education. They will be heard by people who have given the matters discussed serious thought over the years, people who are used to reasoning about virtue. They will be slowly digested, as part of general education, not suddenly imposed on people who have a tendency to be easily persuaded by what philosophers say. In other words, it would be a mistake to try and understand the preambles as isolated pieces of philosophical argumentations designed to persuade any reader, no matter what their background might be.[25] They are to be read and understood as part of a context which Plato sets out with great care in books III and IV.

The second conclusion is that Plato is obviously confident in placing the future of Magnesia in the hands of ordinary, good willing men. He believes that – under the guidance of a wiser man, the Athenian – they will become sufficiently virtuous to understand why their laws are good laws, and should be obeyed. Clinias and Megillus are clearly not as virtuous or as wise as the citizens they hope to produce once they have founded the colony. But they, together with the Athenian, believe that it is possible for them to lay the foundations for a better political future, that it is possible for ordinary men, under the guidance of (divine) reason, to rule themselves in a just manner. This is an incredibly optimistic belief for Plato to hold, compared with the almost eugenic selection of the rulers in the *Republic*, and the recommendation that no one try to meddle with existing laws in the *Statesman*. Here, ordinary men, who have received an ordinary, far from perfect education, are to be trusted to make laws for a city that is expected to produce citizens more virtuous than have existed anywhere.

The two conclusions are linked. That neither education nor preludes are in themselves considered sufficient is a sign that Plato is thinking in terms of what can realistically be done for ordinary citizens. That is, no amount of education, no matter how authoritarian and isolationist the city in which it is dispensed, is going to produce fully rational and virtuous citizens. Citizens will always need reminding; in order to have a good chance to live virtuously, they will need explaining over and over again, in different contexts, at different stages in their lives. Thus the very repetitiveness of what counts as persuasion, its cumbersome aspect, is in fact a virtue – an acknowledgement on Plato's part that he cannot mould human nature in the way suggested in the *Republic*. No matter how good a program of education he sets up, people will not become fully virtuous, fully rational agents; their education will be ongoing, and probably, unfinished.

4. Are the preambles paternalistic?

Now that we have seen how the preambles are supposed to work, and what the motivations for their existence is supposed to be, we are in a better position to reflect on the interpretation of the *Laws* as overly paternistic, or even authoritarian. More specifically, we can ask whether in his last work, Plato is at all able to resolve some of the more pressing problems that his previous dialogues raised, namely, is it possible for a state to be ruled by virtue, and if so, would this state have to be authoritarian? I have suggested, in the previous section, that how one saw the intended audiences of the preambles made a great deal of difference as to whether the preambles were in fact authoritarian. In this section, I want to consider a specific case which may seem to resist even the interpretation proposed in the previous section, namely the preamble for the law on impiety.

In the prologue for the laws on impiety of Book X, the Athenian suggests that atheists should be argued out of their beliefs, and given the chance to argue back for their own:

> Either he must show us that we are wrong in pronouncing the soul the primary source of things, and in the further consequences we drew, or, if unable to get the better of our reasoning, he must yield to us and live henceforth a believer in gods. (899c–d)

The argument is not just for show, and the Athenian appears to be taking very seriously the possibility that the atheist might win the argument. When Clinias congratulates him on his arguments he replies that 'the source of this zeal was apprehension that if they get the better of the argument, the wicked may fancy themselves free to act as they will' (907c). But what the Athenian does not take seriously is the possibility that the atheist might turn out to be right. If the atheist wins the argument, it will be because the Athenian was not thorough enough in putting forward his reasons, not because his arguments are based on false or dubious premises. More worryingly is the fact that if the atheist fails to be convinced, he will be put to death (909a).

That the laws coerce, however, is not a fault with the preambles. If the preambles are genuinely concerned with obtaining a rational agreement from citizens that the laws should be obeyed, then they do promote some freedom to choose for oneself whether to obey the law. That the laws may then retract this freedom is not an objection to the value of the preambles. If Plato does in fact believe that citizens should be rationally persuaded that they should obey the laws, this answers, to some extent a common worry philosophers have about virtue ethics in general and Plato's politics in particular: that an appeal to good character, and learning through habituation encourages paternalism.

For example, we saw in Chapter 6 that the *Statesman's* ideal government was one in which a virtuous king ruled without laws, deciding for each individual what is better for them. By contrast, in the *Laws* Plato is concerned that citizens should be in a position to understand truly that certain laws are good for them, rather than having to accept that they are because somebody wiser than them says so. This seems to answer to the worry about paternalism to some extent.

But this preamble raises another, possibly more disturbing worry: are the preambles appealing to the subjects' rationality in the right way? A genuine attempt to persuade rationally would engage the subject's reason in a dialogue. The subject would be encouraged, or at least allowed to respond to the arguments, object, and make up their own mind whether they are good arguments. Yet, the law on atheism, we saw, requires that a subject who is not persuaded by the arguments of the preamble should be put to death. It may seem that such a response makes a mockery of the attempt at rational persuasion. Still, as I pointed out earlier, what is objectionable here is the law, not the preamble. The preamble does encourage dialogue between the subject and the legislator, and the Athenian *is* serious about the possibility of being refuted – although he believes this could only happen if he did not put his arguments forward convincingly enough, not because his arguments might not be as good as those of the atheist.

This second worry, then, is not immediately related to the question whether the preambles are a good institution, although it may suggest that Plato is not entirely convinced that citizens ought be in charge of their own moral destiny. The question we should be concerned with then, is whether the preamble to the atheism law, as a genuine attempt to engage the subject's rationality, constitutes sufficient evidence that Plato did intend the preambles to persuade rationally, and not pander to our weakened reason while persuading in less respectable ways.[26]

In a sense, there is nothing wrong with a law imposing a sanction once rational persuasion has been tried and failed. If my daughter does not want to go to bed, I shall first spend (a little) time going over the reasons with her why she must get an early night. But if she does not listen to reason, I shall exercise my parental authority and pack her to bed. This would not make the attempt at rational persuasion a farce. I did try to reason with her, but she was unwilling/unable to understand my arguments so I had to resort to force. And although she probably knew that this would happen, she also would have appreciated the chance to argue with me, and to be treated like a rational being (and to spend a little extra time up). Also, she knows she hasn't completely lost her time arguing against me: next time bed times are up for family discussion, she might remember some of her arguments and push for a slightly later curfew.[27]

The main difference between my exercising parental authority when reasoning with my daughter has failed, and the rulers of the Cretan colony putting the atheist to death if he has not 'come to his right mind' is that the nature of the punishment is such that in the second case, but not the first, it will impinge on the rational process of the offender such that he or she will not engage in unrestrained rational debate. The threat of the death penalty is just too big for somebody to be able to engage in calm, philosophical dialogue, defending ideas that may get him or her killed! Even if the atheist has decided to stick to his/her guns, that does not mean he or she will be willing to argue for it. In fact, the death penalty makes this particular law into one that Plato decries in 719e, one which operates through the threat of penalty.

Because of the exceptional nature of this law, it seems that a good response to Plato would be, rather than dismiss the thought that preambles are a good institution, ask that the penalty attached to the law on impiety be changed. But the harshness of the penalty does not cast any doubt on the seriousness of Plato's intent to persuade rationally.

5. Persuading the laws

In Chapter 2, I argued that the key to Plato's proposal in the Crito was that laws should be obeyed provided first that they did a good job of promoting and protecting virtue, and secondly that citizens should be in a position to attempt to persuade the state to change a particular law or set of laws if that law or set of laws failed to promote or protect virtue.

The second clause is there for two reasons. The first reason is that no legal system is perfect. A system can on the whole promote and protect virtue but fail to do so in a particular set of cases. For example, US laws in the 1960s were as good as any except for the segregation laws. Secondly, Plato believes that one essential aspect of promoting virtue is the promotion of wisdom through philosophical dialogue. So unless citizens are able to engage in philosophical dialogue with and about their laws, they do not have a real chance of becoming virtuous. It follows from this that it matters tremendously whether the persuasion proposed in the *Laws* is a one way or two way procedure. If the laws of the new colony are to be truly virtue-promoting, then citizens need to be able to 'persuade' the laws to change when the laws fail to persuade them that they should be obeyed. In other words, it has to be possible for the laws to be changed.

This applies not only to the laws, but also to the preambles. For if a preamble's persuasion is linked to the level of education of the citizens, it must be possible to change the preamble as the level of education grows. Also, it would be paradoxical for a law to change if the preamble were to remain the same: the contention that the preamble is meant to persuade citizens that the law is just could not be taken seriously if the law could change independently of the preamble! In what follows I will consider an objection from Stalley to the effect that the *Laws* do not allow for any changes, either in the laws or the preambles.

That the preambles should appeal to citizens' reason, and persuade them to obey the laws rather than obey simply because they fear punishment, is, perhaps what saves the *Laws* from the accusations of authoritarianism levied against the *Republic.* Citizens are not coerced into obedience by a ruler who claims to have access to knowledge of what is good for everyone. Instead, citizens are invited to consider the arguments propounded by the law-maker, and to agree freely that the suggested laws should in fact be obeyed.

But free agreement is only a real possibility if there can also be free disagreement. In other words, in order to judge the seriousness of Plato's intent regarding the preambles, we must ask what happens in cases where the preambles fail to persuade the citizens of the new colony. Is any provision made for disagreement? Not according to Stalley who writes that the laws of the new colonies will have exactly the same authority as the philosopher kings do in the *Republic.* They are unchallengeable and unchangeable: 'When the new state is founded the legislator will establish a code of laws which thereafter will be more or less unchangeable.'[28]

If Stalley is right, then we have serious reason to doubt whether Plato ever genuinely intended the preambles to persuade. However, Stalley, unusually for him, does not offer any textual support for his claim. Stalley's comment could arguably be true of the *Statesman,* in which Plato puts forward one argument why we should not seek to change laws.[29] But Stalley's claim does not fit the *Laws.* Indeed, in several places in that dialogue, Plato makes the point that the laws of the new colony will need to be revised for several reasons (769d, 772a, 846c). The main reason is that legislators, like anyone else, are bound to make mistakes. Law writing is a complex matter, and it is unthinkable that one group of people should come up with a perfect finished product. Plato even goes so far as to say that if the laws remain unchanged, the city will deteriorate (769d).

Of course, here Plato is talking about changing the laws, not rewriting the preambles, and nowhere does he specifically mention that the preambles are revisable. So we could reasonably ask whether anything he says in that passage, and in the others discussed below, can be taken to mean anything about the preambles. There are two replies to be made to this objection. First, new laws clearly (sometime) require new preambles. Indeed at 723d, Plato tells us that it should be left to the judgment of individual legislators whether a particular new law needs a preamble or not. Secondly, if the provisions of a law are to be changed, then citizens will be to be persuaded of something different, and for the revised law to be accepted on the same term as it previously was, i.e. through persuasion, not compulsion, the preamble will also have to be changed.

There is an apparent exception to my second point: the law on atheism. I discussed, in Section 4, the thought that if Plato's proposal is to be taken seriously, the sentence attached to the law on impiety would have to be changed. The death sentence is too big a threat for anything that comes before to be truly persuasive.

But if the death sentence is indeed replaced, be it by a fine, or exile (both common Greek sentences) it does not follow that the preamble ought to change. The Athenian's attempt at rational persuasion would most likely be more effective if the sentence was changed, and therefore would not need to be modified (at least not on that account). But note that the proposed change in the sentence does not amount to a change in the provisions of the law. The law still says that citizens must not be atheists. A change in the provisions of the law would amount to saying, for example, that citizens must not propagate atheistic beliefs – in which case the preamble would have to be changed as citizens would have to be persuaded not to display their beliefs publicly, but not to discard these beliefs.

As well as the passage at 769d, Plato cites two more arguments for the need to modify laws, which we will take to apply to preambles as well. First, legislators do not know their audience; if laws are not written in consultation with those who will be in charge of applying them, mistakes will not be spotted. He cites the examples of the laws concerning physical education, and argues that it will better if those who dispense that education, i.e. choirmasters, are consulted as to the adequacy of the laws (772a).[30] Secondly, he says, there will be a large number of laws applied to specific cases which should be derived from more general laws. In order to come up with these laws, young legislators should 'experiment', and settle only when they are confident that the laws are as they should be (846c).

These three passages show not only that Plato did not think the laws should be immutable, but maybe more importantly, that changes to the laws could and should be wrought by citizens who are not the main law-makers; these would be junior legislators, or even professionals specifically affected by the laws. This admittedly falls short of the thought that any citizen should be in a position to change the law should they fail to be persuaded by the preamble.

We must ask, however, whether this would be a reasonable expectation of any state. Perhaps it would be enough that citizens be able to change legislation if they are trained law-makers (but not necessarily the original, or even an older law-maker), or if their profession makes them knowledgeable about whether a particular set of laws is effective (as in the case of the choir maker and physical education laws; other examples might include health professionals and health regulations). In any case, the objection levied by Stalley is not supported by the text. One might conceivably object that for the preambles to be truly persuasive, any citizen should be in a position to change the laws, but this objection is not as strong as the one Stalley makes.

It seems enough that the laws are in fact open to revisions to confirm that the 'persuasion' discussed in the dialogue is really a proposal that citizens should reflect philosophically on their legal system, and engage with it when they do not believe that it promotes virtue as well as it should. This completes the project started with the *Crito* of offering an account of the law in terms of jurisprudence. Plato has now shown us how it is possible to obey the law, judge and legislate in a way that promotes and preserves virtue. In the process, we have encountered many obstacles in the form of virtue ethics' apparent incompatibility with laws, and of paternalism, but it seems that most of these obstacles can be overcome in some way or other and that, for the most part, Plato gives us the tools we need to overcome them (which is not to say that he succeeds in overcoming them himself, or even that he always wants to). The Laws provide the last step in the project, and closes the circle by showing how philosophical dialogue has to be central to a system of virtue-centred law, not just from the point of view of the citizens being able to persuade the laws to change, but because the laws themselves must persuade the citizens that they are just and should be obeyed.

Chapter 8

Towards Virtue-promoting Democratic Institutions

1. A flourishing environment: from laws to institutions

I have argued that Plato has a well-developed account of laws as enabling citizens to flourish, through the promotion and protection of an environment in which it is possible for them to become virtuous. I have emphasized that what we can most profitably extract from Plato's proposal is that laws should be wisdom-promoting. This is in large part because this would enable us to avoid the worst of the paternalistic threat that comes with putting laws and virtue together.

What I want to do in this concluding chapter is outline how one might go about applying Plato's account of wisdom-promoting laws to a democracy. Throughout the book I have striven to give examples drawn from contemporary problems. Now I want to adopt a more wide-ranging perspective and ask what kind of things we could do, within a democratic society, to reap the benefits of wisdom-promoting laws, and increase flourishing without departing from a non-paternalistic democratic ethos. I will begin by summarizing the main points of Plato's project, giving a distilled version of the account developed over the previous chapters. Next I will reply to the objection that Plato's anti-democratic stance makes the project of applying his theories to the modern world futile. Following this, I will concentrate on one particular aspect of this objection – is it possible, on Plato's or any account, for a democracy to produce wisdom-promoting laws? Last, working from two examples, I will show how democratic institutions might attempt further flourishing along Platonic lines.

Laws that are wisdom-promoting will most probably focus on three things. First, they will legislate primarily on education. Plato, despite charges of gerontocracy, does seem to believe that acquiring wisdom is something that the young, rather than the old, are capable of doing. And he believes that the way for the young to become wise is to have access to a soundly legislated educational system. The young adults who go through such a system may not be wise – and indeed, they may not achieve wisdom until they are much older, and in that sense, the charges of gerontocracy do stick a little – but they will be wiser than those who have not benefited from that system, and indeed, they stand a much greater chance of achieving wisdom than if they had not received such an education.

What this emphasis on education entails is not only that legislators should concentrate on getting education right, but that if they do, they will have much less to do in other domains – at least this is what Plato believes. For if the younger citizens are wise, he says, they will not need to be controlled in their everyday interactions with each other, in the way that laws control us. As reasonable beings, they will be in a position to solve conflicts without appealing to the law.

We probably do not want to go quite as far as Plato, though. Even if schools were so good that all school leavers became sufficiently wise as to need fewer laws, society would not, for a long time, be populated solely by adults who had benefited from this educational system. Moreover, some disputes are not to be resolved without the intervention of a third party. And this third party had better be a judge, dealing in laws.

But when laws are needed to resolve disputes between two reasonable citizens, or between a reasonable citizen and the state, the laws had better be reasonable themselves, i.e. they had better be such that a reasonable citizen would be satisfied by a verdict drawn from them. This is the second point on which Plato places emphasis: good laws must be accepted by rational citizens. The way to ensure that this is so, is to require that important laws should be prefaced by an argumentative, persuasive speech: a prologue designed to persuade wise citizens that a particular law is a good law and that they should obey it.

Third and last, wisdom-loving citizens, no matter how good an education they have received, will not remain wisdom-loving, let alone attempt to pursue other virtues if they live in an environment that counteracts the effect of their education. This could happen in one of two ways. First, it could be clear that even though education favours wisdom, adult society does not, that it rewards the greedy, the lazy, the unjust, instead of the wise. Secondly, the society one lives in as an adult could simply be too unsafe for anyone to think of nurturing the virtues. Would Socrates have philosophized in the market place had it been filled with murderers and thieves, rather than nice young men wanting intellectual conversation? And would these young men have been so eager to converse with Socrates, had it not been the case that Athenian society encouraged a certain kind of idleness among the young aristocrats?

What matters is not simply that the young should be educated into wisdom, but that the environment they live in as adults should protect and nurture their wisdom. This will depend not simply on laws, but on the institutions which form a large part of the environment we live in. Government bodies which are responsible for upholding certain laws also have a responsibility to the public with regards to how they themselves relate to the laws and how active they are in making sure that the law is observed in every layer of society's life, not just the superficial ones. So for example, an institution employing only white males would fail to nurture anti-discrimination laws. Again, institutions who do not investigate and control the many ways in which businesses can discriminate, beyond those specified explicitly by the law, would fail to protect anti-discrimination laws. So what is crucial, if wisdom-promoting laws in education are to make a difference to the kind of society we live in, is not just the laws regulating that society, but the institutions who should protect and promote these laws.

2. Can democratic institutions be wisdom-promoting?

Before we go any further in our attempt at outlining a modern application of Plato's ideas, we need to pause and ask whether it makes any sense to try and apply any of Plato's political theories to democratic societies. After all, we know that Plato's attitude to democracy leaves much to be desired, and it might be simply impossible to apply any of what he has to say to a democratic model. So we must ask whether Plato's views on wisdom-promoting laws are in principle anti-democratic, and that means looking at some of his views against democracy and seeing whether they would influence his views on wisdom-promoting laws.

What makes us think that Plato's ideas could not be applied to democratic institutions? There are three major points we should consider here. First, Plato criticizes democracy, and we shouldn't expect that his theories would be tailored to fit a type of government he condemns. But although Plato might think that the ideal government for laws to promote virtue is not a democracy, he certainly does not think that laws cannot promote virtue in democracies. If my interpretation of the *Crito* is correct, he does think that the laws and institutions of Athens promote virtue. Socrates would not have been in a position to live the only life worth living, seeking virtue through philosophy, without the laws on marriage and education, and without the protection afforded for his lifestyle by the laws of Athens in general. This is the gist of the position I defended in Chapter 2.

Secondly, Plato's proposals are always highly elitist – so much so that we are led to suspect that for him, laws should promote virtue only in those who are capable of becoming virtuous. Those who are not should be contained. This is in fact a misrepresentation of what Plato says in the *Republic*: he does think that laws should promote virtue for all – but that for some, it will only be possible to promote temperance and courage, and wisdom can only be promoted for the few, the philosopher kings. It is Aristotle who believes that some people are hopeless cases and should be contained rather than habituated:

> But doubtless it is not enough for people to receive the right nurture and discipline in youth; they must also practice the lessons they have learnt, and confirm them by habit, when they are grown up. Accordingly we shall need laws to regulate the discipline of adults as well, and in fact the whole life of the people generally; for the many are more amenable to compulsion and punishment than to reason and to moral ideals.[1]

Aristotle goes on in the next sentence to attribute this view to Plato in the *Laws* 722, however, this attribution strikes me as a misreading of the free/slave doctor analogy. Plato describes slave doctors as treating their patient differently than free doctors treat theirs, but does not go on to say that there should be a parallel in law. Indeed, what he does argue, is that law should be modelled on the free doctor, instead of the slave one.

So although the proposal of the *Republic* is elitist, and deeply unsatisfactory for that reason, at least, it is in principle adaptable to a democratic set up, whereas Aristotle's claim that not everyone is capable of becoming virtuous and that some of us should simply be contained, is less easily adaptable. We could try and understand Aristotle to mean hardened criminals and to say that they have to be imprisoned, as there is no real hope that they can be reformed. But it seems that what Aristotle is actually saying is that the 'base' and 'incorrigible', i.e. those who could not be habituated into virtue, simply cannot be taught, and that this should be at least apparent before they have become criminals, so that we can give up on them even if they have committed no crime.

Thirdly, even in the *Laws*, which is possibly the least elitist of Plato's proposals, there is one group of people whom the laws should not try to persuade: the slaves.[2] It is tempting to think that Plato would want to treat the least privileged members of our society either as slaves because they tend to do menial work or be too poor to be in a position to engage in political or philosophical debates. But this is Aristotle's position, not Plato's – it is Aristotle who claims, in Book I of the *Politics*, that those who are intellectually weak and physically strong, so better suited for manual labour, are slaves by nature.

Although Plato does have strong anti-democratic views, it is not the case that what he says about laws could not be applied to a democratic society. In the last section, we shall look at some possible ways in which Plato's theory of virtue-promoting laws could be applied to democratic institutions.

3. Can wisdom-promoting laws be produced democratically?

Whatever Plato may think of democracy, it seems that one big problem we need to address is whether a democratic people is capable of producing wisdom-promoting laws, or whether this is a job best left to philosopher rulers, or the true king of the *Statesman*. In the previous chapter, part of my argument was that in the *Laws*, Plato is trying to show that ordinarily wise men can together produce laws that will promote wisdom in a new city, provided these laws can be revised as the citizens become wiser. In order to complete this thought, and make the point, as clearly as possible that democracies are in principle capable of producing wisdom-promoting laws, I want to appeal to an Aristotelian doctrine, that of the wisdom of the multitude:

> For the many, of whom each individual is not a good man, when they meet together may be better than the few good, if regarded not individually but collectively, just as a feast to which many contribute is better than a dinner provided out of a single purse. For each individual among the many has a share of excellence and practical wisdom, and when they meet together, just as they become in a manner one man, who has many feet, and hands, and senses, so too with regard to their character and thought. Hence the many are better judges than a single man of music and poetry; for some understand one part, and some another, and among them they understand the whole.[3]

Aristotle uses this argument to suggest that democracy is a better form of rule than monarchy, or even then aristocracy, in that the combined judgments of the many will contain more wisdom than the single judgment of the wise monarch, or even of the wise few. If Aristotle's argument is sound, then our problem disappears: wisdom-promoting laws are more likely to be produced by democratic than any other form of legislation.

However, it is not the case that Aristotle is saying that whenever the many get together, they will come up with a better judgment than the few. There are two important qualifications. First, the many's characters must not be corrupted (1282a), and secondly, there might conceivably be an individual so outstandingly virtuous that his judgments are always better than those of the multitude (1284a).

Nonetheless, despite this second qualification, Aristotle thinks it is a serious possibility that the many will have certain virtues which will enable them to produce wiser judgments than the few or the single ruler. The virtues that the many need to possess for this to be the case must be virtues both of compassion and rhetoric.[4] These virtues are needed for each individual to be capable both of expressing his or her views clearly to the community, and to understand the views of others.

The many do not produce wisdom simply by aggregation, i.e. it is not the case that what makes a multitude wise is the aggregation of each individual's wisdom. If this was all Aristotle was saying, then it would be easy to counter him by saying that just as a multitude's knowledge is the sum of the knowledge of the individuals that compose it, the same is true of a multitude's prejudices! The point is that simple aggregation does not distinguish between the good and the bad, which means that if the individuals composing the multitude are not wiser than those composing the few, then the multitude itself cannot be wiser than the few simply by aggregation.

So how can the multitude end up benefiting from each member's knowledge without being affected by the prejudices? The difference between accepting someone's truthful opinion and accepting someone's prejudice is the reasoning that is required, both from the person defending it and the one listening. A lot of rhetorical skill may be required in order to persuade somebody to accept one's prejudices, but more actual reasoning will be required to reject a persuasively put falsehood than to accept it. So what constitutes the wisdom of the multitude is in part the reasoning that goes on in discussing each other's beliefs and deciding which to adopt. As Jeremy Waldron put it:

> [Aristotle's] view is that deliberation among the many is a way of bringing each citizen's ethical views and insights of each of the others, so that

> they cast light on each other, providing a basis for reciprocal questioning and criticism, and enabling a position to emerge which is better than any of the inputs and much more than an aggregation or function of these inputs.[5]

So it turns out that deliberation of the many produces wisdom in that individuals come out of such deliberations wiser than they previously were. Also, of course, the process of debating and exchanging ideas means that the result of the deliberation will be significantly better than what one might expect the individuals involved to produce if they deliberated alone.

Is this interpretation of Aristotle doctrine at all compatible with the arguments we have extracted from Plato in the previous chapters? It seems that the thought that a multitude would be wiser than the few had not occurred to Plato. Yet, he possessed the necessary premises. The view that wisdom is produced by engaging one's opinions in a philosophical debate with others is certainly not new to Plato. This is the very justification for the Socratic elenchos, i.e. that opinions will be validated or not as they are debated philosophically, and that the interlocutors will come out of an elenctic debate wiser, even if they do not accept any of the opinions offered for debate. Thus it seems reasonable to suggest that if we want Plato's arguments to apply to democratic institutions, we should and can appeal to Aristotle's doctrine of the wisdom of the multitude.

4. Two examples: racism and sexism

To conclude, I want to give a brief illustration of what we might expect to say if we choose to apply Plato's account of wisdom-promoting laws to the running of democratic institutions. Let us start by looking at two cases:

Case 1
A young adult A from an underprivileged suburb of Paris, fresh out of school, wants to find employment and thereby avoid the life of crime predicted for him by statistics.

Case 2
A young woman B has worked hard to obtain a good diploma so that she could have a career that would enable her to choose the best life for herself and not depend on dubious choices made for her by her family.

Why are these stories relevant? In both cases school has taught them that they can better themselves, that they are capable of leading a worthwhile life, and that there is more in them than either a petty criminal or a down-trodden housewife. So the wisdom-promoting laws have done their jobs as far as education is concerned, and it is now up to society's institutions to pick up and not undo what education has achieved. But in fact, it is far too easy for institutions to fail these young adults.

Case 1

He sends his C. V. to various employers, quoting good references from school teachers, good exam results, possibly even work experience. But he also has to send a photograph, which, together with his name reveals that he comes from North African origins. His address indicates that he comes from a high crime area. He will not be interviewed.

Case 2

She gets a low level job and male colleagues get promoted ahead of her. She takes time off to have a baby. When she comes back from maternity leave, she finds that she is offered a new, less rewarding job with even less chances of promotion. She finds that she cannot afford child care, and that her job is not flexible enough to allow her to pick up her child from nursery. Her family pressures her to give up work to be a full time mother. Eventually she caves in.

So what can institutions do in order to protect what has been achieved by a good education?

First, they can make it illegal to request photos for job applications, But they can also recommend that review of applications should be blind, i.e. name, sex, racial origin and address removed; they can reward employers who employ a larger proportion of people from underprivileged areas. They should offer career counselling services (including rejection letter counselling) and follow up on the fate of school leavers in those areas.

In order to avoid second case scenario institutions should develop child care, encourage flexible working hours, reward paternity leave as an alternative to maternity leave, reward companies that employ women and parents.

But as we said earlier, institutions should not merely concentrate on protecting school leavers from bad practice in the rest of society, they should ensure that they do not discourage them from pursuing virtue by giving a bad example themselves. So for instance, they should not reinforce prejudice by employing mostly workers from privileged areas themselves, employing people who are prejudiced or at least insensitive to the problems faced by those coming from underprivileged areas, issuing guidance that is either patronizing, or demeaning, or insufficiently well informed.

There are some of the ways in which institutions can promote virtue in society, if they follow the principles set forth by Plato. Of course, the society we end up with could not be more different than what Plato had in mind.

Notes

Introduction

[1] See Anscombe, E. (1958), 'Modern Moral Philosophy' and Slote, M. (1995a), 'Agent-Based Virtue Ethics' (reprinted), both in Crisp, R. and Slote, M. (eds) (1997), *Virtue Ethics*, Oxford: Oxford University Press, 26–44 and 239–262 respectively; Hursthouse, R. (1999), *On Virtue Ethics*, Oxford: Oxford University Press; Annas, J. (2005a), 'Virtue Ethics: What Kind of Naturalism', in Gardiner, S. (ed.) (2005), *Virtue Ethics, Old and New*, Ithaca, New York: Cornell University Press, 11–29.

[2] See Coope, C. (2006), 'Modern Virtue Ethics', in Chappell, T. (ed.) (2006), *Values and Virtues*, Oxford: Oxford University Press; and Nussbaum, M. (1999), 'Virtue Ethics: A Misleading Category?', *Journal of Ethics*, 3: 163–201.

[3] Indeed, according to Coope, what Hursthouse and Slote call 'virtue ethics' has very little in common with anything proposed by Anscombe and Foot, whose ethics are, according to him, better characterized as 'good sense ethics', p. 21.

[4] It maybe unfair on Philippa Foot as Anscombe, 20 years earlier in 'Modern Moral Philosophy' failed to mention Plato more than once (in conjunction with Aristotle) when she discusses ancient moral philosophy.

[5] Hursthouse, R. (1999), 8.

[6] Slote, M. (1995); Slote, M. (1998), 'Nietzsche and Virtue Ethics'; and Swanton, C. (1998), 'Outline of a Nietzschean Virtue Ethics', both in *International Studies in Philosophy*, 30: 3; Baier, A. (1994), 'What do Women Want in a Moral Theory' in Crisp and Slote (eds) (1997), *Virtue Ethics*, Oxford: Oxford University Press, 263–77; and Wiggins, D. (1996), 'Natural and Artificial Virtues: A Vindication of Hume's Scheme', in Crisp, R. (ed.) (1996), *How Should One Live?*, Oxford: Oxford University Press, 131–40.

[7] With a few exceptions such as Michael Slote (1999), 'Virtue Ethics', in, Baron, M., Slote, M., and Pettit, P. (1999), *Three Methods of Ethics: A Debate*, Oxford: Blackwell, 175–238; Julia Annas (2005), whose discussion of the concept of wickedness is based on a reading of Books 8 and 9 of Plato's *Republic* in 'Wickedness as Psychological Breakdown', *Southern Journal of Philosophy*, 43 (supp.): 515–36, and of Christine Korsgaard, (1999), 'Self-constitution in the Ethics of Plato and Kant', *Journal of Ethics*, 3: 1–29, who bases her discussion of self-constitution on Plato.

[8] See for example G. Santas (1971), 'Socrates at Work on Virtue and Knowledge in Plato's *Laches*', in Gregory Vlastos, (ed.) (1971), *The Philosophy of Socrates*. Modern Studies in Philosophy, Garden City, New York: Doubleday, Anchor Books, 177–208.

[9] *Nicomachean Ethics*, 1145a2. Irwin in his translation (1985, Indianapolis: Hackett.) prefers to call this view 'the reciprocity of virtue' as 'unity' suggests that

there is only one virtue – Plato sometimes says that to be virtuous is to be wise (*Protagoras*) or to be just (*Republic*) – but Aristotle takes care to distinguish between the virtues. Still, if his view is that one cannot have one virtue without having them all, it is not essentially different from Plato's view.

10 Neera K. Badhwaar (1996), 'The limited unity of virtue', *Nous*, 30: 306–29; and Susan Wolf (2007), 'Moral Psychology and the Unity of the Virtues', *Ratio*, 20: 145–67, both argue that the Unity of Virtue thesis has been interpreted more strongly than it was ever intended by Plato or Aristotle, and that a weaker version of the thesis is in fact acceptable.

11 Roger Crisp and Michael Slote (1997), *Virtue Ethics*, Oxford: Oxford University Press.

12 See my (2007), 'Virtue Ethics, Politics, and the Function of Laws: The Parent Analogy in Plato's *Menexenus*', *Dialogue*, 46, 2: 211–30, and Ryan K. Balot's arguments for the modern relevance of Ancient Virtue Politics in the last chapter of his new book (2006), *Greek Political Thought*, Oxford: Blackwell.

13 Coope, 41.

14 I owe this point and the example to Tim Chappell.

15 Part of my discussion of this challenge will aim to establish that Plato was indeed concerned with a form of autonomy.

16 David Bostock (1990), 'The Interpretation of Plato's *Crito*', *Phronesis*, 35, 1: 1–20; and Gregory Vlastos, (1994), 'The Historical Socrates and Athenian Democracy', in Vlastos (1994), *Socratic Studies*, Cambridge: Cambridge University Press, 87–108.

17 See Roslyn Weiss (1998), *Socrates Dissatisfied: An Analysis of Plato's* Crito, New York: Oxford University Press; Verity Harte (1999), 'Conflicting Values in Plato's *Crito*', *Archiv fur Geschichte der Philosophie*, 81, 2: 117–47; and Melissa Lane (1998), 'Argument and Agreement in Plato's *Crito*', *History of Political Thought*, 19, 3: 313–30.

18 *Statesman*, 294a–297b.

19 *Statesman*, 297b–300c.

Chapter 1

1 R. Hursthouse (1999), 8.

2 Roger Crisp (ed.) (1996), *How should one live?*, Oxford: Oxford University Press, Introduction, 2–3.

3 Virtue Theory, more generally, can in some cases simply make the claim that we need to talk about the virtues when we do moral philosophy. This is case of Julia Driver's virtue consequentialism. See her 'The virtues and human nature', in Crisp (1996), 111–30.

4 Although Annas (1995) denies that Epicureanism is a proper form of consequentialism, *The Morality of Happiness*, Oxford: Oxford University Press, 37.

5 Martha Nussbaum certainly believes so and she uses the Stoics and Kant interchangeably, and at times together, to defend her arguments for cosmopolitanism. Cf. Nussbaum, M. (1996), *For Love of Country, Debating the Limits of Patriotism*, Boston: Beacon Press, 2–20; Nussbaum, M. (1997a), 'Kant and Stoic

Cosmopolitanism', *The Journal of Political Philosophy*, 5, 1: 1–25; Nussbaum, M. (1997b), *Cultivating Humanity*, Cambridge, MA: Harvard University Press; Nussbaum, M. (2000), 'Duties of Justice, Duties of Material Aid: Cicero's Problematic Legacy', *The Journal of Political Philosophy*, 8, 2: 176–206; Nussbaum, M. (2003), 'Compassion and Terror', *Daedalus*, Winter 2003: 10–26.

6 Chris Coope in 'Modern Virtue Ethics' offers different reasons why we should not see virtue ethics as a revival of ancient ethics. According to him, what Foot and Anscombe originally proposed was not that.

7 Although we often think of Plato's intellectual legacy to Aristotle as contained in the many footnotes in the *Politics* criticizing the arguments of the *Republic*, Aristotle does in fact borrow extensively from Plato's arguments. Perhaps the most obvious source of borrowing for Aristotle is the *Statesman*. Aristotle was in the Academy while Plato was writing it, and several of the themes developed in that dialogue are central to Aristotle's philosophy, such as for example the idea that there are three main constitutional forms (three correct, three deviant) which Aristotle develops in *Politics* I.7. I will show later on that Aristotle's concept of habituation is also borrowed from Plato.

8 This is also of course a central question for the Stoics, the Epicureans and the Sceptics.

9 In Book 10 of the *Ethics*, Aristotle seems to settle on a different answer to the question how one should live. The good life, he now says, consists in the life of theoretical activity and nothing else. Richard Kraut in his book *Aristotle on the Human Good* has argued that Aristotle neither changes his mind, nor contradicts himself. He is merely offering alternatives. The very best life is the contemplative life but one could also settle for the political life in which all these other things (honour, friendship, wealth, etc.) also matter. In this he does disagree with Plato, as for Plato, the truly political life does not require that one should be materially successful, in fact, these qualities seem to belong to the life of the rhetor, which for Socrates is a travesty of public life (*Gorgias*, 527b–d).

10 The claim that life is not worth living if one is diseased need not imply that virtue is not sufficient for happiness. Maybe Plato, like Aristotle, believes that certain external goods, in this case bodily health, are necessary in order to develop the virtues. Given that for them courage can be shown mostly on the battlefield, this makes a certain amount of sense.

11 Recently, Gilbert Harman following social psychologists has argued that the concept of character is a myth and that it makes no sense to ground an ethical theory on the virtues. I will address this objection in Chapter 4.

12 On this see Miles Burnyeat, 'Aristotle on Learning to be Good', in Amely Rorty (ed.) (1980), *Essays on Aristotle's Ethics*, Berkeley and Los Angeles: University of California Press, and Nancy Sherman (1989), *The Fabric of Character*, Oxford: Clarendon Press, chapter 5.

13 See *Nichomachean Ethics*, 1105b29–1106a9 and 1103a18–b2.

14 Terrence Irwin (1977), *Plato's Moral Theory*, Oxford: Clarendon Press, 305–06. This is in fact an objection to the Vlastos text cited below.

15 G. Vlastos (1981b), 'The Unity of Virtue in Plato's Protagoras', in his *Platonic Studies*, Princeton: Princeton University Press, Second Edition, 221–69, p. 225.

16 Articles on *Republic* I tend to focus on Plato's other arguments against Thrasymachus, and on Thrasymachus' arguments and character.
17 For the significance of that passage see D. Wiggins (1986), 'Teleology and the Good in Plato's *Phaedo*', Oxford Studies in Ancient Philosophy.
18 Michael Slote (1995b), 'Law in Virtue Ethics', in *Law and Philosophy*, 14, 91–113. See in particular pp. 91–93. See also his (1995a), 'Agent-based Virtue Ethics', *Midwest Studies in Philosophy*, 20: 83–101.
19 *Nicomachean Ethics*, 1176a16.
20 *Republic*, 444c–e.
21 *Republic*, 443d–e.
22 See Watson (1990), 'On the Primacy of Character', in Flanagan and Rorty, for a version of the dilemma.
23 See Harman (1999), 'Moral Philosophy Meets Social Psychology' Proceedings of the Aristotelian Society, 99, and Doris (1998), 'Persons, Situations and Virtue Ethics', *Nous*, 32.
24 The Stoics are political thinkers, but this is through an appeal to universalism so they are not virtue ethicists in that respect.
25 Especially Lawrence B. Solum, (2003), 'Virtue Jurisprudence a Virtue-centred Theory of Judging' and R. A. Duff, (2003), 'The Limits of Virtue Jurisprudence', both in *Metaphilosophy*, 34, 1: 2. See also Roger Shiner, (1994), 'Aristotle's theory of Equity', *Loyola of Los Angeles Law Review*, 27.
26 As far as Plato is concerned, I have in mind the analogy between the laws and parents given in both the *Crito* and the *Menexenus*, where Plato argues that the purpose of the law is to provide an environment in which citizens may flourish, i.e. live virtuous lives. I have argued in my (2007), 'Virtue Ethics, Politics and the Function of Laws: The Parent Analogy in Plato's *Menexenus*', *Dialogue*, 46, 2: 211–30, that we should take the parent analogy in both dialogues seriously as a proposal for a virtue ethical conception of the role of laws. For Aristotle, see *Nichomachean Ethics*, 1179b20ff, where he argues that laws are needed to encourage the habituation process in children, parental authority being insufficient for that purpose, and *Politics* book VIII, where he gives a detailed description of the legislator's role in education.
27 This is what Duff suggests on p. 215.
28 Lawrence B. Solum, (2003), 182.
29 See for instance Marcia Baron (1985), 'Varieties of Ethics of Virtue', *American Philosophical Quarterly*, 22, 47–53 and Julia Driver (2001), *Uneasy Virtue*, Cambridge: Cambridge University Press.
30 *Nicomachean Ethics*, 1137b26–32.
31 Roger Shiner (1994), 'Aristotle's theory of Equity', *Loyola of Los Angeles Law Review*, 27.

Chapter 2

1 An earlier version of part of this chapter was printed as Berges, S. (2004), 'Virtue and the Laws: The Parent Analogy in Plato's *Crito*', Yeditepe'de Felsefe.

[2] It is also possible to read the *Crito* as an aporetic dialogue, one in which Socrates does not seek to persuade Crito through the Laws' speech, but where he simply engages in the elenchos with his friend. See Verity Harte and Roslyn Weiss. I find their approach unconvincing for at least two reasons. First, the ending of the dialogue is very unlike that of so-called aporetic dialogues, at the end of the *Crito*, Socrates is in no doubt as to what he should do. Secondly there is very little real elenctic dialogue in the *Crito* and more argument than there is typically in aporetic dialogues.

[3] Inconsistency is only a concern, of course, for those who do not believe that the *Crito* is an aporetic dialogue.

[4] *Apology*, 37e–38a and 32b–d.

[5] Tim Chappell in his (2001), 'Socrates and Antigone: Two Ways to be Martyred', *Prudentia Special Issue*, (May 2001): 161–70, argues that in order to understand Socrates' refusal to escape, we need first to understand how his imprisonment and then death fit in with the overall narrative of his life. In his view, Socrates is looking back to his own past, and trying to make sense of it, rather than looking forward to the future of his fellow citizens.

[6] See Anscombe, E. (1958), 'Modern Moral Philosophy', in Crisp, R. and Slote, M. (eds) (1997), *Virtue Ethics*, Oxford: Oxford University Press, 26–44.

[7] With the notable exception of Michael Slote. See his contribution to, Baron, M., Slote, M. and Pettit, P. (1999), *Three Methods of Ethics*, Blackwell. Of course, commentators on Plato know fully well that his focus is on virtue. My comments apply to virtue ethicists who fail to recognize the significance of Plato's work for that discipline.

[8] Slote (1995a), 91.

[9] At a push we might apply the theory to the city, as Plato does in the *Republic*, i.e. a just city is one in which the parts are working together in harmony. As a city is made up of people, the anthropomorphism is less worrying.

[10] *Statesman*, 294b, Edith Hamilton and Huntington Cairns (eds), (1989), J. B. Skemp (trans.), *Plato, The Collected Dialogues*, Princeton: Princeton University Press.

[11] *Nicomachean Ethics*, 1137b26–32, translation Richard McKeon (1941), *The Basic Works of Aristotle*, New York: Random House, 1020. See also *Politics*, 1286a9–10.

[12] This emphasis on the universality, and the rigidity of laws may obscure the fact that a good judge will always need to put some work into deciding which laws apply to a particular case and how they apply. In this sense, it is possible to overemphasize the difference between laws and judgments. But I believe that when they are talking of laws as being rigid, both Plato and Aristotle have in mind the distinction between the work of the legislator, who cannot possibly be aware of the many different cases his or her laws will be applied to, and of the judge, who, on the other hand, is working with these cases. In this way should the distinction be understood.

[13] Bostock, D. (1990) and to some extent Vlastos, G. (1994).

[14] See Weiss, R. (1998); Harte, V. (1999); and Lane, M. (1998).

[15] A second claim is also somewhat relevant. It is Socrates attitude to the opinions of the many stated at 48a. The passage states that the many are not in a position to form correct judgments about right and wrong. It follows that as Athens is a

democracy, and its laws are the laws of the many, Socrates has reason not to accept the laws' advice blindly in deciding what it is just for him to do. Hence it follows from this passage that Socrates does not believe it would be just for him to obey the laws no matter what. He would have to ascertain that what they did order him to do was just.

This argument is open to two objections which require lengthy responses. The first cites the fact that the opinion of the many often serves as the starting point of the elenchos, from which it follows that Socrates cannot be so dismissive of it. The second refers to the second half of the passage at 48a which states that instead of the many one should turn to the expert. Taking into consideration Socrates' well known reluctance ever to name an expert, one may well wonder if the whole statement is thereby nullified, i.e. Socrates does not believe there is an expert, so we might as well listen to what the many say. I have answered these objections in my Ph.D. dissertation 'Plato's defence of Justice – Socrates contra Nietzsche', chapter I.

16 For this point see Santas, G. (1979), *Socrates: Philosophy in Plato's Early Dialogues*, London: Routledge and Kegan Paul, 286.

17 Kraut, R. (1984), *Socrates and the State*, Princeton: Princeton University Press, 12–13, footnote 22.

18 See Kraut (1984), 11.

19 Bostock (1989), 19.

20 Hobbes *Leviathan*, chapter 20.

21 I do not dispute that the Laws' speech is on the whole authoritarian – but that in this particular passage, Plato is trying to convey the idea that certain aspects of the laws' speech are in fact compelling, i.e. that they give the person who cares about virtue good reasons to obey.

22 Kraut (1984), 49.

23 Would Socrates be harming the Laws if he were to escape? Would it matter? To answer the second question, yes, it would matter, for when Socrates talks of harming the Laws, he talks of harming the Athenians (48c1–2; 48e; 50a1). What harm would he cause? If the Laws are to promote flourishing, they must act as a deterrent, i.e. they must prevent citizens from acting in such a way as would threaten their flourishing. If they are a deterrent, then examples matter. In particular, if the convict were to disobey and get off free in a highly publicized case, then the Laws' power to deter would be diminished. So yes, Socrates would be harming the laws by escaping.

24 Weiss (1998), 99, footnote 9.

25 Were attitudes to family relationships so different in ancient Greece that adult children would feel they owed it to their parents to carry on obeying them? It is hard to tell. Sophocles' heroes and heroines do tend to take orders from their parents as a matter of course. Aristophanes, on the other hand, portrays parents despairing of getting their adolescent children to do anything. This is of course partly due to the difference between tragedy, portraying strong but flawed characters, and comedy, portraying weakness in everyday life. Yet, One is tempted to say that it is unlikely that the Greek attitude would have been one of unconditional obedience of adults towards their parents.

[26] Weiss's own interpretation of Socrates' reasons for not escaping is that first, he agreed with the laws' death sentence, and the agreement was just, and secondly, if he escapes, he will be engaging in stealth and paying bribes, thus behaving deceitfully. But this is unsatisfactory for the following reasons: if Socrates agreed with the laws' sentence, then we must know why he agreed. The most likely answer has to be that he thinks that on the whole, the laws of Athens are just, and therefore must be respected. And although Weiss's second reason is certainly very plausible, it cannot stand on its own. Had Socrates felt no qualms about obeying the laws, Crito would certainly have found a way to escape which minimized deceitfulness. See Weiss (1998), 80–81.

[27] Weiss (1998), 99, footnote 9.

[28] The following argument and the Oedipus example are largely inspired by Bostock (1989), 11.

[29] It may be countered that there is some element of the sacred in the relationship between citizen and the city – after all, one of the accusations raised against Socrates at his trial was that he did not recognize the city's gods. But I would reply that even if there is a sacred relationship, it is not a blood link. Plato does try to show, in the *Menexenus*, (236d–239a) that there is something akin to a blood link between citizens and land, but his argument is far from convincing, and in any case, it does not show (or even try to show, to Plato's credit) that there is a blood link between city and citizen.

[30] Of course, I am not claiming that religious considerations are inconsistent with good psychological insight, or that Plato was free from religious beliefs, even implausible ones. The theory of recollection in the Meno, is an example of both how Plato appears to hold beliefs about the supernatural, and how he uses these beliefs to develop a psychological theory. Nonetheless, there is a marked preference, in Plato, for psychological explanations which do not involve direct intervention from the gods, but deal more clearly with human agency. This is perhaps why he deemed Euripides and not Sophocles, the wisest tragedian (*Republic*, 568a).

[31] *Apology*, 21a.

[32] *Laws*, 788a–c.

[33] *Nicomachean Ethics*, 1179b36–1180a4.

[34] *Nicomachean Ethics*, 1180a19–21.

[35] Martin Luther King (1963), 'Letter from Birmingham Jail', http://www.stanford.edu/group/King/popular_requests/frequentdocs/birmingham.pdf (last accessed 6 October 2008).

[36] Raz, Joseph (1979), *The Authority of Law: Essays on Law and Morality*. Oxford: Clarendon Press, 272–23.

[37] Thoreau, H. (1849), 'On the Duty of Civil Disobedience', http://www.gutenberg.org/files/71/71-h/71-h.htm (last accessed 6 October 2008).

Chapter 3

[1] An earlier version of part of this chapter was printed as Berges, S. (2007), 'Virtue Ethics, Politics, and the Function of Laws: The Parent Analogy in Plato's *Menexenus*', *Dialogue*, 46: 211–30.

2 This is what the Personified Laws of Athens suggest at 50ab.

3 In Section 5, I shall argue that the parent analogy as it is used by Plato is not viciously paternalistic in that its emphasis is on the flourishing of children and citizens rather than on expectations of obedience.

4 Michael Slote (2001), 'War Crimes and Virtue Ethics', in A. Jokic (ed.), *War Crimes and Collective Wrongdoings*, Oxford: Blackwell, 77–84.

5 Nussbaum (1992), 'Human Functioning and Social Justice: In Defence of Aristotelian Essentialism', *Political Theory*, 20.

6 Winnicott, D. W. (1976), *The Maturational Process and the Facilitating Environment*, London: Hogarth Press, 223, 239.

7 Nussbaum (2004), *Hiding from Humanity*, Princeton: Princeton University Press, 223–25.

8 Nussbaum (2004), 282.

9 Lawrence Blum (1996), 'Community and Virtue', in Crisp (ed.), *How should one live*, OUP, 231–53, 238.

10 Nussbaum (2004), 226.

11 Machiavelli (1983), The *Discourses*, chapter 2, 112.

12 Slote (2001), 77–84.

13 Slote (2001), 79.

14 Here one may object that Slote's argument is best understood as a methodological point than one about sufficient conditions. The best way to ensure that just laws are passed is to have just law-makers. Close reading, I think, does not bear this out as Slote's claim is phrased in such a manner as to suggest he is looking for sufficient conditions: 'if the law is passed justly [. . .] then it is a just law'. If, however, Slote is making a methodological claim, then his point is question begging as far as the present inquiry is concerned (although this is not to say that it is a question begging point taken in its own context, i.e. the treatment of war criminals) because it does not tell us what makes a law a just law independently of our appraisal or the law-maker's character, merely that just law-makers make just laws.

15 The fact that Socrates claims he is merely repeating a speech written by Pericles' mistress may also be contrasted to his denunciation of recitation in the *Ion*. However, as in the last lines of the *Menexenus* it becomes clear that the speech is very probably of Socrates' own composition, the contrast is not necessarily significant.

Also introduced are grounds for thinking that the speech to follow is going to be to some extent a parody of Pericles' funeral oration as reported by Thucydides. For textual and historical support for the parody view, see Pamela Huby (1957), 'The *Menexenus* Reconsidered', *Phronesis*, 2.

Charles Kahn (1963), 'Plato's Funeral Oration: The Motive of the *Menexenus*', *Classical Philology*, 58, and Sara Monoson (1998), 'Remembering Pericles: The Political and Theoretical Import of Plato's *Menexenus*', *Political Theory*, 26, 4: 489–513. All three recognize that there is some amount of parody in the dialogue directed at Pericles and Thucydides, but at the same time, they do not share A. E. Taylor's view that the whole dialogue must be read ironically (1960), *Plato, the Man and his Work*, London: Methuen and Co. All seem to agree that at least the last part of the dialogue is meant to be taken as a serious piece of philosophy.

16 Pamela Huby read this as a political pamphlet designed to shame Athens' recent policy, in particular, laws seeking to cut down the state support for war orphans.

17 Huby, and Kahn agree that it is.

18 That there should be such an argument is compatible with the view that the dialogue criticizes Athenian policies if Plato thought that those policies no longer supported the virtuous life in Athens. In particular, the strong injunction at 248d–249a that the city should care for the children of the dead as parents would, i.e. that it should give them the means to become virtuous citizens – 'she places in their hands the instruments of their fathers' virtues' (249a) – can be read both as a reminder that Athens has a duty towards the children of the dead (especially relevant if Athens was in the process of revising the relevant laws) and as part of an argument designed to elucidate what it is for a law to be a just law.

19 This and other passages quoted was translated by Jowett, in *The Collected Dialogues*, Edith Hamilton and Huntington Cairns (eds) (1989), Princeton: Princeton University Press.

20 See Huby for the historical note regarding the proposed reforms.

21 Sara Monoson suggests a different role for the analogy of motherhood and land, i.e. that it is used by Plato to derive a conclusion that all Athenians are related. While this is a plausible interpretation, it seems that it does not preclude a role for the mother/land analogy in determining the city/parent analogy.

22 Here I follow Locke, *Second Treatise*, chapter six, 55: 'Their parents have a sort of rule and jurisdiction over them when they come into the world, and for some time after, but it is but a temporary one. The bonds of this subjection are like the swaddling clothes they are wrapped up in and supported by in the weakness of their infancy; age and reason, as they grow up, loosen them, till at length they drop quite off and leave a man at his own free disposal'.

23 This is supposed to be reminiscent of Mill's harm to others principle, cf. J. S. Mill, (1991), *On Liberty and Other Essays*, Oxford: Oxford University Press, 14.

That the only purpose for which power can be rightfully exercised over any member of a civilized community, against his will, is to prevent harm to others. His own good, either physical or moral, is not a sufficient warrant. He cannot rightfully be compelled to do or forbear because it will be better for him to do so, because it will make him happier, because in the opinions of others, to do so would be wise or even right.

One way of supporting Mill's position (though not Mill's own) would be to apply to Locke's view: parents have dominion over children's choices just because children are not fully rational. So given a mature adult, there are no reason why anyone should dictate to her what is best for her.

Another argument is available for this particular anti-paternalistic position. To impose life choices on individuals over and above their expressed preferences is wrong because we have no real way of knowing what is good for people beyond what they claim to prefer. See Alan Hamlin (1993), 'Welfare', in B. Goodin and P. Pettit (eds), *A Companion to Contemporary Political Philosophy*, Oxford: Blackwell, 653–54.

24 Joseph Raz (1986), *The Morality of Freedom*. Oxford: Oxford University Press, 154.

25 I do not want to underestimate how significant a threat to autonomy censure might be – my point is that it is distinct from the threat of laws.

[26] The contrast is less obvious if we consider non-coercive forms of paternalism of the kind defended by Raz (2000), 'Legitimacy, Unanimity, and Perfectionism', Philosophy and Public Affairs, i.e. where the laws aim to encourage certain choices without coercion, by providing subsidies, tax exemptions and education. However, such laws are also more difficult to challenge than one's culture. Imagine for instance that you are a smoker in a part of the world where cigarettes are very expensive and there are important tax breaks for non-smokers. Schools also teach people to demonize smokers and so if you do want to carry on indulging in smoking, you feel as though you have to stand up against a culture that is state-sanctioned if not state-created. This makes it doubly hard to challenge it.

[27] One crude objection to the claim that laws should be virtue-promoting is that this proposal would license locking people up for not leading virtuous lives. Not so: virtue-promoting laws would have to educate the character, and, as Aristotle has shown, this is best done through repetition, and then conscious and willing habituation. A spell in prison is not that. More insidious, perhaps, is the objection that virtue-promoting laws would license the jailing of people on grounds that they were bad examples for other citizens. But this would have the same effect of forcing people to behave in a certain way because they were afraid of being punished – again, this effort at pretence would probably prevent their character from maturing as it should.

[28] One could also make a case for the other virtues. Arguably, courage is needed for autonomy: one needs to be courageous to stick to the choices one believes to be the right ones. Temperance may also be necessary if one is to weigh the pros and cons of a life style, or course of actions without being swayed by temptation of short term enjoyment. And of course, one could argue that no choice is the right one unless it is just, and that all we need in order to make the right choices is to be able to avoid injustice.

[29] *Laws* III, 688a.

Chapter 4

[1] *Crito*, 47e–48a.

[2] Julius Moravcsik (2000), 'Health, Healing, and Plato's Ethics', *Journal of Value Inquiry*, 34, also argues that Plato takes the medical analogy seriously. His purpose in discussing the analogy, however, is to show that Plato uses it to support an understanding of ethics as techne. Thus, Moravcsik's discussion is not entirely relevant to mine.

[3] Mike W. Martin (2006), *From Morality to Mental Health*, Oxford: Oxford University Press, argues that the use of medical terms in Plato is no 'mere metaphor', p. 17.

[4] *Republic*, 444c–e.

[5] *Republic*, 443d–e.

[6] For an argument that healthiness can serve as a model for understanding goodness, because moral goodness and physical healthiness have the same ontological and epistemic status, see Paul Bloomfield (1997), 'Of Goodness and Healthiness: a Viable Moral Ontology', *Philosophical Studies*, 87.

[7] Kenny (1973), 'Mental Health in Plato's *Republic*', in *The Anatomy of the Soul*, Blackwell, Oxford, 1–27. See also Flew (1954), 'Crime or Disease?' *The British Journal of Sociology*, 5, 1 (Mar.): 49–62.

[8] See Kenny's synopsis of what is wrong with Plato's health analogy in Kenny, 23–24. Ruttenberg (1986) offers a successful systematic refutation of Kenny's interpretation, claiming that most of his references are radically misinterpreted.

[9] *Apology*, 30a–b.

[10] Socrates claims that Callicles has three things which make him a good 'touchstone': knowledge, goodwill and free speaking – but it is obvious that Callicles has none of these.

[11] Note that according to Plato, the best cure for vice is, at least some times, litigation: if one does wrong one should pay for it. (see *Gorgias*, 480a–b). He believes that the process of being punished for what one has done can sometimes correct the tendency which led us to do wrong in the first place. It is interesting that he believes in the curative power of punishment in the light of his critics' interpretation that all the non-virtuous are simply mad and must be restrained.

[12] I will not refer to the Good Samaritan experiment, another experiment in helping behaviour as it does not appear to show anything more than the dime helping experiment does.

[13] Milgram (1963), (1965), Good Samaritan; Darley and Batson (1973), Dime helping; Isen and Levin, 72 and 75.

[14] Gleitman, 465 says that social psychologists did not mean to reject personality wholesale.

[15] J. Block, 71 and 77; Gleitman, 465.

[16] See for example Christian Miller (2003), 'Social Psychology and Virtue Ethics', *The Journal of Ethics*, 7: 365–392, Diana Fleming (2006), 'The Character of Virtue: Answering the Situationist Challenge to Virtue Ethics', *Ratio*, XIX: 24–42.

[17] J. M. Doris (1998), 'Persons, Situations, and Virtue Ethics', *Nous*, 32: 504–30 and (2002), *Lack of Character: Personality and Moral Behavior*, Cambridge: Cambridge University Press.

[18] Stephen Crane (1994), *The Red Badge of Courage*, Penguin Popular Classic, 19.

[19] See Rex, S. and Gelsthorpe, L. 'The Role of Community Service in Reducing Offending: Evaluating Pathfinder Projects in the UK', *The Howard Journal*, 41: 331–25.

[20] Rex and Gelsthorpe, 320.

[21] See Rex and Gelsthorpe.

[22] Community service fits with several views of what punishment should be. It can be seen as retributive (the work is a 'fine on time'), restorative (giving back to the community, or even to the victim, some of what one has taken), a morally justified sentence (less objectionable than prison sentences with respect to the treatment of offenders), and finally, as rehabilitative (reducing recidivism, and increasing rehabilitation).

[23] See Rex and Gelsthorpe.

[24] See Rex and Gelsthorpe, and also Gill McIvor (1998), 'Pro-social Modelling and Legitimacy: Lessons from a Study of Community Service', in S. Rex and

A. Matravers (eds), *Pro-social Modelling and Legitimacy: The Clarke Hall Day Conference*, Cambridge: Institute of Criminology, University of Cambridge.

25 Of course, I'm not suggesting that offenders should learn to meditate on the form of the good and forget about the fact that they have no money, or no roof over their heads. A certain adaptability in the interpretation is needed here, one which pulls away from an almost Stoical reading of Plato, but which retains the sense in which emotional and intellectual development are essential for a pro-social outlook on life.

26 See McIvor 'In many instances, it seems, contact with the beneficiaries gave offenders an insight into other people, and an increased insight into themselves; the acquisition of skills had instilled in them greater confidence and self-esteem; the experience of completing their community service orders placed them in a position where they could enjoy reciprocal relationships – gaining the trust, confidence and appreciation of other people and having the opportunity to give something back to them', 55–56.

27 Richard Brandt (1995), 'Conscience (rule) Utilitarianism and the Criminal Law', *Law and Philosophy*, 14: 65–89.

28 See Brandt, 83.

Chapter 5

1 J. S. Mill (1991), *On Liberty and Other Essays*, Oxford: Oxford University Press, 14.

2 For a detailed version of the view that education is a central concern of the *Republic*, see Scholfied, M. (2006), *Plato: Political Philosophy*, New York: Oxford University Press, 32–37, and Burnyeat, M. (1999), 'Culture and Society in Plato's Republic', *The Tanner Lectures on Human Values*, 20: 215–324.

3 I will focus here on censorship rather than lies. Plato says that the rulers may tell lies to the others at 389b. At 414b–c he proposes himself to lie to the rulers and the rest.

4 Kenny, A. (1973), 'Mental Health in Plato's *Republic*', in Kenny (1973), *The Anatomy of the Soul*, Oxford: Blackwell, 1–27.

5 See Kenny's synopsis of what is wrong with Plato's health analogy in Kenny. 23–24. Ruttenberg (1986), 'Plato's Use of the Analogy Between Justice and Health', *Journal of Value Inquiry*, 20: 145–56, offers a successful systematic refutation of Kenny's interpretation, claiming that most of his references are radically misinterpreted.

6 See Lidz, J. (1994), 'Medicine as Metaphor in Plato', *Journal of Medicine and Philosophy*, 19: 527–41.

7 *Republic*, 425d–e.

8 Cf. Primary National Strategy: excellence and enjoyment, social and emotional aspects of learning. http://www.standards.dfes.gov.uk/primary/publications/banda/seal/pns_seal137805_guidance.pdf (last accessed 6 October 2008).

9 http://www.education.gouv.fr/cid323/contre-les-derives-communautaristes-reaffirmer-les-principes-de-la-laicite-republicaine.html (last accessed 6 October 2008).

Chapter 6

1 *Statesman*, 294b, Edith Hamilton and Huntington Cairns (eds) (1989), *Plato, The Collected Dialogues*, J. B. Skemp (trans.), Princeton: Princeton University Press.

2 See Lane's comment on the statement of the incompatibility between virtue and laws at *Statesman* 294b, Melissa Lane (1995), 'A New Angle on Utopia: the Political Theory of the Statesman', in Christopher Rowe, (ed.) *Reading the Statesman, Proceedings of the III Symposium Platonicum*, Sankt Augustin: Academia Verlag, 276–91, 284.

3 The emphasis in each part seems to be at least on the demonstration of the method used as it is on the conclusions it reaches. In this sense the dialogue is as much (or more) a debate on philosophical methodology as it is on political philosophy. Stanley Rosen (1995), *Plato's Statesman: the Web of Politics*, New Haven: Yale University Press, vii; and Brisson and Pradeau, 20. That said, the part I propose to concentrate on has clearly philosophical content and seems to be intended as a contribution to political philosophy, i.e. a contribution to the debate on the art of political science.

4 Although towards the end of the dialogue it is not clear whether it is the role of the Statesman in particular, or political science in general that is being discussed – see Luc Brisson and Jean Francois Pradeau's (2003) introduction to their translation *Le Politique*, Paris: Flammarion, 18, and also Jim Dratwa (2003), 'Le Statut de la Philosophie dans le Politique', *Revue de Philosophie Ancienne*, 1: 23–50, 31. It seems that the dialogue is about both: the *Statesman* representing political rule at its best, and political science being a necessary pursuit in the absence of a statesman, like laws.

5 A similar myth is told in the *Laws* (713b–714a) but with a different conclusion, that we should imitate the rule of Kronos and organize our lives according to immortal and godlike reason, and its social expression, law. This is in keeping with the different conception of the role of law put forward in the *Laws* more generally, and the belief that it is always better to be ruled by laws than by men (751b, and *Epis*.7, 334c). On this see also Charles Kahn (1995), 'The Place of the *Statesman* in Plato's Later Work', in Rowe, 49–62, 52.

6 With one important difference: in the *Statesman*, Plato emphasizes that only a select few receive the gift of political wisdom, 297b–c.

7 *Statesman*, 311a. See also Dratwa, 31 and Lane in Rowe, 281–84 for comments on the role of autonomy in this passage.

8 *Statesman*, 294a–297b.

9 *Statesman*, 297b–300c.

10 *Nicomachean Ethics*, 1137b26–32, translation Richard McKeon (1941), *The Basic Works of Aristotle*, New York: Random House, 1020. See also *Politics*, 1286a9–10.

11 This emphasis on the universality, and the rigidity of laws may obscure the fact that a good judge will always need to put some work into deciding which laws apply to a particular case and how they apply. In this sense, it is possible to overemphasize the difference between laws and judgments. But I believe that when they are talking of laws as being rigid, both Plato and Aristotle have in mind the distinction between the work of the legislator, who cannot possibly be aware of the many different cases

his or her laws will be applied to, and of the judge, who, on the other hand, is working with these cases. In this way should the distinction be understood.

12 Incidentally, Rosen's suggestion that the Young Socrates finds this claim difficult to accept is because of his mathematical training being a bit far fetched – who would not be uncomfortable at the thought of being a the mercy of a lawless king? See Rosen, 156.

13 But presumably, the Stranger's view is that if they have been meddled with, it is still best not to interfere with them any further.

14 For a full text of the current code (in French) see http://codes-et-lois.fr/codes/code_civil (last accessed 6 October 2008).

For extracts of the original code (in English) see http://www.historyguide.org/intellect/code_nap.html (last accessed 6 October 2008).

15 England has many such laws, some of which (for example the law requiring taxi drivers to carry a bail of hay in their cab) have been repealed, some others (taxi drivers are also required by law to ask all passengers whether they have small pox or the plague) not yet. The British Parliament passes repeal bills every few years, each time getting rid of hundreds of pages of obsolete laws.

16 There is little evidence, because little said, that the young Socrates is in fact defending a constitutionalist position. But Lane notes that this is not an accurate representation of how the Athenians understood the role of law, i.e. as a restraining framework for politics, p. 151.

17 Christopher Gill (1995), 'Rethinking Constitutionalism in *Statesman* 291–303', in Rowe, 292–305, 293.

18 See Brisson and Pradeau (2003), 255, footnote 291, on the relative importance of Young Socrates' comment.

19 Melissa Lane (1998), *Method and Politics in Plato's* Statesman, Cambridge: Cambridge University Press, 163.

20 *Statesman*, 268d–277e.

21 Rosen, 175.

22 *Statesman*, 555b–558c. See also Vlastos (1993), 'The Theory of Social Justice in the Polis in Plato's *Republic*', *Studies in Greek Philosophy* Vol. 1, Princeton: Princeton University Press, 69–103.

23 This is not an implication that Rosen considers as he believes that for Plato the true king, who can rule without laws, is *Phronesis* itself, p. 149. and therefore not something that a human being can imitate.

24 *Statesman*, 293e.

25 See Dratwa, 31, who comments that the myth and the weaving paradigm point to an argument for self-rule.

26 *Statesman*, 301e.

27 *Statesman*, 311a.

28 Brisson and Pradeau discuss this in p. 255, footnote 291. They suggest that Young Socrates misunderstands the Stranger and that it is wrong to place a great emphasis on his comment at 293e.

29 *Statesman*, 295b.

30 *Statesman*, 295c.

31 The Stranger uses an analogy with a physical trainer who chooses to train everybody according to the same rules, starting and finishing at the same time under

the assumption that this will benefit the largest number of people at once. Presumably, if one person were to respond badly to this group training, he or she would be easy to pick out among the people who trained successfully. Arrangements can then be made for that person to train differently. *Statesman*, 294a–295a.

32 The belief that laws should never be changed is not typical of Plato. In the *Laws*, certainly, the Athenian claims that any law-maker is bound to make some mistakes, even if they are only minor, and that these mistakes will only become apparent to those who experience the laws in practice. Therefore, rulers should regularly amend the laws, even when they were not the original legislators (772a). One might think that this shows that, by the time he wrote the *Laws*, Plato had acquired a more relaxed view about the role of laws, and accepted that citizens could intervene and modify them. However, I will argue that the contrary is true. In the *Statesman*, Plato believes we should not change the laws because it is possible to rule partly outside the laws, whereas in the *Laws* he refuses the very thought of lawless government (cf. *Epis.* 7, 334c).

33 *Statesman*, 295d.

34 Equity in this sense, i.e. doing justice in the particular case, is to be distinguished from equity as a distinct body of legal rules (equity laws) or as a consideration of distributive justice.

35 Solum (2003), 'Virtue Jurisprudence: A Virtue-centred Theory of Judging', *Metaphilosophy*, 34: 178–213, 204–205. See also Roger Shiner (1994), 'Aristotle's theory of Equity', *Loyola of Los Angeles Law Review*, 27, and Kraut (2002), *Aristotle: Political Philosophy*, Oxford: Clarendon Press, 108–11.

36 Solum, 205–06.

37 Although arguably, the concept of equity is rooted in neither, but in the practice of Athenian democracy. The Athenians tended to prefer judgment over laws, and regarded laws more as general guidelines than absolute dictators. It is this tendency that Aristotle is criticizing in *Rhetoric* I, 1354b. On the Athenians' attitude to laws and reliance on equity see Danielle Allen, 'Punishment in Ancient Athens', http://www.stoa.org/projects/demos/punishment.pdf (last accessed 6 October 2008) and Victor Bers and Adriaan Lanni, 'An Introduction to the Athenian Legal System', http://www.stoa.org/projects/demos/article_intro_legal_system?page=1&greekEncoding (last accessed 6 October 2008).

38 Roger Shiner believes that a theory of equity can be extracted from the texts mentioned, and he has written on how the theory in question differs from most jurisprudential accounts of equity, in particular, that it does not fit in the natural law, *vs* positive law divide. However, as he himself notes, p. 1247, to extract a theory from those short texts amounts to analysing a few very dense remarks. Because of this it is not clear that we are better off looking at Aristotle than Plato in order to get an idea of what a virtue theory of law would look like. See Shiner (1994).

39 *Rhetoric*, 1354a–b.

40 *Nicomachean Ethics*, 1229b20–24.

41 *Nicomachean Ethics*, 1229b13.

42 *Rhetoric*, 1374a.

43 *Nicomachean Ethics*, 1137b23, 'what the legislator would have said himself, had he been present'.

[44] *Rhetoric*, 1374a.
[45] See Kraut (2002), *Aristotle: Political Philosophy*, Oxford: Clarendon Press, 108–10 for a discussion of these points.
[46] Solum, 206.

Chapter 7

[1] Trevor Saunders in his commentary on Plato's *The Laws* (translation 1970, London: Penguin Classics.) argues that there is in fact no change of heart but that the *Republic* and the *Laws* are 'opposite sides of the same coin', with the *Republic* setting the ideal, and the *Laws* focusing on the practicalities, p. 28. I am sympathetic to Saunders' view and will argue that the *Republic* is only meant as a model for understanding justice, whereas the *Laws* offers a way in which actual ordinary people may govern themselves following the ideals of the earlier dialogues. See also Andre Laks (1990), 'Legislation and Demiurgy. On the Relationship between Plato's Republic and the Laws', *Classical Antiquity*, 9: 209–29.
[2] For such a view see Charles Kahn (1995), 'The Place of the *Statesman* in Plato's Later Work', in C. Rowe (ed.) *Reading the* Statesman, Sankt Augustin: Academia Verlag, 49–62. Kahn argues that what has happened between the *Republic* and the *Laws* is a change in 'Plato's understanding of the realities of power' brought about by his trips to Sicily, p. 54. See also G. E. L. Owen (1953), 'The Place of the *Timaeus* in Plato's Dialogues', *Classical Quarterly*, n.s. 3: 79–95; G. Vlastos (1981a), 'Review of J. Gould *The Development of Plato's Ethics*', in his *Platonic Studies*, 204–17, Princeton: Princeton University Press; and C. Gill (1979), 'Plato's Politics: The *Critias* and the *Politicus*', *Phronesis*, 24: 148–67.
[3] But it would be wrong to call it autonomy without qualifications, if only because that would constitute an anachronism.
[4] I will address the concern whether to the modern reader this is a sufficient protection against paternalism in Section 4.
[5] This is described as a source of mirth to an outside observer. Plato seems to be telling us that it is unusual for an individual in a position of authority to be seen as a teacher. Yet even a free doctor would not have the status of a legislator. So what Plato seems to be saying is that he expects his proposal that legislators should persuade to be very badly received.
[6] The question whether this preamble does take the form of an elenctic debate is complicated by the absence of the supposed interlocutor, i.e. the young atheist. However, his role in the debate is made fairly clear by the Athenian who says at 899c–d that 'either he must show us that we are wrong in pronouncing soul the primary source of all things, and in the further consequences we drew, or, if unable to get the better of our reasoning, he must yield to us and live henceforth a believer in gods'. This is clearly an invitation to refutation. Also, when Clinias is asked to take on the role of interlocutor, at 891c, the Athenian begins by asking him to state his opinion – a common feature of other elenctic dialogues.
[7] K. Popper, *The Open Society and its Enemies*, Vol.1, but also, see M. Scholfied (2003), 'Religion and Philosophy in the *Laws*', in S. Scolnicov and L. Brisson

(eds), *Plato's Laws: From Theory into Practice*, Sankt Augustin: Academia Verlag, 1–13, 13.

8 Glen Morrow (1960), *Plato's Cretan City*, Princeton: Princeton University Press; Richard Stalley (1994), 'Persuasion in Plato's *Laws*', *History of Political Thought*, 15, 2: 155–77.

9 Indeed, it has been argued that references to doctors in the *Gorgias* and the *Laws* anticipate the view that consent is necessary for a medical treatment to beacceptable. See P. Dalla-Vorgia, J. Lascaratos, P. Skiadas and J. Garanis Papadotos (2001), 'Is Consent in medicine a concept only of modern times?', *Journal of Medical Ethics*, 27: 59–61.

10 Stalley (1994), 163.

11 Stalley (1994), 172.

12 Stalley (1994), 171.

13 I return to this worry in Section 4.

14 Stalley (1994), 173.

15 Christopher Bobonich (1991), 'Persuasion and Compulsion in Plato's *Laws*', *Classical Quarterly*, n. s. 41, 365–88; (1996), 'Reading the Laws', in Gill and McCabe (ed.) *Form and Argument in Late Plato*, New York: Oxford University Press; (2002), *Plato's Utopia Recast*, Oxford: Clarendon Press.

16 See Bobonich (2002), 103 for a comment on autonomy in the *Republic*.

17 Bobonich (1996), 264.

18 Bobonich (1996), 264.

19 Bobonich (2002), 104.

20 I take Clinias to be in charge or legislating for the new colony on the basis of the following passage: 'Our instructions are further to frame a legislation from such local Cretan laws as have our approval or laws from other quarters; we are not to concern ourselves with their foreign origin, so long as we judge them superior.' 703c.

21 The *Laws* is often accused of promoting gerontocracy both because throughout the dialogue, references are made to the age and experience of Clinias and Megillus, and also because, when the new city is discussed, it is made clear that elders should be in charge of it, simply because their experience makes them wiser. See Scholfied (2003).

22 See J. Cleary (2003), 'Paideia in Plato's *Laws*', in Brisson and Scolnicov (2003), 165–73, 166.

23 Although the education program proposed in the *Laws* is not as thorough as the education received by the philosophers in the *Republic*, it is inclusive of all the colony's citizens and not merely its elite. See Cleary (2003), 165.

24 Bobonich (1996) makes a similar point about the intended audience of the preamble for the law on atheism, 268.

25 An anonymous referee has suggested that the reader constituted the third audience for the *Laws*. This is particularly enlightening when it comes to resolving the following puzzle: if Clinias and Megillus are not intellectually sophisticated enough to deal with complex preambles, then how do we explain the presence in Book X of the preamble on Atheism? The answer could well be that this preamble is offered to the reader as an example of what a fully developed preamble might look like. But although the idea that there is a third

audience is enlightening in that sense, I argue that the balance between the two audiences of Clinias and Megillus on the one hand, and the new colonists on the other , can explain the apparent contradictions of the *Laws*.

26 This worry was raised by an anonymous referee.

27 This example was suggested to me by Bill Wringe.

28 Stalley, (1994), 165.

29 *Statesman*, 297b–300c.

30 At 772b Plato specifies that a time limit of 10 years is to be imposed on the revision period for laws on physical education. So although this passage supports the view that laws can be changed, it does not provide compelling evidence that the need for change will come from the education of the new citizens, as only a few (i.e. those who would have come as older children) will have benefited from the new colony's education system in time to be old enough to become young legislators allowed to assist the older ones. But there is no suggestion that this 10 years limit will apply to any set of laws other than the ones concerned with games and songs.

Chapter 8

1 *Nicomachean Ethics*, 1180a1.

2 There is a discussion of Plato's treatment of slaves in the Laws by Amir Meital and Joseph Agassi (2007), 'Slaves in Plato's Laws', *Philosophy of the Social Sciences*, 37, 3: 315–47. In particular they argue that philosophers, post-Popper, have made too many excuses for Plato's proposed treatment of slaves. Here I am not interested in making excuses – I agree with them that what Plato says in the *Laws* about slavery is a moral outrage (p. 13). What I want to show is that there is no evidence that Plato's account of slavery would translate to a modern society. The same cannot be said, of course, of Aristotle's natural slavery argument.

3 Aristotle, *Politics*, 1281a43–b9.

4 Jeremy Waldron (1995), 'The Wisdom of the Multitude. Some Reflections on Book III Chapter 11 of Aristotle's Politics', *Political Theory*, 23: 563–84, 575.

5 Waldron (1995), 569–70.

Bibliography

Annas, J. (1995), *The Morality of Happiness.* Oxford: Oxford University Press.

—(2005a), 'Virtue Ethics: What Kind of Naturalism?'. In Gardiner, S. (2005), *Virtue Ethics.* Ithaca, New York: Cornell University Press, 11–29.

—(2005b), 'Wickedness as Psychological Breakdown'. *Southern Journal of Philosophy,* 43 (supp.): 513–36.

Anscombe, E. (1958), 'Modern Moral Philosophy'. In Crisp, R. and Slote, M. (eds) (1997), 26–44.

Badhwaar, N. (1996), 'The Limited Unity of Virtue'. *Nous,* 30: 306–29.

Baier, A. (1994), 'What do women want in a moral theory?' In Crisp, R. and Slote, M. (eds) (1997), 263–77.

Balot, R. K. (2006), *Greek Political Thought.* Oxford: Blackwell.

Baron, M. (1985), 'Varieties of Ethics of Virtue'. *American Philosophical Quarterly,* 22: 47–53.

Baron, M., Slote, M. and Pettit, P. (1999), *Three Methods of Ethics: A Debate.* Oxford: Blackwell.

Begley, A. (2006), 'Facilitating the Development of Moral Insight in Practice: Teaching Ethics and Teaching Virtue'. *Nursing Philosophy,* 28: 57–62.

Benson, H. (ed.) (2006), *A Companion to Plato.* Malden, MA: Blackwell.

Berges, S. (2007), 'Virtue Ethics, Politics, and the Function of Laws: The Parent Analogy in Plato's *Menexenus*'. *Dialogue,* 46, 2: 211–30.

Block, J. (1971), *Lives Through Time.* Berkeley: Bancroft Books.

Bloomfield, P. (1997), 'Of Goodness and Healthiness: A Viable Moral Ontology'. *Philosophical Studies,* 87: 309–32.

Blum, L. (1996), 'Community and Virtue'. In Crisp, R. (ed.) (1996), 231–50.

Bobonich, C. (1991), 'Persuasion and Compulsion in Plato's *Laws*'. *Classical Quarterly,* n. s. 41: 365–88.

—(1996), 'Reading the Laws'. In Gill and McCabe (1996), 249–82.

—(2002), *Plato's Utopia Recast.* Oxford: Clarendon Press.

Bondanella, P. and Musa, M. (1979), *The Portable Machiavelli.* New York: Penguin.

Bostock, D. (1990), 'The Interpretation of Plato's *Crito*'. *Phronesis,* 35, 1: 1–20.

Brandt, R. (1995), 'Conscience (rule) Utilitarianism and the Criminal Law'. *Law and Philosophy,* 14: 65–89.

Brisson, L. and Pradeau, J-F. (2003), *Platon: Le Politique.* Paris: Flammarion.

Burnyeat, M. (1980), 'Aristotle on Learning to be Good'. In Rorty, A. (ed.) (1980), *Essays on Aristotle's Ethics.* Berkeley and Los Angeles: University of California Press, 69–92.

—(1999), 'Culture and Society in Plato's Republic'. *The Tanner Lectures on Human Values,* 20: 215–324.

Chappell, T. (2001), 'Socrates and Antigone: Two Ways to be Martyred'. *Prudentia Special Issue,* (May 2001): 161–70.
Charlton, W. (2006), 'Goodness and Truth'. *Philosophy*, 81: 619–32.
Cleary, J. (2003), 'Paideia in Plato's *Laws*'. In Scolnicov, S. and Brisson, L. (eds) (2003), 165–73.
Coope, C. (2006), 'Modern Virtue Ethics'. In Chappell, T. (ed.) (2006), *Values and Virtues.* Oxford: Oxford University Press, 20–52.
Crane, S. (1994), *The Red Badge of Courage.* London: Penguin Popular Classics.
Crisp, R. (ed.) (1996), *How Should One Live?* Oxford: Oxford University Press.
Crisp, R. and Slote, M. (eds) (1997), *Virtue Ethics.* Oxford: Oxford University Press.
Dalla-Vorgia, P., Lascaratos, J., Skiadas, P. and Garanis Papadotos, J. (2001), 'Is Consent in Medicine a Concept Only of Modern Times?'. *Journal of Medical Ethics*, 27: 59–61.
Danzig, G. (2006), 'Crito and the Socratic Controversy'. *Polis*, 23: 21–45.
Darley, G. M. and Batson, C. D. (1973), 'From Jerusalem to Jericho: A Study of Situational and Dispositional Variables in Helping Behavior'. *Journal of Personality and Social Psychology*, 10: 202–14.
Devigne, R. (2006), '"Cultivating the Individual and Society": J. S. Mill's Use of Ancient and Romantic Dialectics'. *History of Political Thought*, 27: 91–121.
Doris, J. M. (1998), 'Persons, Situations and Virtue Ethics'. *Nous*, 32: 504–30.
—(2002), *Lack of Character: Personality and Moral Behavior.* Cambridge: Cambridge University Press.
Dratwa, J. (2003), 'Le Statut de la Philosophie dans le *Politique*'. *Revue de Philosophie Ancienne*, 2003, 1: 23–50.
Driver, J. (1996), 'The Virtues and Human Nature'. In Crisp (ed.) (1996), 111–30.
—(2001), *Uneasy Virtue.* Cambridge: Cambridge University Press.
Duff, R. A. (2003), 'The Limits of Virtue Jurisprudence'. *Metaphilosophy*, 34: 214–24.
Fleming, D. (2006), 'The Character of Virtue: Answering the Situationist Challenge to Virtue Ethics'. *Ratio*, 19: 24–42.
Flew, A. (1973), 'Crime or Disease?' *The British Journal of Sociology*, 5, 1 (Mar.): 49–62.
Foot, P. (1978), *Virtues and Vices.* Oxford: Blackwell.
Gill, C. (1979), 'Plato's Politics: The *Critias* and the *Politicus*'. *Phronesis*, 24: 148–67.
—(1995), 'Rethinking Constitutionalism in *Statesman* 291–303'. In Rowe, C. (1995), 292–305.
Gill, C. and McCabe, M. M. (eds) (1996), *Form and Argument in Late Plato.* New York: Oxford University Press.
Gill, M.-L. and Pellerin, P. (eds) (2006), *A Companion to Ancient Philosophy.* Malden, MA: Blackwell.
Gleitman, H. (1992), *Basic Psychology*, Third Edition. New York, London: Norton.
Hamilton, E. and Cairns, H. (1989), *Plato: The Collected Dialogues.* Princeton: Princeton University Press.
Hamlin, A. (1993), 'Welfare'. In Goodin, R. and Pettit, P. (eds) (1993), *A Companion to Contemporary Political Theory.* Oxford: Basil Blackwell, 651–62.
Harman, G. (1999), 'Moral Philosophy Meets Social Psychology'. *Proceedings of the Aristotelian Society*, 99: 316–31.

Harte, V. (1999), 'Conflicting Values in Plato's *Crito*'. *Archiv fur Geschichte de Philosophie*, 81, 2: 117–47.

Hinchliffe, G. (2006), 'Plato and the Love of Learning'. *Ethics and Education*, 1, 2: 117–31.

Hobbes, J. (1989), *Leviathan*. London: Penguin.

Huby, P. (1957), 'The *Menexenus* Reconsidered'. *Phronesis*, 2: 104–14.

Hursthouse, R. (1999), *On Virtue Ethics*. Oxford: Oxford University Press.

Irwin, T. (1977), *Plato's Moral Theory: The Early and Middle Dialogues*. Oxford: Clarendon Press.

—(1985), *Aristotle: Nicomachean Ethics*. Indianapolis: Hackett.

—(1995), *Plato's Ethics*. New York & Oxford: Oxford University Press.

Isen, A. M. and Levin, P. F. (1972), 'The Effect of Feeling Good on Helping: Cookies and Kindness'. *Journal of Personality and Social Psychology*, 34: 384–88.

—(1975), 'Further Studies on the Effects of Feeling Good on Helping'. *Sociometry*, 38: 141–47.

Janssens, D. (2006), 'The Law of the Stranger: Waldenfels, Plato and the Origin of the Legal Order'. *Ethical Perspectives*, 13, 3: 383–410.

Kahn, C. (1963), 'Plato's Funeral Oration: The Motive of the *Menexenus*'. *Classical Philology*, 58: 220–54.

—(1995), 'The Place of the *Statesman* in Plato's Later Work'. In Rowe, C. (1995), 49–62.

Kenny, A. (1973), 'Mental Health in Plato's *Republic*'. In Kenny (1973), *The Anatomy of the Soul*. Oxford: Blackwell, 1–27.

Keyt, D. (2006), 'Plato and the Ship of the State'. In Santas, G. (2006), 189–213.

King, M. L. (1963), 'Letter from Birmingham Jail'. http://www.stanford.edu/group/King/popular_requests/frequentdocs/birmingham.pdf (last accessed 6 October 2008).

Korsgaard, C. (1999), 'Self-constitution in the Ethics of Plato and Kant', *Journal of Ethics*, 3: 1–29.

Kraut, R. (1984), *Socrates and the State*. Princeton, New Jersey: Princeton University Press.

—(1989), *Aristotle on the Human Good*. Princeton, New Jersey: Princeton University Press.

—(2002), *Aristotle: Political Philosophy*. Oxford: Clarendon Press.

Laks, A. (1990), 'Legislation and Demiurgy: On the Relationship Between Plato's *Republic* and the *Laws*'. *Classical Antiquity*, 9: 209–29.

Lane, M. (1995), 'A New Angle on Utopia: The Political Theory of the Statesman'. In Rowe, C. (ed.) (1995), 276–91.

—(1998a), 'Argument and Agreement in Plato's *Crito*'. *History of Political Thought*, 19, 3: 313–30.

—(1998b), *Method and Politics in Plato's* Statesman. Cambridge: Cambridge University Press.

—(2006), 'Plato's Political Philosophy: The *Republic*, the *Statesman*, and the *Laws*'. In Gill, M.-L. (2006), 170–91.

Lidz, J. (1994), 'Medicine as Metaphor in Plato'. *Journal of Medicine and Philosophy*, 19: 527–41.

Machiavelli, N. (1983), *The Discourses*. London: Penguin Classics.

Martin, M. (2006), *From Morality to Mental Health*. Oxford: Oxford University Press.

McIvor, G. (1998), 'Pro-social Modelling and Legitimacy: Lessons from a Study of Community Service'. In Rex, S. and Matravers, A. (eds) (1998), *Pro-social Modelling and Legitimacy: The Clarke Hall Day Conference*, Cambridge: Institute of Criminology, University of Cambridge.

McKeon, R. (1941), *The Basic Works of Aristotle*. New York: Random House.

McPherson, C. B. (1980), *Locke: Second Treatise of Government*. Indianapolis: Hackett.

Meital, A. and Agassi, J. (2007), 'Slaves in Plato's Laws'. *Philosophy of the Social Sciences*, 37, 3: 315–47.

Meyer, S. (2006), 'Plato on the Law'. In Benson, H. (ed.) (2006), 373–87.

Milgram, S. (1963), 'Behavioral Study of Obedience'. *Journal of Abnormal and Social Psychology*, 67: 371–78.

—(1965), 'Some Conditions of Obedience and Disobedience to Authority'. *Human Relations*, 18: 57–76.

Mill, J. S. (1991), *On Liberty and Other Essays*. Oxford: Oxford University Press.

Miller, C. (2003), 'Social Psychology and Virtue Ethics'. *The Journal of Ethics*, 7: 365–92.

Monoson, S. (1998), 'Remembering Pericles: The Political and Theoretical Import of Plato's *Menexenus*'. *Political Theory*, 26, 4: 489–513.

Moravcsik, J. (2000), 'Health, Healing, and Plato's Ethics'. *Journal of Value Inquiry*, 34: 7–26.

Morrow, G. (1960), *Plato's Cretan City*. Princeton: Princeton University Press.

Nussbaum, M. (1992), 'Human Functioning and Social Justice: In Defence of Aristotelian Essentialism'. *Political Theory*, 20: 584–612.

—(1996), *For Love of Country, Debating the Limits of Patriotism*. Boston: Beacon Press.

—(1997a), 'Kant and Stoic Cosmopolitanism'. *The Journal of Political Philosophy*, 5, 1: 1–25.

—(1997b), *Cultivating Humanity*. Cambridge, MA: Harvard University Press.

—(1999), 'Virtue Ethics: A Misleading Category?' *Journal of Ethics*, 3: 163–201.

—(2000), 'Duties of Justice, Duties of Material Aid: Cicero's Problematic Legacy'. *The Journal of Political Philosophy*, 8, 2: 176–206.

—(2003), 'Compassion and Terror' *Daedalus*, Winter 2003: 10–26.

—(2004), *Hiding From Humanity*. Princeton: Princeton University Press.

O'Hear, A. (2006), 'Democracy and Openness'. *Philosophy*, 58 (supplement): 39–56.

Owen, G. E. L. (1953), 'The Place of the *Timaeus* in Plato's Dialogues'. *Classical Quarterly*, n. s. 3: 79–95.

Popper, K. (1945), *The Open Society and its Enemies*, Vol.1. London: Routledge.

Purshouse, L. (2006), *Plato's Republic: A Reader's Guide*. New York: Continuum.

Raz, J. (1979), *The Authority of Law: Essays on Law and Morality*. Oxford: Clarendon Press.

—(1986), *The Morality of Freedom*. Oxford: Oxford University Press.

—(2000), *Engaging Reason: On the Theory of Value and Action*. Oxford: Oxford University Press.

Rex, S. and Gelsthorpe, L. (2002), 'The Role of Community Service in Reducing Offending: Evaluating Pathfinder Projects in the UK'. *The Howard Journal*, 41: 311–25.

Rosen, S. (1995), *Plato's Statesman: The Web of Politics*. New Haven: Yale University Press.

Rowe, C. (ed.) (1995), *Reading the* Statesman, *Proceedings of the III Symposium Platonicum*. Sankt Augustin: Academia Verlag.

Ruttenberg, H. (1986), 'Plato's Use of the Analogy between Justice and Health'. *Journal of Value Inquiry* 20: 145–56.

Santas, G. (1971), 'Socrates at Work on Virtue and Knowledge in Plato's *Laches*'. In Vlastos, G. (ed.) (1971), *The Philosophy of Socrates. Modern Studies in Philosophy*. Garden City, New York: Doubleday, Anchor Books, 177–208.

—(1979), *Socrates: Philosophy in Plato's Early Dialogues*. London: Routledge and Kegan Paul.

—(2006), *The Blackwell Guide to Plato's Republic*. Malden, MA: Blackwell.

Saunders, Trevor J. (trans.) (1970), Plato's *The Laws*. London: Penguin Classics.

Scholfield, M. (2003), 'Religion and Philosophy in the *Laws*'. In Scolnicov, S. and Brisson, L. (eds) (2003), 1–13.

—(2006), *Plato: Political Philosophy*. New York: Oxford University Press.

Scolnicov, S. and Brisson, L. (eds) (2003), *Plato's Laws: from Theory to Practice*. Sankt Augustin: Akademia Verlag.

Sherman, N. (1989), *The Fabric of Character*. Oxford: Clarendon Press.

Shields, C. (2006), 'Learning about Plato from Aristotle'. In Benson, H. (ed.) (2006), 403–17.

Shiner, R. (1994), 'Aristotle's Theory of Equity'. *Loyola of Los Angeles Law Review*, 27: 1245–64.

Slote, M. (1995a), 'Agent-based Virtue Ethics'. *Midwest Studies in Philosophy*, 20, 83–101.

—(1995b), 'Law in Virtue Ethics'. *Law and Philosophy*, 14: 91–113.

—(1998), 'Nietzsche and Virtue Ethics'. *International Studies in Philosophy*, 30: 3.

—(2001), 'War Crimes and Virtue Ethics.' In Aleksandar Jokic (ed.), *War Crimes and Collective Wrongdoings*. Oxford: Blackwell, 77–84.

Solum, L. B. (2003), 'Virtue Jurisprudence: A Virtue-centered Theory of Judging'. *Metaphilosophy*, 34: 178–213.

Stalley, R. (1994), 'Persuasion in Plato's *Laws*'. *History of Political Thought*, 15, 2: 155–77.

Swanton, C. (1998), 'Outline of a Nietzschean Virtue Ethics'. *International Studies in Philosophy*, 30: 3.

Taylor, A. E. (1960), *Plato: The Man and His Work*. London: Methuen.

Thoreau, H. (1849), 'On the Duty of Civil Disobedience'. Gutenberg Project. http://www.gutenberg.org/files/71/71-h/71-h.htm (last accessed 6 October 2008).

Vlastos, G. (1981a), 'Review of J. Gould *The Development of Plato's Ethics*'. In Vlastos, G. (1981), *Platonic Studies*. Princeton: Princeton University Press: 204–17.

—(1981b), 'The Unity of Virtue in Plato's *Protagoras*'. In *Platonic Studies*, Second Edition. Princeton: Princeton University Press, 221–69.

—(1993), 'The Theory of Social Justice in the Polis in Plato's Republic'. In Vlastos, G. (1993), *Studies in Greek Philosophy, 1*. Princeton: Princeton University Press, 69–103.

—(1994), 'The Historical Socrates and Athenian Democracy'. In Vlastos (1994), *Socratic Studies*. Cambridge: Cambridge University Press, 87–108.

Waldron, J. (1995), 'The Wisdom of the Multitude. Some Reflections on Book III Chapter 11 of Aristotle's Politics'. *Political Theory*, 23: 563–84,

Watson, G. (1990), 'On the Primacy of Character'. In Flanagan, O. and Rorty, A. (eds) (1990), *Identity, Character, and Morality*. Cambridge, MA: M.I.T. Press, 449–83.

Weiss, R. (1998), *Socrates Dissatisfied: An Analysis of Plato's* Crito. New York: Oxford University Press.

Wiggins, D. (1986), 'Teleology and the Good in Plato's *Phaedo*'. Oxford Studies in Ancient Philosophy.

—(1996), 'Natural and Artificial Virtues: a Vindication of Hume's Scheme'. In Crisp, R. (ed.) (1996), 131–40.

Winnicott, D. W. (1976), *The Maturation Process and the Facilitating Environment*. London: Hogarth Press.

Wolf, S. (2007), 'Moral Psychology and the Unity of the Virtues'. *Ratio*, 20: 145–67.

Index